The Public School Advantage

WHY PUBLIC SCHOOLS OUTPERFORM PRIVATE SCHOOLS

+ + + + + + + + + + + + + + + + + + +

CHRISTOPHER A. LUBIENSKI AND
SARAH THEULE LUBIENSKI

THE UNIVERSITY OF CHICAGO PRESS
CHICAGO AND LONDON

Christopher A. Lubienski is professor in the Department of Education Policy, Organization, and Leadership at the University of Illinois at Urbana-Champaign. He is coeditor of *The Charter School Experiment: Expectations, Evidence, and Implications* and *School Choice Policies and Outcomes: Empirical and Philosophical Perspectives*. **Sarah Theule Lubienski** is professor of education and associate dean of the Graduate College at the University of Illinois at Urbana-Champaign.

The University of Chicago Press, Chicago 60637
The University of Chicago Press, Ltd., London
© 2014 by The University of Chicago
All rights reserved. Published 2014.
Printed in the United States of America

23 22 21 20 19 18 17 16 15 14   1 2 3 4 5

ISBN-13: 978-0-226-08888-4 (cloth)
ISBN-13: 978-0-226-08891-4 (paper)
ISBN-13: 978-0-226-08907-2 (e-book)

DOI: 10.7208/chicago/9780226089072.001.0001 (e-book)

Library of Congress Cataloging-in-Publication Data

Lubienski, Christopher, author.
    The public school advantage : why public schools outperform private schools / Christopher A. Lubienski and Sarah Theule Lubienski.
        pages ; cm
    Includes bibliographical references and index.
    ISBN 978-0-226-08888-4 (cloth : alkaline paper) —
    ISBN 978-0-226-08891-4 (paperback) —
    ISBN 978-0-226-08907-2 (e-book)   1. Academic achievement—United States. 2. Public schools—United States. 3. Private schools—United States. 4. Education—United States.   I. Lubienski, Sarah Theule, author.   II. Title.
LB1556.5.L93   2014
371.010973—dc23

                                        2013017873

♾ This paper meets the requirements of ANSI/NISO Z39.48-1992 (Permanence of Paper).

To our children, and other people's children
CAL & STL

Contents

Acknowledgments

The authors gratefully acknowledge the contributions of several individuals and organizations in completing this project. A number of scholars provided valuable help and feedback on this work at various stages, including (in alphabetical order) Henry Braun, Eric Camburn, Chris Forman, Jerry Janczy, Jin Lee, Matt Linick, Jane Loeb, Martha Makowski, Bekisizwe Ndimande, Joe Robinson, Marcus Weaver-Hightower, and Peter Weitzel. Corinna Crane gave valuable research assistance throughout the earlier stages of this project and allowed us to draw upon her dissertation findings as part of a chapter of this book. We are also grateful for the feedback offered by graduate students at seminars we led at the University of Illinois, as well as discussants and participants at academic conferences where this material was presented. Our editor at the University of Chicago Press, Elizabeth Branch Dyson, offered the necessary enthusiasm and guidance critical for the completion of this project. Sarah would personally like to acknowledge her gratitude to Jan and Sy Ellens, who generously paid for her to attend a Christian high school—reminding us that there are other reasons besides test scores that people attend different schools. Finally, we note that this work was completed with the support of the National Center for Education Statistics (NAEP Secondary Analysis Grant R902B05017) and the University of Illinois at Urbana-Champaign. Of course, these individuals and organizations are not responsible for the interpretations or analyses, or any errors of fact, in this book.

Portions of Chapter 4 were drawn with permission from Sarah T. Lubienski and Christopher Lubienski, "School Sector and Academic Achievement: A Multi-Level Analysis of NAEP Mathematics Data," *American Educational Research Journal* 43, no. 4 (2006): 651–98.

Preface

We are living in a historic era where the irresistible power of markets is eroding established boundaries between the public, private, and civic sectors. Markets now shape many areas of life previously thought to be beyond the purview of private sector arrangements—the traditional state responsibility of incarcerating criminals and the civic duty of national defense are being shifted to for-profit companies; the "right" to put pollution into the atmosphere is determined by emissions markets; life-forms are being patented.[1] Around the globe, policymakers increasingly draw on market mechanisms to redefine social policy, introducing consumer-style choice to citizens using public services, encouraging competition between state and for-profit organizations, or privatizing public entities, for instance. Many argue that markets should be used as a model not only for economic transactions, but for understanding and organizing traditionally non-market endeavors. For instance, market ideals like consumer choice serve as standards for assessing public services such as public schooling, or for evaluating optimal access (or lack thereof) to public goods like clean air. Even interpersonal relationships are understood through the lens of market assumptions: predicting human or animal behavior in "mating markets," conceiving of marriage as a series of economic-style transactions, or assessing the economic value of the name a parent gives to a child.[2]

While free markets can be credited with alleviating poverty for untold millions, they also have threatened the world economy with catastrophe. Nevertheless, understanding that communism was an inherently failed system, and that even moderate state socialism appears to produce stagnation, we continue to move in the direction of deregulation, diminishing—for better or for worse—state oversight and participation in many areas of life. Instead, we seek to quantify, measure, and assign value to mundane things in order to incentivize behaviors for organizations and individuals in pursuit of market goals of efficiency and effectiveness. Thus, market arrangements have come to be, often implicitly, elevated as the optimal, if imperfect, approach to organizing and assessing key areas of life: health care, security, knowledge production, and education.

This current global trend stands in stark distinction to the era starting in the mid-twentieth century, when nations accelerated their efforts to build a better welfare state. Following the disaster of the Great Depression, policymakers designed state institutions to address areas of perceived market failure. In the postwar consensus, governments on the liberal/left side of the spectrum expanded state programs in health, safety, nutrition, and education. When conservative/right governments assumed power, they tended not to dissolve those programs, but instead, at most, diminished the rate of their growth. Yet in the last three to four decades, state provision in developed countries came to be associated with economic stagnation and even moral decay. In the Western market democracies, the postwar consensus was supplanted by a remarkable new consensus in the policy arena.

It is now a widely accepted truism that the private sector is preferable to public. This is a notion that is obviously true in many private consumer markets. But is it also the case with previously nonmarket endeavors, such as universal education? Politicians seem to think so. While they argue endlessly about seemingly arcane issues, they appear to embrace the idea that using private-style organizational models, especially in areas such as public education, represents the best approach to solving difficult problems.

Indeed, this new consensus is perhaps most apparent in discussions on how to reform schools—an area of remarkable bipartisanship in an era of intractable ideological differences and gridlock. While the political parties battle over the size and role of government around a number of key issues, they have found common ground on the idea of rolling back the direct state control of education governance for more effectively educating the next generation of citizens. This area of consensus reflects a widespread view that the current state of U.S. public schooling is leading to endemic failure[3] and that the fix can be found in applying market mechanisms to the structures of American education—how schools are governed and operated, how educators are trained and compensated, and how students are placed in particular schools.

Since the inception of choice-oriented reforms in the early 1990s, both major American political parties have continuously embraced such measures, differing not in principle on the issue but only in the extent to which the idea would be advanced through specific programs (ironically, giving voters little choice on the question of school choice). With the exception of general—but hardly universal—Democratic opposition to sporadic Republican proposals to expand the number and scope of voucher programs, policymakers accept the idea that choice and competition in education will lead to greater innovation and better outcomes. Presidential candidates, senators and congressional representatives, state governors and lawmakers, mainstream think tank figures, philanthropists, and opinion makers in the media have largely promoted the expansion of school choice for families, and especially disadvantaged students, believing that the resulting competition will force schools to be more effective and generate better academic outcomes.

The question is, will it? While there has been an apparent consensus of policymakers and idea shapers, is there a similar consensus around the evidence? The idea of choice fits squarely into the American vocabulary of values and appears to create better options and outcomes in many areas of American life. Yet, while we know that competition between Apple and Microsoft creates better technology for consumers, should we force PS 97 to compete with the higher performing Excellence Charter School and Our Lady of Perpetual Help School? Certainly, families often appreciate the opportunity to pull their children from an underperforming neighborhood school and send them instead to a higher scoring charter or private school. But does that competition lead to better outcomes? Are those private and independent schools—as policymakers assume—necessarily "better?" In fact, these questions have been central to an ongoing debate in American education, a debate in which there has been much heat but surprisingly little light. While assumptions abound and often guide policymakers and parents, the debate has often been characterized by a failure to use evidence, an abundance of unsupported assumptions, and an excess of ideologically inspired misinformation. Here we offer evidence that provides illumination.

On a Tuesday morning right before the beginning of the 2004 school year, the front page of the *New York Times* reported on a study of achievement in charter schools in the United States. Questions about these new schools reignited a controversy that had long been dormant.[4] Charter schools are one of a number of reform models that embrace autonomy, choice, and competition to improve America's public schools. In a field plagued by continuous reform, charters themselves are a relatively fresh model of schooling, publicly financed but managed by private or independent managers free of most bureaucratic regulations and very popular with the current crop of reform proponents. Many of the new generation of reformers had expressed an admirable faith that the greater operational autonomy granted to charters in return for market-style accountability would produce the higher levels of achievement seen in private schools, so much so that they had persuaded the federal government to collect data on a representative sample of charter schools as part of the National Assessment of Educational Progress (NAEP)—the gold standard of achievement measures often referred to as the "nation's report card."[5] However, the results reported in the *Times* directly contradicted the hope that these autonomous schools, modeled after private schools, would outperform public schools.[6]

Almost immediately, some policy advocates and associated academics went on the offensive, attacking the study. In days, one prominent and well-funded education reform group placed a full-page advertisement in the *Times*, signed by some thirty prominent choice proponents, condemning the research and reprimanding the *Times* for carrying the piece.[7] Their concerns centered on the limited methods used in the analysis—the authors of the study did not adequately consider differences in students' family backgrounds. The critics, many of whom were affiliated with provoucher and charter think tanks, were also bothered by the fact that the study had been conducted by the American Federation of Teachers (AFT)—a teachers' union known to be critical of charters. They pointed out that the AFT had an announced position on charter schools that might influence the findings and that the study had not been reviewed by independent experts before the *Times* reported the results.[8]

By coincidence, we were completing an in-depth study of the NAEP data when this story broke—a study that addressed those methodological concerns and would be vetted by experts in the field and published in a leading research journal. We watched in amazement at the hostility as advocates and opponents of charter schools fired verbal volleys at each other through the media and across the blogosphere. We checked the politically charged claims regarding the AFT results against our own initial findings on charter school achievement (which had yet to be released). More importantly, we had already decided to go beyond simple comparisons of achievement in charter and district-run public schools. Since charter schools are designed to emulate private schools in many important ways, and since private schools themselves are the fulcrum of another important debate—the efficacy of programs that provide vouchers to move students from public schools—we chose to include the different types of private schools in our analyses. Readers will find the results reported in the following pages to be intriguing; many will find them to be surprising or counterintuitive; others will find them to be provocative or controversial.

While it is not the debate itself that motivates us to write this, the passionate nature of the discussions that follow the release of reports such as these is telling. Many foundations, policy advocates, interest groups, and philanthropists have invested substantial effort and resources in competing plans vying to reform America's schools, so it should not be surprising that empirical research results typically challenge one ideological agenda or another and are in turn attacked. Although these debates are often fought on methodological grounds, using research terms as weapons, the actual battle lines are too often ideological, determined by implicit assumptions about the appropriate ways to organize education in a democratic society. And these competing ideas—and associated research studies—often produce more friction than illumination for solving deeply rooted social problems. Our goal in this book is to take a step back from the battles over ideologies, to provide a clearer picture of the assumptions and empirical evidence around efforts to remake American education.

Incentives and Education

Of the many competing plans to improve America's schools, one overall agenda distinguishes itself in terms of its logical potential for fundamentally changing education. The innovative strategy of giving parents more choice of schools, of encouraging competition between those schools, and of granting schools more autonomy to satisfy parents—in short, "incentivizing" education—has taken hold as perhaps the most prominent and promising idea for improving American education at its core. This approach is evident in efforts such as charter schools, vouchers and tax credits for private schools, private management of schools, and privatization. All such "incentivist" approaches draw on market mechanisms modeled after the private sector, including the private education sector.[9]

The reason reformers look to the private sector is obvious. The beauty of the logic is its simplicity. Governments and the bureaucracies they generate are thought to lead to overspending and ineffectiveness—whether the U.S. Postal Service, military procurements, or public schools. This is because governments typically administer enterprises on a monopoly basis, setting up barriers to potential competitors in order to protect their own entities in areas such as education. Hence, virtually all public funding goes only to "public" schools that are traditionally regulated by government bureaucrats, run by administrators who have obtained an official endorsement from the state, and staffed by teachers who have been certified by state-approved teacher training programs. As with all monopolies, this may lead to complacency, and even disincentives for employees to innovate or otherwise respond to the needs of their "customers." But the private sector, driven by choice and competitive market incentives, is thought to produce better outcomes, such as those associated with FedEx, eBay, or private schools. There, school employees have built-in incentives to work harder, or at least more effectively, at providing a better education, for fear of losing students, losing tuition funds, losing their jobs, or even seeing their school "go out of business."

At least that is what we thought. Indeed, that is the narrative of the market and, increasingly, public policy in the United States and around the globe. Yet the evidence reported in this book tells quite a different story than what theorists and the current crop of self-proclaimed reformers assert. Specifically, it points to a new, emerging view of the academic performance and impact of public schools in contrast to the outcomes of their more autonomous counterparts in the charter and private sectors.[10] And the question of the impact of different types of schools, or schools in different sectors, is paramount in this era of choice, charter schools, and vouchers for private schools.

Yet, despite the significance and timeliness of this issue, this topic was not really on the research agenda for either of us. We were each happily ensconced in our own work—one studying mathematics instruction and achievement, the other examining school organization and innovations. While the question of achievement in different types of schools had occasionally appeared on the radar of the wider research community in recent years, it was usually around the hotly contested voucher debates—often vicious arguments that seemed to be geared more toward personal acrimony than enlightenment when it comes to social policy. Indeed, like many researchers, we believed the question of a beneficial private school effect on achievement had been essentially settled by the seminal studies of the 1980s and '90s, and we had virtually no inclination to delve into that area. And then, while examining data on mathematics instruction from the 2000 NAEP, Sarah added "private school" as a control variable, and some surprising results appeared.

We were both skeptical when we first saw the initial results: public schools appeared to be attaining higher levels of mathematics performance than demographically comparable private and charter schools—and math is thought to be a better indicator of what is taught by schools than, say, reading, which is often more influenced directly and indirectly by experiences in the home. These patterns flew in the face of both the common wisdom and the research consensus on the effectiveness of public and private schools. Immediately, we checked to see what had happened in the analysis, whether "public" and "private" had been "reverse-coded" or some other such error was involved. But after further investigation and more targeted analyses, the results held up. And they held up (or were "robust" in the technical jargon) even when we used different models and variables in the analyses. We eventually posted a technical paper on a respected website and published a short article, which received some attention.[11] And then, like any good researchers, we applied for funding to study this issue in more depth using the most recent, comprehensive databases. As we describe in this book, the results across datasets are consistent and robust—indicating that these patterns are substantial and stable, regardless of changes in the details of the analyses.

These results indicate that, despite reformers' adulation of the autonomy enjoyed by private and charter schools, this factor may in fact be the reason these schools are underperforming. That is, contrary to the dominant thinking on this issue, the data show that the more regulated public school sector embraces more innovative and effective professional practices, while independent schools often use their greater autonomy to avoid such reforms, leading to curricular stagnation. Considering the substantial amounts of resources that special interests have devoted to advancing their agendas around such issues in education, we completely expect that our findings will create some controversy.

Inquiring minds may want to know a bit about our own backgrounds and preferences with regard to education. We were educated at both public and private schools—parochial in one case, Christian in the other. Our respective families send their children to schools that are public, Lutheran, or evangelical, or they homeschool. We have volunteered our time and efforts in both public and private schools, and one of us served on the board of directors at an urban Christian school. While we see a role for both public and private schools, as of this writing, our own children currently attend public schools—including our neighborhood school and a magnet high school—owing more to convenience than conviction on our part. (While we were writing this book, our children also attended state-funded Catholic, Christian, and public schools overseas.) Regardless of our particular school choices and commitments, we share with many of the reformers and advocates (even those whose agendas are questioned by our findings) a deep concern for equitable, quality education, especially for the most disadvantaged students.

Yet far from the "panacea" that some of those advocates promised, the evidence presented in the following pages indicates that the choice and competition associated with private education may not by themselves be the best route to effective and equitable educational opportunities for all. In fact, as we note in the conclusion, education may be unique in that it embodies essential elements that resist the easy application of simple structural remedies from the private sector, and it may corrupt the competitive incentives thought to promote improvements in schools. Indeed, despite the bipartisan popularity of choice and charter schools with policymakers, it appears that the major reform movements premised on the assumption of school sector remedies may be misguided.

This book examines the underlying assumptions of those structural reforms; it was not written to offer a simple prescription for the myriad problems facing America's schools—and, indeed, we believe those problems to be tragically widespread, substantial, and deeply engrained in the American system of education. However, these analyses indicate that public schools have no monopoly on the problems that inhibit student growth. Reform remedies that rely on structural changes in school sectors, while relatively easy and appealing, are (to paraphrase H. L. Mencken) simplistic and probably the wrong response to the complex and deeply embedded problem of academic disparities. Which is not to say that those problems cannot be addressed. Solutions are available, and (while not the point of this book) some are affirmed in the evidence we present. But those approaches tend to be difficult to implement, particularly in terms of mustering the political will to bear the substantial costs they entail.

Authors' Note

Although the data and analyses on which this book is based are rather technical, the questions and findings at the center of this work are highly relevant and are of interest to a broad audience. Therefore, we present this analysis as much as appropriate in a manner that is accessible to interested observers, even if they do not have experience with the arcane details of logistic regression or multilevel modeling. Consequently, the technical details and supporting information for our analyses are included but relegated to the appendices and endnotes for those interested.

The book's seven chapters are structured and sequenced to be accessible to a wide variety of interested readers. In the following introductory chapter, we outline some of the main issues regarding the role and organization of schooling in a democratic society and highlight the recent move toward the use of market mechanisms to improve education. Then, in Chapter 2, we focus on the theoretical perspective undergirding much of the current education reform movement. Thus, these two initial chapters have more of a theoretical and even philosophical bent and are in that way distinct from the more empirical sections that then follow.

Chapters 3 through 6 move into more empirical terrain. Chapter 3 offers an overview of some of the challenges and possibilities in examining student achievement in different schools and different sectors. In Chapters 4 and 5 we analyze achievement by school sector using two different and quite distinct nationally representative data sets. The supporting technical details for these analyses are available in the appendices. Chapter 6 goes a step further and examines potential reasons for patterns in school achievement, considering such issues as school size, class size, school climate, teacher qualifications, and instructional practices. Finally, in Chapter 7, we focus on the policy and political implications of our findings, identify reasons for continued confusion about these issues, and discuss some of the virtues and inherent limitations of markets in education.

1 Conflicting Models for Public Education

Societies based on the idea of liberty have two primary templates for organizing their institutions. For many enterprises, free markets are best suited for advancing both individual and collective interests through the private or nongovernment sectors. For other undertakings, especially those needed to nurture or sustain freedom and individual autonomy, government action is often used to initiate, support, or administer essential services. Each of these organizational models evinces specific advantages for recognizing and meeting the needs and preferences of citizens, and each has its own purview of institutions where it is deemed more appropriate and useful.

And yet, while democratic or bureaucratic "politics" and economic "markets" are often presented as contrasting ideals, the line between these arenas is often less defined than it may first appear, with government action often necessary for supporting effective market mechanisms and private interests frequently playing a pivotal role in the public arena. Indeed, individual institutions themselves—for example, the military or the federal courts—can often include elements of both politics and markets, so that there is more of a spectrum than a stark boundary between government action and private economic activity. Some concerns can be addressed largely through one organizational model, while the other plays a lesser, perhaps supporting, role in providing goods and services to citizens in that sector. And it is in the area between pure market and government models—on issues such as health care, transportation, the environment, and education—where the most interesting debates play out on the appropriate and optimal roles of the government and the market in social organization.

Where one model is less effective, the other may serve as a better primary template for organizing institutions. For instance, the free market ideals of voluntary participation and individual choice may not be the best tenets for organizing, say, national security. Instead, collective and coercive government action may be better suited for administering that public good, which all then enjoy. Likewise, government's ability to gather and redistribute resources and enforce equity standards may not be useful in all areas. State control over the media and food production led to disastrous results in the Soviet Bloc; people prefer individual freedom and choice in many areas of their lives, and the aggregate of individual choices can lead to the best outcome when articulated through market mechanisms in many areas. The problem comes when one model systematically fails to produce an important good or service that is placed in its purview, yet there are reasons to resist the obvious remedy of shifting production toward the other model.

That is, there are many examples of "market failure" or "government failure" evident in a number of areas. We all know of instances where the state fails to effectively deliver a service, such as filling potholes or policing the streets. And we know of cases where markets produce drastic inequality in wages or limit access to essential goods based on people's ability to pay. In these cases, people often react by seeking to move the endeavor into the other model. Governments could easily limit CEOs' pay or distribute important goods to the poor, many would claim; and private companies may be better prepared to provide security services, for instance.

In this knee-jerk tendency to look to alternative models, markets have been ascendant in particular in recent years as a means to address the social problems that are increasingly associated with popularly perceived government failure. Problems of government ineffectiveness and social malaise tied to public programs such as welfare help explain why markets have become increasingly paramount, seen as a commonsensical solution to seemingly intractable problems of government ineffectiveness. Whether it is promoting individualized retirement accounts (instead of federally administered Social Security), privatized medical savings accounts (instead of government health insurance programs), or even privatized military services (for functions previously performed by the armed forces), markets make sense on many levels.

The same is true in the area of schools, where market-style organization has an inherent appeal. Particularly in the case of public schools,
which—as we will show—are the site of multiple tensions and competing demands, markets represent a very attractive solution because of
their apparently neat delineation of producers responding to the needs
of consumers, namely, the children. But closer scrutiny of these issues
raises important questions about the efficacy of simplistic solutions
such as these.

Indeed, the idea of education for all may be the best example of the
unforeseen difficulties of moving to a market model. In fact, schools
were not always a state function, as is evident in the history of most
Western democracies. Instead, they were often left to a range of private providers, including religious, charity, for-profit, and family-based
models. Education became a state concern in the United States only
when reformers in the nineteenth century argued that a laissez faire
approach to education led to too much variation, too much inequality,
and not enough access to a service that was crucial to the young republic (and, according to some perspectives, not enough uniformity when
the nascent Industrial Revolution required workers with a reliable set
of skills and values).

The Continuing Crisis

The U.S. public education system was created because of perceived
failures in how schools were suited to respond to social and economic
upheaval. Yet, since that time, America's system of public education
has seemingly been in a chronic state of crisis. Reports on the state of
the public schools are familiar to anyone concerned about the quality
of U.S. education:

· In New York City, "only 24 per cent of 1135 tenth graders tested for
  arithmetic performed at their grade level;" half of the students
  performed at a sixth grade level.
· The nation suffers from a shortage of qualified teachers: "One out
  of every seven teachers in this country cannot meet even the mini-
  mum requirements."
· Teachers are underpaid, and the U.S. education system, once the
  envy of the world, is falling further behind its global competitors.

- Even the students who make it through this failing system are notably unprepared for college—a solid majority of college freshman cannot identify even the most famous U.S. presidents.

So the failure of America's public education system threatens not only to induce economic decline: as one report concluded, "Our democracy is at stake."

Interestingly, these seemingly dead-on indictments were all leveled *before* the Soviets launched Sputnik in 1957 and even *before* the 1954 Supreme Court called for the end of a two-tiered education system.[1] Yet those students and teachers were also part of the "greatest generation," which produced unparalleled economic growth, extended democratic rights, developed incredible technical innovations, and spread prosperity like never before (or since). Were the critics wrong?

While we do not pretend to answer that question, the familiarity and resonance of these admonitions about the state of public education illustrate that anxiety regarding the state of public schools is not new. Such crisis factoids have always been popular with reform advocates seeking to advance their own policy agendas. As Meredith Wilson comically illustrated in his 1957 slice of Americana, *The Music Man*, Americans may not be motivated to buy into change unless they see signs of substantial trouble, especially in their own backyards. Economist Milton Friedman made the same causal connection regarding the potential of an apparent crisis to effect drastic changes in social policy: "only a crisis—actual or perceived—produces real change."[2]

In fact, continued concerns about school quality and inequality led to major efforts to improve education, including the National Defense Education Act of 1958 and the Great Society programs such as Head Start and Title 1, where the federal government directed unprecedented resources toward education starting in the 1960s. Yet consternation about America's educational performance has only intensified since then. The fact that the warnings of the 1940s and 1950s reverberate so clearly now only strengthens the claim that these immense and expensive efforts have done little to turn around a stagnant public education system.

Now a new generation of reformers has taken up the familiar refrain of failure in public education, noting, for instance, that no country currently spends more on education but gets less in the way of results.[3] These reformers raise the alarm when U.S. students score near or at the bottom in international rankings or when results on some standard-ized tests appear to be stagnant.[4] In view of this widespread mediocrity, it should be no surprise that every year well over one million students quit school; some critics note that actual graduation rates vary from 60% to only 70% across states, with students in some urban areas just as likely to graduate as to flee these "dropout factories."[5] While billions have been spent on marquee social programs such as Title I for poor children, we are told that fewer than six of ten high school graduates can read at a level necessary to succeed in daily life.[6]

Perhaps most alarmingly, the gaps in achievement between rich and poor children, and between white and minority students, are stub-bornly persistent in a nation that holds education as the primary route to equal opportunity. A half-century after *Brown v. Board of Education* supposedly broke down legal barriers to equitable educational oppor-tunity, the typical African American student was still scoring below 75%–85% of white students on standardized tests. In the eighth grade, fewer than one out of twenty English language learners can read at a proficient level.[7] The litany of such concerns has been so constant for so long that the crisis in public education is now a permanent attribute of the educational landscape in the United States. Parents, policymak-ers, employers, and taxpayers all see good reasons to demand vastly improved outcomes from the school system.

And reformers have been trying many things. Just as earlier gen-erations tried to fix the schools with a plethora of new curricula, re-sources, and programs, the chronic concern with the state of American education has spawned a slew of new efforts at the local, state, and na-tional levels. Theoreticians, policy analysts, columnists, and corporate CEOs have all advanced various plans to improve America's schools. Some of these are quite specific, focusing on a particular pedagogical approach such as phonics-based reading or block scheduling to recon-figure instructional time. Others are grander in scale, such as whole-school reform packages, the No Child Left Behind legislation, or efforts to universalize prekindergarten education.

In view of the constant flow of reforms directed at schools, con-trasted with the generations of failure, it is hardly surprising that peo-ple lose patience with the constant tinkering around the edges.[8] Indeed, in light of the myriad short-lived and misguided reform efforts, many observers suggest that K-12 education in America may be deteriorating not only in spite of, but at least partly *because of,* this barrage of often

misguided efforts to improve public schools. That is, instead of con-
centrating on imparting core academic skills to the next generation,
some worry that educators are too distracted by the next new thing,
whether it be "professional development schools" or whole-language
instruction or multicultural education or Reading First.

And the apparent failure of massive reform efforts to spur substantive change in a system "institutionally opposed to significant structural reform" has fueled a new generation of reformers who look to
change the structures of the system itself.[9] These policy advocates
point to persistent evidence of public school failure in advancing an
agenda structured around choice and competition—giving families
the option of attending a private school or using competitive pressures
associated with private schools to force public schools to improve. They
have forcefully moved beyond the considerable evidence on the substantial difficulties of educating at-risk children to focus on school and
teacher accountability—arguing that educators too often fall back on
demographics as an excuse, when we now have models from the charter sector that demonstrate that poor children can learn if given the
effective instruction that is apparently evident in private schools.[10] The
watershed 1990 book, *Politics, Markets and America's Schools*, from Brookings scholars John Chubb and Terry Moe is still probably the most ar-
ticulate and compelling statement of the problems and root remedies
for public education since Milton Friedman published his proposal for
vouchers in the 1950s. They identified politicized governance—"direct
democratic control"—as the institutional flaw of American public education and presented empirical evidence on market mechanisms of
choice, competition, and school autonomy as the panacea for lagging
school performance.

Politics, Science, Markets, and School Failure

Once only on the periphery of education reform, the insight from
Chubb and Moe on the structural problems in public education has
gained prominence in its appeal as an alternative perspective for in-
ducing fundamental change in schooling. This idea is premised on the
notion that the public education system is inherently incapable of improving itself. According to this line of thought, and echoing Ronald
Reagan about government in general, these "existing institutions cannot solve the problem, because they *are* the problem."[11] Wave after wave

of ultimately unsuccessful reforms demonstrate that schools resist and repel even the best, most well-intentioned efforts at substantive change.

In the 1970s, radical scholars argued that, like it or not, this is exactly the way that the system is supposed to function in a market society. According to this "social reproduction" perspective, schooling is an institution in capitalist society that perpetuates social and economic advantages for elites. Since a hierarchical economic structure needs a certain number of people to fill less prestigious and less rewarding positions, schools serve the role of sorting students based on their social class origins or race or gender and not on their actual abilities. Consequently, although schools may go through the motions, adopting the rhetoric and symbols of reform in order to maintain their popular legitimacy, they in fact avoid substantive efforts to make education more effective, since increasing equitable outcomes would actually undermine their true function.[12]

In more recent times, theorists of quite a different ideological bent have also argued that the institutions of schooling are structured to resist substantive change. Reforming the internal policies and processes of schools will not go very far, according to these self-avowed "market theorists."[13] Contemporary curriculum and instructional practices reflect a remarkable continuity with earlier eras because, unlike schools in the private sector, public schools themselves have no incentive to become more innovative or responsive to the needs of students.[14] Educators may half-heartedly adopt ideas that could work, only to cast them aside when the next fad appears. More likely, they may adopt nominal changes to please their bureaucratic supervisors but will continue doing what they always do once the classroom door is closed. So the strategy of targeting the internal processes of public schools is destined to fail because the external environment—the institutional framework in which schools have operated—essentially inhibits real change, according to this logic. Rather than focusing on educating children, these institutions are instead geared toward serving the needs of powerful interest groups, most notably the teachers unions in the current expressions of this thinking. To change public schools, these theorists argue that we need to change that institutional framework in ways that encourage schools to adopt the more effective educational practices that drive the private school sector.

At least that is the logic of the reform agenda we examine in this book. However, the evidence presented later in this volume suggests that market models may also face challenges owing to the complexities and uniqueness of education as a social endeavor; in fact, market mechanisms such as deregulation or greater autonomy for schools may even be *causing* some of the problems they are purported to address. Indeed, Americans put multiple (and often conflicting) responsibilities on their public schools by enabling schools to avoid effective practices in response to misguided market demand. America's schools are supposed to promote social tolerance, train students in employable skills, provide nutrition, teach social skills, offer athletic programs, and boost academic achievement. And the idea of *public* education means doing all this and more for very diverse groups of people who often have very different conceptions about what schools should be doing and how they should be doing it. Few would say that public schools are succeeding at these multiple missions. Indeed, market theorists offer a cogent and compelling critique of the myriad failures of public schools, but we will see that it is not at all clear that market models would do any better in this regard. In light of this potpourri of demands on public schools, the question that has emerged as the central consideration is whether public schools can still "work" in enhancing academic outcomes for diverse students.

But this was not always the defining question. In fact, as the radicals of the 1970s argued, it could be that schools are working, but simply towards other ends besides academic achievement. In perhaps the most insightful analysis of this issue, David Labaree noted that schools are burdened with conflicting goals as they strive to serve both collective and individual interests.[15] According to Labaree, a democratic society has a commitment to equal educational opportunity for all, but an individual family seeks additional opportunities for its own child, so that he/she may have a competitive advantage in education and the economy. But providing everyone with such additional advantages is inefficient from a broader resource standpoint, since schools are also asked to sort students based on ability, with the only the best and brightest going on to further education. If schools focus on a single goal, it can only be to the detriment of other widely endorsed purposes for public schools and the constituencies that support those goals. Thus, schools may be effective at meeting some goals, but purposes set out for public schools are inherently contradictory and therefore self-defeating.

Just as many goals for education are incompatible with each other, the ways in which we organize education are also fraught with contradiction and therefore ineffectiveness. In fact, following Friedman, Chubb, Moe, and others, we often hear arguments about politics and markets in social policy. Yet American education reflects not two but at least three competing organizational models: political, scientific, and commercial—each representing particular perspectives on the best way to configure educational services. Here we discuss the strengths, weaknesses and contradictions of these three paradigms in order to illustrate how the competing forces shape education as well as the calls to reform it.

When educational systems adopt elements of these different models, deep-seated tensions emerge, leading not only to overt arguments about values but also to underlying institutional pathologies that hinder the effectiveness of school systems. While theorists often discuss the tension between two of these models in education—between "politics" and "markets"—we also need to consider the role of the "technocratic" or scientific approach to organizing education as well, that is, the model of schooling as a science delivering state-of-the-art practices as determined by empirical inquiry.[16] These models do not necessarily weigh the core *purposes* of education, at least explicitly, but instead represent three distinct *means* through which education is most appropriately and effectively organized in a democratic society. As we will see, there has been a significant shift in the models through which education is organized.

PUBLIC EDUCATION AS POLITICS

First, the idea of *politics* as an organizing principle certainly conveys some negative connotation because of the word's association with power, corruption, and wastefulness. And yet, phrased differently, the notion of democratic control of schooling is a core tenet of American public education. The broader public exerts a claim on education not only because public schools are funded through tax revenues but also because of a legitimate societal interest in education, both for communities and individuals. On a wider scale, inasmuch as education is a public good, negative social consequences such as ignorance, crime, or other social ills can emerge from the failure to provide education to all;

just as positive societal outcomes such as economic growth, social co-hesion and stability, and a more informed electorate result from a wider distribution of education. But the public also has an interest in educa-tion for individuals, since the failure to offer a child an adequate educa-tion offends democratic ideals of fairness and equal opportunity.

Typically, the public expresses its interest in education through mechanisms of democratic governance. The public funds schools for all and compels all children to receive an education of some sort. The public then also creates and administers schools to do this, although Friedman and others have raised legitimate questions as to whether private schools might be a more efficient vehicle for this goal. While there are conflicting explanations for understanding the growth of the state in education management in the nineteenth century, the fact is that approximately nine of every ten students are now educated in publicly run schools—as has been the case in the United States for de-cades. Traditionally, local public school districts, controlled by demo-cratically elected school boards, administer these public schools (or "government schools," according to Friedman and others),[17] although they may be regulated by the individual states and the federal govern-ment. Private schools, on the other hand, are thought to be largely apo-litical—removed from the vagaries of politics because they are essen-tially free of direct bureaucratic oversight from the government.

The tradition of lay leadership in public education reflects a sense that education is not a highly technical endeavor; it is open to public scrutiny and guidance and best administered through democratic or political mechanisms that should advance the values of the local com-munity. However, lest we romanticize the idea of democracy, remember that the majority is not always right: segregation in Southern schools was not repealed by the will of the majority expressed in the polling booth but in courts through litigation. Indeed, because the geographic communities that make up school districts play host to internal con-flicts between different constituencies with competing visions of edu-cation, an administrative apparatus has emerged around education to mediate these conflicts and run schools. Yet, as economists like Fried-man and "public choice" theory adherents such as Chubb and Moe have noted, such bureaucracies can also represent the preferences of special interests, rather than citizens within the community. And inasmuch as democratic politics are majoritarian and defy consensus making, the political organization of public schooling can marginalize the needs of those with little political power. So, depending on one's perspective, people are motivated to participate in democratic or political models of public schooling either out of a sense of civic responsibility or out of a desire to exert power and control (or both).

Thus, despite any connotations of the term, the idea of *political* control is appealing on a basic level, particularly in its emphasis on the public good aspects of education and the central role afforded to citizens through voting. But because it is manifest through bureaucratic structures, even "direct democratic control" blunts the power of citizens to effect change in schools, and their preferences can be trumped by the power of better organized special interests. It can be argued that private schools, by eschewing political control, offer a more direct link between the school organization and the preferences of the consumer. Hence, although the political governance of public schools give the citizen, voter, and taxpayer a role in the governing process, they have relatively little immediate recourse for leveraging any dissatisfaction with the public schools they are compelled to support.

THE SCIENCE OF SCHOOLING

In a second model, education can be viewed as a science, not unlike medicine in its capacity to address problems by leveraging evidence-based remedies. In its purest form, such a system would be run along technocratic lines, with skilled experts making decisions according to specialized knowledge of social and organizational ills and their appropriate solutions. In this line of thinking, education itself can best be thought of as a "treatment" administered by these experts according to professional perspectives on specific individual and community needs. (Indeed, many of the early advocates of public schooling saw universal education as the remedy to wider societal ills.) As in other professions, practitioners are largely accountable to the professional norms of their field, rather than to political pressures, commercial considerations, or popular opinion. They are motivated largely out of a sense of responsibility to their work or passion and commitment for what they do (although they may also be paid quite nicely in some fields). And the decisions of these education experts are informed by research on educational problems and treatments. Inasmuch as education is a profession, there would be a body of unique, specialized knowledge available to practitioners, and entry into the ranks would be limited to those demonstrating the necessary capabilities or mastery of that knowledge. For this more meritocratic model in education, people would be given positions in school systems based on their abilities, instead of political affiliations or personal connections.

Largely because of the corruption that was associated with political control of early public schooling, reformers in the last century looked to rationalize public education systems in the United States. Progressives sought to limit the influence of special interests by moving from political control of school governance to more professional models. School administration became a field of study in universities where experts could train new cadres of leaders and practitioners in the arcane knowledge of their profession. Reformers attempted to organize schools on state-of-the-art principles from administrative science, where "best practices" would prevail. These ideas are very much in evidence in many ways. The continued quasi-monopolies granted to education schools—acting as gatekeepers of access to education careers—reflect the effort to professionalize teaching and administration, for instance, not unlike medical schools. The field of special education represents another prime example of this medical-style model, where individual students are diagnosed, the diagnosis being drawn from research on various conditions, and then specific treatments are applied to those conditions. More recently, the emphasis on scientifically based research in the No Child Left Behind legislation and the creation of the Institute of Education Sciences in the Federal Department of Education also echo this perspective.

Yet while it makes sense to entrust the education of our children to the people who are most knowledgeable and capable in this area, a reliance on experts also implies other factors that may not be so appealing. For example, professional expertise in a mass endeavor such as education is distributed in somewhat of a hierarchical fashion, with front-line educators often taking direction from school and district officials, who in turn implement state and federal directives—not to mention the advice of professional and research organizations and reform advocates. Hierarchy and top-down regulation breed bureaucracy, which can shift power away from local considerations, or even from popular sentiments. And "best practices" administered by bureaucracies leave little room for tailoring a service around individual needs and preferences. If the consensus of expertise guides education, distinctions between "public" and "private" delivery systems might be less consequential in terms of substance, if not funding and governance. However, such a consensus would also guide public funding, leaving experimental or outdated educational approaches that fall outside of expert-designated best practices to private schools.

Yet people often resent being told what to do by experts, whether in regards to diet and nutrition, art appreciation, or the environment. Indeed, experts are often wrong.[18] And popular resentment is especially evident in an area such as schooling where virtually everyone has some experience with the system and has preferences and opinions about the correct way of doing things. If education is a science akin to medicine, we would value the critical judgments of elite cadres of experts, just as we do with oncologists and surgeons making decisions about cancer treatment. But if education is a more common and accessible enterprise, then self-professed experts are simply usurping the power of the average citizen regarding the best use of his or her tax money or of the parent regarding the best education of his or her child. Inasmuch as there is a body of knowledge on the field of education that is not readily accessible to the average person, that elevates the importance of expert opinions over the desires of nonexperts, including voters, taxpayers, and parents. However, this is problematic when one considers the intimate knowledge a parent has regarding his or her child, and the scientific model denigrates this personal knowledge, as it is trumped by the trained expert who has much less familiarity with an individual child's circumstances.

SCHOOLING THROUGH MARKETS

When we consider schooling in a business paradigm, where schools have to compete with each other to attract consumers, education markets offer a third model for school governance. Although such markets can be configured in various ways, they all share the two basic tenets of consumer choice and competition between providers.[19] For instance, charter schools and private schools—including those supported through vouchers and tuition tax credits—often exhibit elements of competition for students. The intriguing aspect of this approach is that it does not dictate curriculum packages or instructional approaches to failing public schools. Instead, frustrated by failed efforts to micromanage reforms, this approach advances from the desire to capitalize on the ideas of many on-the-ground actors—advancing from the insight that people are motivated by self-interest and that their behaviors (and those of the organizations in which they work) can be shaped to meet particular objectives if the appropriate incentive schemes are in play. Consequently, it establishes structural incentives, changing the institutional environment of the floundering public school sector to better reflect the efficiency and effectiveness of the private sector. Rather than assuming that one set of best practices will fit all students, this approach localizes governance so that parents can find the right educational experience that fits their child.

The appeal of these arrangements is often highlighted in juxtaposition to other models of schooling. Technocratic and political paradigms for education are thought to engender top-down directives, bureaucratic control, standardization, inefficiency, and ineffectiveness; however, market forces—as evident in other sectors—are thought to promote innovation and responsiveness to diverse consumer preferences. People do things out of self-interest, according to this logic. Once this is acknowledged, proponents contend that we can then structure incentives around education to shape desired behaviors. Thus, by trading bureaucratic sticks for economic carrots, markets can promote freedom in education: the opportunity for a small group of educators or community activists to start a new school around a fresh idea, for instance; and the right of parents to select the best school for their children, regardless of political/bureaucratic boundaries or administrative directives.

The multitude of school reforms of the last few decades demonstrates the various shapes that education markets can assume. Charter schools and vouchers, for instance, incorporate essential aspects of education markets, including consumer choice and provider competition. And there is a more established market in schooling in the United States. While we may not immediately think of markets when we consider our local private school, these religious, independent nonprofit or for-profit schools rely on the choices of consumers, since the schools are usually funded largely through tuition. And private schools in the United States are much more autonomous than public schools and must compete, increasingly so, with other private schools, with public (and charter) schools, and even with the homeschooling option. Indeed, even nonprofit schools have had to adopt business-style practices such as marketing in order to compete.[20] Actually, as some reformers have noted, the idea of markets for education is not so exotic as it may seem. Markets for higher education (which include both public and private institutions) have been in operation for years, with prospective students enjoying a range of options, and colleges competing through marketing and other practices, for the attention of those students.[21]

Indeed, as many advocates for market models in education have bluntly noted, market arrangements are the preferred paradigm in many, if not most, other aspects of our lives. We want to choose between competing vendors when we select our food, clothes, cars, homes, and entertainment. And that competition works well in many areas—consider consumer electronics, for instance—to simultaneously drive down prices and ramp up quality by forcing producers to develop innovations. While the U.S. Postal Service may have a (perhaps overstated) reputation for mediocrity and inefficiency, Federal Express, United Parcel Service, DHL, and a number of other private operations compete to rush your package to "the right place at the right time" and for the right price. Thus, it seems commonsensical that markets offer distinct advantages for consumers, and since the superior outcomes of private schools suggest that these same forces can effectively leverage improved performance in education, market advocates have offered a number of reforms to harness these forces in improving educational options for children. Charter schools, although technically public schools, are modeled on private schools in that they are largely independent and must compete to attract students to choose them. Voucher and tuition tax credit programs go even further, using public (or, in some cases private) funds to send children from failing public schools to private schools, thereby embracing the private sector to create more market-like competition for the public sector.

Yet, while markets for education can harness structural incentives to encourage greater effectiveness, efficiency, and innovation in education, critics have noted that markets are also associated with inequality.[22] For instance, inner-city communities may have less access to affordable credit or fresh groceries when the market is left to its own devices, just as rural communities often have access to fewer services if delivering such services to a thinly populated geographical region is not profitable for providers. And the invisible hand has done little to level out generational chasms of wealth and poverty—indeed, it may widen these gaps. Consequently, critics have expressed some concerns about the potential of liberated choice and competition in education. Could it be that markets for education would make the academically rich even richer, while the disadvantaged could fall further behind? Would wealthier, whiter, and more ambitious families use choice to avoid sending their children to schools attended by minority and economically disadvantaged children? As motivated parents pull their children out of poorer schools, will the students left behind sink further in a declining academic environment? Or will the market open up opportunities for students trapped in failing schools and put competitive pressures on schools to improve, even for nonchoosers? While there has been much hypothesizing about the potential pitfalls of choice and competition, the growing numbers of studies on these questions do not appear to have answered all these questions but only seem to fuel the politicized debates about the appropriateness of markets in education.[23]

Still, in a sense, debates such as these illustrate where one of the main advantages of education markets comes to the foreground. While researchers and other experts can argue about the relative benefits or drawbacks of different types of schemes, and while politicians and other officials can battle over whose agenda will win out, markets bypass these squabbles and give the ultimate power to the consumer. In that regard, markets are seen as apolitical in that they can preempt the political conflicts around standards or textbooks, for instance, that mire much of our education system in inefficiency and bureaucracy. Rather than one group getting its way, many different preferences can be satisfied as multiple options become available in a market system. Moreover, instead of faceless experts declaring policy diktats that affect a child, education markets have a popular-democratic element in that those decisions would be placed in the caring hands of those who best know the child's needs. In light of the generations of targeted and incremental tinkering with the school system that have failed in the past, markets for education get to the heart of the matter—bypassing the political and technical remedies and reconfiguring the actual incentive structures that shape schooling. For many observers, this explains the relative success of private schools and justifies the expansion of private models for public schools.

The Chronic Tension of Conflicting Models

The fact that Americans have never settled on a single model for their school system suggests one of the primary reasons for the chronic dissatisfaction with education in this country. While each model for school governance has its advantages, any one model cannot predominate without invalidating important values and upsetting important constituencies associated with the other two competing models. For instance, politicians love to point out problems with the schools and often advance plans that would give more power to . . . well, politicians. Congressionally mandated federal interventions, or state and mayoral takeovers of city school systems, may appear to be appropriate reactions to entrenched failure in local schools. Yet it is important to keep in mind that these kinds of government-based measures also represent a challenge to popular and professional models of schooling, since—whatever the rhetoric—such politics-driven reforms actually sideline the views of local parents as well as educational experts.

Similarly, technocratic administration of school systems is attractive in many respects. It seems obvious that we would want knowledgeable professionals with expertise in the issues inherent in complex educational systems to run our schools and districts. However, ceding control to specialists comes at the cost of disempowering the citizens who pay for public schools and the families that use them. "Putting parents in charge" of their children's education sounds like a self-evidently excellent idea.[24] After all, parents seem better positioned than any bureaucrat or expert to know what is best for their children, and some then make a moral argument that they should thus be empowered to make educational choices on behalf of their children. Yet there is also a moral argument that other citizens should not have to pay for those choices, through taxes or through other social costs that could follow from poor choices. Moreover, there is a case to be made that the larger society owes each child the best educational experience possible, based not on a parent's preferences or background but on the most state-of-the-art knowledge on teaching and learning.

Although some might argue that these conflicts can produce creative tensions that balance the different societal impulses we place on our schools, the fact remains that these tensions have also led to the rise of institutions that embody essential contradictions, leading to ineffectiveness.[25] As one prime example, local school boards are structured to channel democratically expressed preferences of voters regarding the function of the community's schools. But school boards and district officials are also expected to consider the cumulative expertise of research on teaching, learning, and organizations—knowledge that is often manifest through state and federal requirements that limit local district autonomy. Moreover, market-like forces are also at play. Dissatisfied citizens have another option besides the political mechanism of voting to remove their offending representatives; they can also "vote with their feet," in the famous observation of Charles Tiebout.[26] They exercise this economic-style behavior in the political realm in many instances by pulling their children from the district's schools to attend a private school or a public school in another district when the option is available.

In fact, the lay leadership design of districts may position public school boards to address education issues in the community, yet this governance structure is highly susceptible to the efforts of even small groups of well organized voters. Relatively few community members from the larger public participate in school board elections (especially compared with, say, presidential politics, in which individuals or small groups are much less likely to have an impact). While the broader public is forced to pay for the schools, they largely leave the field of educational governance to officials, bureaucrats, teachers unions, and other groups that may organize around topical questions such as abstinence education or intelligent design. So the institutions of "direct democratic control" of schools create a disconnect: the people actually funding schools exercise little control, while organized groups see the opportunity to control or "capture" those resources and institutions. Meanwhile, those most directly affected by school policies—families with children in the schools—often exercise no more influence on how or what their children are taught than does the indifferent, childless retiree down the street.

So an institution such as the local school board, which epitomizes America's commitment to local democracy in action, illustrates the schizophrenia of school governance in the United States. Similar pathologies are evident around other institutions and aspects of public education: curriculum development groups, teacher colleges, state boards and departments, professional and research organizations, federal agencies, educational management companies, think tanks, and advocacy organizations. While each of these may represent a political/democratic, scientific, or market impulse, they also incorporate elements of the other models. This hodgepodge represents an inherently conservative system of checks and balances. But this messy institutional mixture also hinders efficient decision making and improvement efforts within that system.

As the late political economist Albert O. Hirschman wisely noted almost four decades ago,[27] other institutions besides education also conflate different models in their design, leading to structural compromises that ultimately hinder their efficacy. Yet American public education itself seems to epitomize this conflation, as an institution structured to respond to democratic discontent from the wider voting public that instead provokes market-style reactions by unhappy customers who use pedestrian political behavior: voting with their feet to move to another district. All the while, it assumes, but does not necessarily incorporate, channels for technical expertise. As almost anyone would agree, pathologies will inevitably ensue as a result of public education's position as a "lazy oligopolist"[28]—with multiple districts collusively controlling most of the market, with little incentive to compete with each other or otherwise make effective changes.

In Hirschman's logic, there are two obvious solutions.[29] One is to reform educational governance to make it even more democratic. This could mean making schools more directly accountable not to parents but to the wider voting public on even mundane issues, cutting out intermediate players such as boards, bureaucrats, and unions and also ending the influence of other advocacy groups. There have been radical experiments with this approach in the past, although they tend to be isolated and difficult to sustain.[30] Of course, this would be unwieldy and, as we have seen, would also mean disenfranchising constituencies with legitimate claims on education: teachers, experts, citizen groups, and even parents. In view of the general distrust of state-enforced equality efforts, this option is simply not politically viable on a large scale.

But the second solution in Hirschman's framework has genuine appeal in the current policy climate. In this logic, public education should be moved more squarely into the realm of markets so that we treat schools as businesses and acknowledge that the students and their parents are truly customers who consume the schools' services.

Positioned as such, dissatisfied customers would be encouraged to select other schools that could better meet their needs. And schools would have to strive to attract and satisfy customers. As many economists have pointed out, moving to this market-based model could then create the competitive dynamics that would force schools to innovate and improve their services, even for families who are not active choosers, since a "rising tide lifts all boats."[31] There is evidence of such a dynamic with charter schools and programs that provide vouchers or tax credits to fund children attending private schools.

This book offers some illumination on efforts to move to a singular model based on competitive markets for education. While political and scientific models each present us with their own inherent problems, which are compounded when compromised by the other models, the market solution is said to offer a tidy fix for our schools that bypasses all the political entanglements and expert debates of the other models. As market advocates have noted, market relationships can guarantee that everyone is happy: no one is forced to participate in a market transaction, and people are not likely to participate unless they recognize a distinct benefit for themselves.[32] And just as the common wisdom shows that our public schools have been in a state of crisis, common sense suggests the way forward. The growing bureaucratic and special interest apparatus associated with continued government administration (the "blob" or "direct democratic control") appears to parallel the popularly perceived decline in American education.[33] At the same time, markets demonstrate an undeniable ability to satisfy customers in many sectors of life, including private education. So common sense would dictate that we should apply this model to public schools.

In fact, this is not only a matter of special interests and policy advocates using crisis rhetoric to advance a particular policy agenda. Prominent and respected theoreticians and scholars have outlined a compelling critique of public administration of services such as education. And concurrent with that critique is an attractive prescription for the pathologies of the public sector, which identifies remedies in market-style mechanisms associated with the private sector. We describe this "public choice theory" and its market-theory variant in education, in the next chapter, but it is important to note that the logic outlined in public choice, while applicable to many different sectors, has been particularly influential in the area of education policy. It is the guiding logic behind a slew of popular reform policies, including public school choice, charter schools, tuition tax credits, and vouchers for private schools.

Although public choice recommendations to move toward a more market-oriented model of schooling make sense on many levels, and play to common wisdom on the relative merits of the private sector, they are based on what turns out to be a questionable assumption. The private sector is indeed a superior dynamic for providing a wide range of goods and services, but the question is whether, as public choice theorists assume, this is also true for education. While popular perceptions might hold that the private sector provides a better educational experience, and chronic concerns about a crisis in public school effectiveness appear to affirm the common wisdom, there has been a long and simmering debate in the research community about the extent to which this may be true.

We have known for years that private schools exhibit, on average, higher levels of academic outcomes. But we also know that private schools tend to serve, on average, more affluent families—families that offer many advantages associated with school success. So the question then becomes whether the higher achievement evident in private schools reflects greater private school effectiveness or simply the more advantaged family backgrounds of the students who attend those schools. If it is a matter of more effective organization in private schooling, then such findings would support public choice–inspired policy efforts to replicate or expand private schools, or the attributes they embody, to be available to the greatest number of children. If higher academic performance in private schools is only a matter of more advantaged students, then—since it is impossible for policymakers to replicate those students' backgrounds—they should instead consider efforts to create programs and educational experiences that support equitable educational opportunities.

But this is a very difficult question to address. Student achievement is a result of multiple family and school factors working simultaneously and at a number of levels. It is not just parent income levels but values, resources, peers, and many other factors that shape student outcomes. There are few good ways to disentangle all of this given that students are not randomly assigned to public and private schools. One approach is to try to control for these multiple factors, using sophisticated statistical mechanisms to distinguish student background influences from factors at play in school—factors that school choice seeks to incentivize through competition-based policies. Efforts to control for background factors work best when researchers can compare large and representative samples of students in different types of schools, while controlling for demographic differences in student populations in those schools. If the data on achievement and demographics are comprehensive and reliable, the comparison will then give us a good sense of how much of the variations in achievement are related to differences in schools—between public and private schools, in this case. Another approach is to measure changes in student achievement over time in public and private schools (again, after considering the substantial differences in the populations served by public and private schools). Any differences in the rate of growth between students in public and private schools can then be attributed to differences in effectiveness between the sectors. In the chapters that follow, we do both.

2 *The Theory of Markets for Schooling*

More than any other nation, the United States has placed a profound faith in the idea of public education, and yet at the same time Americans are deeply skeptical of the institutions they created to educate future generations. Well before other countries embarked on similar ventures, Americans created systems to provide virtually universal access to schools, believing that all students have a right to an education and that the larger community benefits when citizens are more educated. Yet, for much of their history, Americans have expressed a widespread and deep consensus that public schools in general are failing. And although many Americans value their local public schools, it seems that few media reports, speeches, or commentaries from policy and opinion makers appear without some harsh mention about the general state of public education. While the basis and standards for this evaluation are not always explicit, the assessment is itself crystal clear and compelling: although Americans support the notion of public education, they belittle the government institutions established to pursue that goal. And much of the evidence on American student achievement reported in both the policy and popular media seems to lend support to this concern.

Indeed, there is ample evidence of widespread failure in the public education system. For instance, perhaps the most influential study of school achievement of the last quarter century reported that performance "on the Scholastic Aptitude Test headed downward year after year . . . [and] American students consistently did worse than students from other nations on international achievement tests."[1] Other policy advocates observe that the stagnation and decline in U.S. achievement is particularly evident in terms of a decreasing number of high-scoring

American students, especially when compared with other nations.[2] More recently, more high-level commissions of business, government, and education interests confirmed that the school system is failing, noting that high school graduation rates have been stagnant for the last four decades, with U.S. student performance mediocre, at best, on international comparisons, despite a tremendous increase in resources and reforms devoted to school improvement.[3] A recent documentary chronicles the "crisis for U.S. schools regarding chronically low scores in math and science indicators."[4] An economic competitiveness guru thus pointed out that "All Americans know that the public education system is a serious weakness. . . . The problem is not money—America spends a great deal on public education . . . The real problem is the structure of our education system."[5] Consequently, it is not at all uncommon to see popular commentators argue that public schooling necessarily "gets terrible results. Private, parochial and charter schools get better results."[6] And the reasons behind public schools' poor results have been laid bare by prominent researchers: "because the schools are owned and operated by the government."[7]

This criticism of public sector institutions is hardly unique to education. It is an established truism that government-run organizations are less effective than their private sector counterparts. Unfortunately for taxpayers and citizens alike, we often see voluminous evidence of waste, corruption, political manipulation, and ineffectiveness in state-administered endeavors. Congressional earmarks for pet projects, Pentagon overpayments for hammers, toilet seats, and other everyday equipment, bloated state and federal bureaucracies that fail to provide basic services—there are innumerable instances of the public sector failing to adequately secure the interests of the public. In the common wisdom, it is not just "city hall" that is unresponsive: FEMA, TARP, and the United States Post Office are also punch lines for governmental ineptitude.[8] On the other hand, the private sector appears to foster venerated traits such as innovation, efficiency, and responsiveness to consumer demand. Consequently, Americans often express preferences for private alternatives to public transportation, state-run health care, government-administered pensions, government insurance, package delivery—and, when possible, education.[9]

In fact, policymakers across the globe have also embraced this perspective on state administration of services for the public. While Soviet-era bureaucracies maintained direct state control of economic func-

... many nations also placed th... "commanding heights" ... l enterprises, as w... many public-service ef- ... ownership or control ... tional airlines, telecom ... es for histori... re administered by gov- ... of comp... from the private sector. the reemergence of the ...sm and governing phi- ...rovision as the default ...ervices. Frustrated with ...trenchment, and stag- and Argentina to New ...se shifted these efforts t the behest of interna- ...terprise could provide ...han could bloated gov-

...ainly have a unifying ...parate sectors and lo- a universal theory of ...around various policy ...ling critique of public ...ng diagnosis of state- ...s the sole remedy for ...med body of research ...ining this theoretical ...on in its definition of the problem and consequent prescription, we focus on three of the key assumptions that guide this perspective.

Should Governments Run Schools?

We have witnessed a continued global shift in the provision of many public services. Policymakers are increasingly drawn to market models for organizing public services because public-sector entities are thought to be inefficient and ineffective at delivering services both to the individual and to the larger community. When we look at the reasons for superior effectiveness of organizations in the private sector compared with government enterprises, a clear and coherent pattern emerges, accompanied by a theory of human behavior to explain these patterns. Theorists have argued that waste and unresponsiveness in government-run entities are symptomatic of pathologies inherent in the public sector. This theoretical perspective has been quite influential, embraced by many policymakers of different political stripes in recent years.

The diagnosis of public sector underperformance centers on the idea of how different incentives for organizations are unique to each sector and suggests an appealing remedy that draws from the success of for-profit organizations. While we explain this perspective in greater detail below, essentially, theorists contend that private sector organizations exist in an institutional environment where—as autonomous organizations not dependent on government—they must compete with each other to survive, recognizing that they have to attract consumers or clients by offering a better quality option than their alternatives. These external incentives then shape the internal structures of these autonomous organizations within that sector, rewarding organizations that are lean, innovative, and focused on pleasing the customer. In this line of thinking, however, government sector organizations do not thrive in the same competitive environment; shielded from competition, they operate under incentive structures that reward bureaucrats who can build up their budgets, expand their power, and enforce dictates handed down from higher levels of the bureaucracy.

Of course, many people assume that certain services, such as public education, are so essential to democratic societies that they cannot be left to the vagaries of private markets and must instead be entrusted to public institutions. Indeed, some values we hold for public education, such as universal access, would seem to defy business models. While we want all children, regardless of background or ability to pay, to have access to quality schooling, businesses are designed to meet the demands and preferences of defined groups of consumers and have the inherent ability to exclude those unable to afford the goods and services they sell. Thus, we have created public education institutions governed by elected representatives and administered by the state to guarantee universal access to education for all.

But an influential school of thought has challenged this common wisdom, especially in areas such as public schooling. As its most prominent public figure, the late economist Milton Friedman is widely recognized as among the first modern thinkers to challenge the accepted wisdom regarding the basic model of public education. Friedman contested the common notion that public education had to be provided by public—or, what he preferred to call "government-run"—schools.[11] Instead, Friedman argued that, while the state has an essential interest in the general *provision* of education for all children, it does not then follow that governments must actually administer the schools. According to this perspective, government is effective at collecting revenue but not managing services. In fact, in view of the popular perceptions of the myriad government failures noted earlier, the actual provision of education to our children might best be removed from the public sector. This perspective, encompassing a diagnosis of the problem with publicly administered education, and the subsequent remedy, has emerged as one of the most prominent theories in political science.

PUBLIC CHOICE THEORY

Friedman's main insight was that, while the externalities or broader effects associated with mass education (or lack thereof) justify public funding, they do not justify public provision or management of a system of public education. Instead, such services could be contracted to private providers who would then serve the public's needs more effectively because they are driven by competitive incentives. He lamented the fact that mass education had developed through state action along nonmarket lines and thus proposed a voucher plan in which the government would provide parents, rather than public schools, with education funding that they could then use to purchase an education at a state-run or private school.

Friedman and his followers believed that thus subverting state monopolistic control of public education would open up the school sector to competitive market forces, which would then lead to greater innovation and better outcomes. This system would expand the notion of "public education" to include private schools, which are thought to be better organized to respond to public demand because they are receptive to competitive market incentives. Then schools will be subjected to competitive incentives to adopt more effective practices in order to satisfy parents' preferences for better academic options. In such a scenario, parents will pull their children from poorly performing schools, which must improve their services or risk "going out of business."[12]

Friedman initially made his argument from a libertarian perspective, arguing against government involvement in order to promote the greater end: individual freedom. But as his critique advanced, it would coalesce with an emerging theoretical perspective on public administration. Public choice theory is an influential approach to public policy, particularly in its diagnosis of the pathologies of the public sector and its prescriptions for reform drawing on market mechanisms.[13]

Public choice theory adopts economic assumptions in assessing government failures, which are viewed as the natural outcome when governments produce goods and services.[14] While market failures are evident in areas such as pollution or overuse of antibiotics, where individual self-interest can lead to less than optimal outcomes overall,[15] public choice theory focuses on government failure as a factor inherent in public administration—echoed in Ronald Reagan's famous dictum that "government is not the solution to our problem; government is the problem."[16]

In applying economic analyses to nonmarket activities that have traditionally been beyond the purview of market-style values, public choice theory embraces on behalf of the public sector the rational-choice assumptions we see with consumers and producers operating in the business world. While more romantic conceptions portray governments as integral to protecting the public from profit-seeking private interests, public choice theorists view government bureaucracies as calculating to advance their own interests or those of the private interests that control them. Thus, bureaucrats typically work to enlarge their budgets or advance the special interests that have "captured" them.[17] Therefore, government agencies are thought to implement rules and regulations to protect corporate interests from competition or litigation, not to protect citizens.

STRUCTURAL PROBLEMS OF THE STATE SECTOR

The component of public choice theory focused on education has been called "market theory" by adherents and detractors alike.[18] Prominent critics of government administration of public education, including diverse figures such as economist Gary Becker, the late historian E.G. West,[19] political theorist Paul Peterson, and education scholar James Tooley,[20] are associated with market-based evaluations of state-administered education. Similarly, public choice logic is evident in the influential Chicago school of economics as it is applied to social policy issues, where Friedman and his colleagues advocated for the privatization of public services, including education—an approach that was embraced with particular force with the Pinochet-era adoption of school vouchers in Chile, as advocated by Friedman's students.[21]

Typically, the analyses of these individuals point to the relative lack of choice, competition, and organizational autonomy in the public sector. According to public choice theory, instead of serving the elusive concept of the "public good," actors in the public sector pursue their own interests by creating "fiefdoms" within and through bureaucracies.[22] Consequently, from this perspective, public education organizations are necessarily geared toward the needs of the adults they represent rather than those of children.[23] As such, instead of promoting the effective and efficient use of public resources, public officials work to extend their authority and thwart any potential competitors[24]—for example, by limiting the profession to unionized teachers trained in state-certified preparation programs or preventing nonstate schools from accessing public funds. Since they are not bound by bottom-line economic imperatives, government administrators are thought to be inherently incapable of taking account of costs, leading to chronic cost overruns, inefficiencies, and lack of responsiveness to the needs of the people—students, in the case of public schools—using their services.[25]

This logic has been both illuminating and influential in diagnosing public education's failings. Politicians, reformers, columnists, and popular documentarians such as those behind *Waiting for Superman* and *The Cartel* put the blame for the apparent shortcomings of schools on the "education establishment" of teachers unions, school administrators, and school boards that have reoriented public education to their own ends. Friedman explicitly encouraged this view, claiming that public schools "are really not public at all but simply private fiefs primarily of the administrators and the union officials."[26] Whereas some historians present a romantic view of the growth of public education as an effort to expand learning opportunities for all, public choice theorists see this instead as an effort by a growing bureaucracy to extinguish competition from independent (and more effective) schools.[27] The result, in this line of thinking, is a self-perpetuating bureaucratic hierarchy where schools have little control over their own resources, have no competition, have no incentive to improve, and are thus mired in mediocrity.

While other sectors flourish because competitive forces drive innovation, the institutionalized monopoly that is public education is its downfall, according to this perspective. As notable public choice theorists John Chubb and Terry Moe argued in their landmark treatise on American schools, public education is governed through institutions of "direct democratic control," with elected school boards attempting to negotiate the conflicting demands on public education.[28] Because Americans have established a system where school districts have essentially divvied up territory between them, they must each consequently accommodate competing special interests within those districts, thus serving none very effectively. Bureaucracies then emerge to mediate between these conflicting claims on topics such as curriculum and instruction, personnel, and resources. Since elected boards and unelected bureaucracies are liable to be "captured" by special interests, according to public choice theory, better organized interests such as teachers unions are able to assert their own interests ahead of those of less organized constituencies such as the parents of poor children, for instance.

Certainly, the bureaucratic establishment still champions reforms to improve schools, but these efforts are more symbolic, according to public choice theorists, designed not to improve the quality of schooling so much as to present the appearance of concern, even while shoring up control of the system. In fact, the established system is inherently incapable of substantive reform on its own, absent external incentives, since its actors will always truly focus instead on their own ends.[29] Friedman noted exactly this in discussing teacher unions: "there is one thing you can depend on everybody to do, and that is to put his interests above yours. That's what we are doing, and that's what they are doing."[30] The key insight of public choice theory, then, is to recognize, acknowledge, and then harness this rational self-interestedness in creating incentive structures that drive systemic improvements.

THE PROMISE OF AUTONOMOUS ORGANIZATIONS IN COMPETITIVE CLIMATES

Of course, when the private sector fails to produce on its own a universal public service such as education (or produces negative outcomes such as pollution that become a public burden), policymakers note these "market failures" and often respond by creating public institutions to meet the need. This is why most market democracies have publicly administered pension schemes, transportation infrastructures, and public safety arrangements, for instance, as well as substantial state involvement in, if not outright authority over, health care systems. Public choice, however, holds that government administration of such institutions is the second-best alternative, since public officials and institutions are susceptible to the influence of defined groups whose interests are not aligned with those of the general public.[31]

Since the lack of competition is thought to lead to a bureaucratic monolith, public-choice logic asserts that market-style institutional arrangements represent the best remedy. This thinking calls for largely deregulated, autonomous public agencies to be managed as business-style enterprises in competition with other providers—public and private—thereby giving citizens or "consumers" an array of options. That is, these prescriptions focus on reorienting organizations so that the self-interested motivation spurs organizational behaviors that have a broader, positive effect.

This may seem like a contradiction. Why would elevating individual self-interest as a driving force lead to broader social benefits? Of course, we all expect that this happens constantly in the private sector. The "invisible hand" of the marketplace allows both consumers and providers to seek their own advantage, which then results in innovation, increases in quality and options, lower prices, better matching of consumers with their preferred goods and services, more effective service providers, economic development, and general prosperity. Public choice theory simply seeks to bring the same forces and benefits to the public sector in areas such as education. That is, it sees both the individual and collective aspects of education as more effectively and appropriately produced by organizations driven by self-interest.

Yet, while public choice theory assumes that private institutions are superior owing to autonomy, choice, and competition, most advocates do not necessarily seek pure market arrangements for public institutions. There is often an acknowledged need for continued state funding for public services, since the potential for free-riders could lead to underproduction of social services if left to individual private payers.[32] Alternatively, government funding can be individualized to users through vouchers, for instance. However, in embracing the economic assumption of individual self-interestedness, public choice theorists follow Friedman in denying that direct government production of public goods is optimal, or even preferable. Consequently, public choice supports decentralization and organizational autonomy to better approximate market-style arrangements.

Instead of mandating specific policies and practices—as is typical in education reform—public choice seeks to fashion external, competitive incentives to guide autonomous organizations into desired behavior and, hopefully, outcomes.[33] In fact, policymakers influenced by this perspective have adopted market-style incentives in a number of areas both to free up consumer-style choice for citizens and to address the problems widely associated with bureaucratic monopolies.[34] In this way, they reject the technocratic/scientific version of education management in favor of the idea that anyone can be an expert in educational matters. Such policies cast the citizen as a consumer empowered to choose between different service providers, as would be seen in the business arena. In order to encourage diverse options, the approach emphasizes the need for an array of small, local, autonomous institutions for delivering public services.[35]

Although this perspective is based on the observation that private, autonomous organizations are more effective because they are free of government oversight, the way to promote these objectives is not necessarily by "privatizing" state-administered entities such as schools (although, in addition to proposing vouchers, Friedman and others also argued that public schools should be made private).[36] Instead, education reformers inspired by public choice thinking argue for creating an institutional environment that causes schools and districts to reorient their focus away from the needs of officials or special interests and toward the needs of the people using the services.[37] This can be accomplished by liberating consumer choice, allowing new providers to open largely independent schools, and deregulating existing schools in terms of supply and operations, which will then create the appropriate opportunities and incentive structures for public schools to respond to demands for improvement. Reformers expect public schools will then emulate private schools by being more effective and responsive to consumers.

By freeing up both the demand and supply side of public services, these policies elevate what political economist Albert O. Hirschman described as the "exit" option where consumers can "vote with their feet" for their preferred service, thereby giving service providers the incentives they need to be efficient and responsive to consumer demands.[38] Although consumers' preferences for services might vary or even conflict—for instance, some may want a more traditional curriculum while others may want an experimental or progressive education for their child—the market gives providers the incentive to offer differentiated options, with consumers then sorting themselves into homogenous "clusters" defined by their common preferences. Policies that promote such arrangements for public organizations are inspired by the insight that, owing to their autonomy and location in a more competitive environment, private organizations are better able to sense the incentive to respond to customers, and government agencies can also be placed in more competitive institutional climates. This insight is rooted in an increasingly popular theoretical perspective that is guiding much of education policy making.

The Theory of Markets for Schooling

Market theory—sometimes referred to as "incentivism" by its proponents—serves as a basis for the diagnosis and prescription for the ills of public administration in schooling.[39] In general, theorists believe that education has been inappropriately positioned outside the purview of market forces and that competitive pressures must be brought into public education in order to incentivize individuals and organizations to act more effectively. This thinking is evident in areas such as merit pay and the removal of tenure for teachers and new efforts to pay students to attend classes or to improve their academic performance.[40]

But market theory has made its greatest impact in the area of organizational incentives. There, incentivist schemes in education advance from the public choice logic that the public school system is inherently incapable of improving itself because it is oriented around the needs of bureaucrats and other interests within the system and is not structured to be externally accountable to consumers.[41] Rather than requiring particular processes and procedures for educators, incentivism endorses general goal setting for schools and then giving these organizations the opportunity and motivation to create the best approaches for meeting those goals for themselves, which may differ based on entrepreneurial creativity, consumer preferences, and local conditions. If we want greater curricular diversity, incentives can be fashioned through policies that encourage schools to adopt new alternatives. If we want to promote social tolerance, policies can shape incentives that entice individual schools to serve different types of students. If we want to improve achievement, incentives can be arranged to encourage educators to do that.[42]

This last objective in particular has enthralled policymakers in recent years. Concerned about the mediocre performance of American public schools, the chronic gap between the achievement of affluent students and poor and minority students, and the incessant failure of the education system to make substantive and lasting improvements on its own, policymakers have sought to refashion the institutions of education by infusing them with competitive incentives. Thus, vouchers for students to attend private schools are intended to raise achievement for students using the vouchers, as well as to generate the competitive effects required to make public schools adopt more effective organizational behaviors that private schools are thought to utilize, or risk losing students and funding. Similarly, charter schools are publicly funded but independently (often privately) managed organizations, separated from traditional, local mechanisms for school governance and accountability in order to provide better alternatives for the families that choose them, as well as to provide competition for other local public schools.[43] Choice plans such as these have been advanced primarily under the logic that reforms of school governance can incentivize schools and improve achievement for students. Indeed, achievement is often the sole measure of the success of these programs, and such incentives can be unleashed through these programs because they allow family choice of schools and competition between schools for students—mechanisms we already admire in the private sector.

Some observers have expressed concern that such choice systems can also have negative consequences, particularly in two areas. First, since market forces generate winners and losers in other sectors, there is concern about students left behind in failing schools because their parents have relatively less access to the information, or less initiative, to make good choices for them.[44] Second, in contrast to this worry about individual failure, there is also some apprehension about organizational losers under a more market-driven system. That is, as some have noted, there is the distinct possibility that competitive forces could prevent failing schools from improving, as the students with higher academic aspirations leave for better schools, sending the failing or "sink" schools into further "spirals of decline."[45] Thus, even if competition and choice drive an overall improvement in quality, some see reason to fear that improvements would be distributed inequitably and that overall gains might come at the expense of further diminishment of opportunities and attainment for the most disadvantaged students.

Yet, according to market theorists, part of the beauty of a system based on competitive incentives is that it generates a self-correcting mechanism that promotes organizational effectiveness on the part of schools, thereby benefiting students. As competitive forces increasingly drive organizational behavior, schools are compelled to improve or risk losing students and funding—thus being closed either by authorizing bodies or by the marketplace when the customers look elsewhere. In fact, it is not even necessary for everyone to be wise and active consumers of educational options. Just as in other sectors—say, consumer electronics or automobiles—where most people are not connoisseurs or technical experts, there are wider benefits from the demand for innovation expressed by a relative few savvy consumers.[46] Similarly, in education, schools are expected to emulate the best practices of successful organizations in order to survive and succeed in the educational marketplace, where "a rising tide lifts all boats."[47] In fact, many market theorists have argued that competitive conditions not only drive overall improvements in quality but leave no child behind. Echoing the Hippocratic oath in medicine, they suggest that no choice program has been shown to cause any harm to students—"everyone wins."[10]

This incentivist thinking is evident to varying extents in an array of prominent policies representing some of the most prominent contemporary instances of school reform. In fact, while often not using the term, the current generation of self-described reformers holds quite fast to the basic elements of market theory.[49] For example, charter schools and voucher programs promote the idea that by injecting the incentive to compete for students, and enabled by their autonomy from district bureaucracies, public schools will then have the incentives and opportunities to act more like private schools in serving students more effectively, particularly in adopting more innovative and effective classroom practices. Merit pay plans assume that providing educators with incentives will encourage them to work harder and more effectively than they would otherwise. The Bush administration's No Child Left

Behind (NCLB) Act, the biggest shift in federal education policy since the 1960s, also focuses on organizational effects, requiring schools to demonstrate effectiveness through improvements in achievement. The sanctions for schools that fail to do this include reorganization and conversion to charter schools, which indicate again a focus on organizational effectiveness, and remedies to the organization as the key to improving achievement. Additionally, the Obama administration's Race to the Top competition uses massive federal resources to persuade states to open up the market for charter schools and adopt mechanisms that can be used for teacher incentive programs.

PRIMARY TENETS OF THE MARKET THEORY OF EDUCATION

Inspired by public choice, the incentivist prescription for schools assumes that organizations in the private sector obtain superior outcomes on metrics associated with consumer demand, such as academic achievement in education. Yet this overall assumption is situated in a sequence of logical, if unstated, presumptions.

Ineffectiveness of Public Administration

First, as noted above, the guiding presumption in this thinking is that private sector organizations—as well as more autonomous public organizations put into more competitive, market-like institutional climates—are more effective because they have an inherent institutional advantage over state-administered organizations. In demonstrating this, public choice theorists typically look to two measurable outcomes for evidence on that advantage: organizational effectiveness and user satisfaction. Taking the latter first, theorists consider the extent to which clients using a service are happy with the level of service they are receiving. In the private sector, businesses can measure this satisfaction simply by looking at the bottom line. Since government agencies are not typically focused on a balance sheet susceptible to loss of consumers, they are thought to be less responsive to the needs of those they are supposed to serve. But by giving people the ability to take their business elsewhere (as with the private sector), these agencies are forced to respond to users' preferences. The success of these policy changes are often determined by measures such as waiting lists or customer satisfaction surveys—both popular in discussions of school reform.[50] However, it is important to note that, while these reforms recast citizens as consumers of public services (an approach very popular with politicians seeking to run government like a business), a crucial difference is that they are not *paying* customers, since public funding is in fact picking up the tab.

But there are problems with these measures. It is not clear how accurate these new consumers are in assessing school quality, which represents a problem for reformers and policymakers seeking to improve the overall effectiveness of schools. Indeed, despite the attempts to equate longer waiting lists with superior school effectiveness, there is much evidence that parents often pick schools of questionable academic quality—a pattern that choice advocates both deny and lament. For instance, at one point the attorney general of Ohio moved to sue underperforming community (charter) schools in order to close them, since they were not closing to a lack of demand (as would have been predicted by market theory).[51] Similarly, several studies have shown that many parents, when given the option, are apt to choose academically inferior schools in some cases, focusing instead on other factors such as a school's racial composition or even simply its use of uniforms.[52] There are different ways to understand these patterns, including a dearth of good information on school quality, the primacy of other preferences besides academic effectiveness, or the possibility that some parents act irrationally (in theorists' terms) in choosing schools. But regardless of the reason, it is important to note that relying on simple measures of demand for a given school is a poor proxy for actual evidence of its effectiveness—especially in an era when policymakers expect that parental demand for better schools will drive quality improvements across the system.

Likewise, measures of consumer satisfaction can be inherently unreliable. Although such measures are often associated with private sector organizations that are concerned with consumer dissatisfaction, in fact, many such surveys of consumers only gauge approval for those currently using a given organization's services—thereby neglecting dissatisfied consumers who have already left for other options. Thus, they cannot be a measure of the success of, or satisfaction with, an organization if they exclude a defined pool of negative responses. And again, there are deeper questions as to whether parents are capable of determining school quality. Indeed, although market theorists often point to such measures for private or independent schools to demonstrate the success of their reforms, they often dismiss exactly such measures when public school parents give high grades to their own children's schools.[53]

So, in light of these concerns, many researchers and policymakers focus on a second measurable goal, academic achievement, which then in turn illuminates some other underlying assumptions of public choice theory.

Focus on Standardized Measures of Academic Achievement

The tendency to elevate academic performance as the ultimate measure of schools has been a prominent feature in American public discourse for the past few decades, going at least back to the famous *Nation at Risk* report of 1983.[54] Reformers and policymakers have focused primarily on standardized tests as measures of the general failures of public schools, as well as to test the potential of various reform efforts. Test scores allow for comparisons across time, space, schools, and students; they appear to be objective measures; they are relatively easy (and cheap) to gather; and they can be used to provide baseline objectives or diagnostic guidelines for schools, districts, states, and the nation. In addition, policy advocates frequently use test scores as a way to prove that the model they champion is superior. For instance, charter advocate Andrew Rotherham points to the disproportionate number of charter schools among the highest scoring schools in Massachusetts as evidence of their more effective institutional model.[55]

This type of thinking aims the focus largely on academic achievement as the primary indicator of school performance. It is fundamental in understanding how Americans look at their schools. Yet in considering the state of American education, it is important to remember that early reformers originally established public education in the fledgling republic in response to many concerns. The founders of "common schools"—the prototype for the American public school—would be puzzled by a singular focus on academic achievement as the primary purpose for public education and the measure of its success. They saw public education as a remedy for numerous societal ills related to new waves of immigration, increased economic diversity, and the emerging issues associated with an industrializing, urbanizing, and expanding America. Popular schooling, it was argued, would instill appropriate character, morals, and dispositions for segments of the population that otherwise lacked such attributes, at least according to the reformers. And, of course, there was also the economic argument, although it differed somewhat from the current focus on national economic competitiveness. In the 1830s and 1840s, education reformers made a direct appeal to business interests regarding the benefits of a workforce that was educated and trained—not simply in specific work skills, but trained in basic skills, attitudes, and values.[56] Thus, indicators of the success of this experiment were to be found not in standardized test scores but in the growing numbers of schools, higher attendance rates, and, hopefully, increasing social stability.

Almost two centuries later, Americans still place multiple, diverse, and sometimes contradictory responsibilities on their schools.[57] Besides reading, writing, and arithmetic, Americans also ask schools to teach civics as well as provide programs to counter bullying and teen pregnancy, to support child nutrition and national economic competitiveness, to offer athletic programs and technology training, and to house social services and career counseling. They ask their schools to nurture civic cohesion in what are distinct and often segregated communities, while training the next generation of workers to compete in the global economy. When these needs are not met, or when other societal challenges emerge, schools or whole school systems are easily—and often appropriately—identified as failing.

But in recent years, the idea of a failing school has come to have a much narrower meaning. Especially in the era since NCLB was passed, policymakers and the public are focusing increasingly and often exclusively on academic outcomes, and particularly academic achievement—usually stated in terms of the percentage of students meeting a level deemed to be proficient on a test—as the main measure of schools' effectiveness or failure. Many critics claim, with some reason, that this singular focus on academic achievement in turn leads to other problems: a school culture of teaching to the test, a narrowing of the curriculum, the diminishment of true learning, and a monolithic conception of education that marginalizes other important goals for schools.[58] For example, some community activists have called for the expansion of charter schools on the grounds that serving minority communities raises achievement. While there is something to be said for focusing on underserved groups, regardless of whether such a focus actually raises achievement, it is also worth remembering that such a focus then neglects the traditional common school objective for schools, which was to promote social cohesion and tolerance through exposure to different people and worldviews.[59]

Although we have some sympathy for these concerns and, like many, embrace multiple goals for schools, it is clear that academic achievement is now the dominant language of education policy and the primary argument used in promoting market remedies for failing schools. And this is due, at least in part, to the fact that indications of academic achievement are relatively easy to measure through standardized tests, compared with measuring, say, creativity or civic values. But as the vocabulary of school success or failure, the achievement orientation not only conveys an easily digestible sense of an individual school's performance but also shapes overall conceptions of what effective education is. Most importantly, the language puts the onus of success or failure almost exclusively on the organizational effects of schools. Schools and school systems are said to be succeeding or failing their students based on the percentage of students achieving proficiency levels on an exam.[60] NCLB confirms this orientation, identifying only schools as the source of academic outcomes. If student academic performance is lagging, schools are sanctioned under NCLB. The law puts these achievement measures squarely in front of the public, so that parents are then better able to compare and choose the best (highest scoring) options for their children.

In fact, the assumption that poor achievement is caused by ineffective schools underlies much of the discussion of education in the United States.[61] While this may make sense at the level of popular debates, we know other factors are also at play. Most any worthwhile researcher would point out that academic performance is a result of several factors, with the school's effectiveness at fostering academic skills only one part—and, contrary to claims by some policymakers and reformers, not the major part—of the equation.[62] Which is not to say that achievement or schools' contribution to it are unimportant, but that understanding school effectiveness involves more than simply comparing raw test scores. Still, test scores themselves are now the coin of the realm, and any serious discussion of the state of American education must adopt the language—if not assumptions—of the achievement orientation to develop and convey an understanding of how public schools are performing.

The Centrality of Organizations

The key element of the incentivist perspective, as informed by public choice theory, is that it holds organizations in the primary role, with the effectiveness of organizations thought to be the main determinant of how well schools can meet a demand for education.[63] Indeed, the incentivist perspective is premised on the idea that the institutional environment is the only force that can provide the motivations necessary to cause change in and through organizations. As bundles of individuals motivated by self-interest, organizations are also thought to be best motivated by institutional incentives that play upon their self-interested impulses, such as profit maximization, growth, or gaining competitive advantages as they compete for consumers. Of course, this premise presupposes that those incentives from the institutional environment are clear, that organizations can sense and respond to them, and that the consequent actions of those organizations can have a significant impact on the issues they are intended to address.

This incentivist premise would also seem to be self-evident in education.[64] Schools are thought to be the primary agent in teaching academic skills to children. In fact, it has become quite fashionable for reformers and educated observers to claim that teaching has the greatest impact on the future chances of a child.[65] So when students are not succeeding academically, we often look to the school as the cause of this problem, or at least to address that failure. But "sometimes adults aren't doing their jobs."[66] When three out of ten freshmen at a high school will graduate in four years, with only 1% demonstrating proficiency in math, it seems to make sense to conclude that something is wrong with the school—for instance, it would appear obvious that we need to scrutinize an organization "that fails 70 percent of the children it's charged with educating."[67]

When we see patterns of chronic failure around specific schools, it makes sense to consider what it is about those schools—as organizations—that makes them so ineffective at addressing these patterns, especially when other school organizations are more successful, given the same challenges. As education writer Jay Mathews suggests, "We have seen enough successful schools in such areas to know that many of those children are just as capable of being great scientists, doctors, and executives as suburban children are. But most low-income schools in the United States are simply bad."[68] Thus, when we see patterns of failure only around specific types of schools, it would be reasonable to assume that there is some pathology specific to that organizational type that leads to systemic failure. Since schools "develop organizations that reflect and are compatible with their institutional environment," according to public choice theorists Chubb and Moe, a pathological institutional environment may precipitate widespread organizational behavior in schools aligned to that environment: "Different types of environments produce different types of schools. . . . when schools turn out to have undesirable characteristics—those conducive to ineffective performance—the most logical culprit ought to be the environment."[69]

This notion of the centrality of organizations is evident in two ways. First, it is quite apparent in terms of diagnosing problems in public schools. But second, it is a primary assumption in fashioning the remedies for individual and endemic academic failure because it looks to the superior organization of private schools. If the effectiveness of the organization is key for questions of academic failure, then creating the right institutional incentives that can compel organizations to increase their effectiveness—usually cast as the dynamics associated with the private sector—is an approach that holds the promise of improving academic outcomes, especially for children chronically underserved by ineffective educational organizations. Again, it seems self-evident that better schools produce better outcomes. And, as organizations, schools can embrace more effective practices that lead to better results, as a number of commentators have noted. Given the right incentives, schools will adopt appropriate "pedagogic skills,"[70] rather than focusing undue attention and resources on, say, abstract societal goals such as "anti-racist math."[71] Moreover, if a certain type of school consistently graduates higher achieving students, then we might conclude that "different institutional forms are likely to have different consequences for school performance."[72] Consequently, as Chubb and Moe famously concluded, bringing the organizational incentives associated with the competitive private sector into the effort to reshape public sector organizations represents the most promising policy approach: "choice *is* a panacea" for fixing schools.[73]

To Test Market Theory

School reform in the United States reflects a global trend toward using market-style institutional environments to create the incentives that will foster more effective organizations, especially for state-run efforts in the bureaucratically administered public sector. The theory of markets for schooling, directly derived from the public-choice diagnosis of the institutional ills of public administration of service, is solidly based on assumptions that appear, at least on the surface, to be commonsensical. Needing a useful metric to gauge results, policymakers have tended toward achievement scores to rate the success or failure of schools. As with many organizations, schools in the private sector see better results than do their counterparts in the public sector. Drawing from the ideas of Milton Friedman and other theorists, policymakers point to characteristics unique to organizations in the private sector— things like choice and competition—to explain those differences and argue that the public sector must be refashioned in order to incentivize public organizations to get better results. This can be done, if not through direct privatization, then by giving schools more autonomy and forcing them to compete for students who can then decide which schools they choose to attend.

By bringing this logic to bear on public education through choice, autonomy, and competition—characteristics drawn from private sector models—the anticipated gains in effectiveness should then lead to greater student achievement, as is already evident in private schools. While this logic is seemingly self-evident, quite popular with policymakers, and is driving the current generation of school reform, two overarching questions linger, each of which gets at the very foundation of this logic and the reform movements it has spawned and are the basis for the remainder of this book.

First, while the beauty and truth of this market-oriented logic is apparent in the production and distribution of consumer goods, public education is sometimes seen as a common or public good. The extent to which education should be treated as a collective or a consumer good is a complex and fascinating discussion—one that has attracted some scholarly attention and disagreement.[74] But a more fundamental issue is not whether education is a public or private good but how well the multiple goals we hold for schools can be met in a market environment.

That is, education markets are now a fixture on the landscape of schooling in America and elsewhere: more than one in ten students attend a private school; charter schools compete for students; voucher programs are proliferating; and millions more families choose public schools for their children, either by deciding to move to a district or taking advantage of a choice program. But markets are premised on certain assumptions regarding supply, demand, and institutional conditions. How does education, as we know it and/or want it to be, align with or resist the market model? Are there central goals of public schooling that can be better advanced through markets, or are there essential attributes of public education that confound the application of market forces? This is an important question, and one we return to at the end of this book.

The second and more immediate question is one of relative performance of schools across sectors. Market theory posits that the private sector is superior because it offers better incentives that induce more autonomous organizations to compete by working more effectively. Thus, students in private schools generally show higher academic achievement than do students in public schools—thus seeming to offer support for the assumption that private-style organizations produce better outcomes. But we also know that other factors are at play that may confound simple conclusions based on raw test scores: student background, resources, classmates, and so on, all differ substantially from the public to the private sector. If we can account for these differences when comparing academic achievement across different types of schools, we could test the assumption of the inherent institutional superiority of the private sector, at least in regard to education. While many past efforts have attempted to make those inherently complex comparisons, we now have both the comprehensive data sets and sophisticated analytical tools to examine this issue in more detail. This is where we now turn.

3 *The Private School Effect*

Parents and policymakers have recognized for some time that there are serious problems with America's public schools. The superior results achieved in private schools—including private schools that serve poor and minority students—strongly suggest that these schools possess particular characteristics that are lacking in the lagging public school sector. The solution proposed by market theorists and policymakers to import organizational attributes such as consumer choice, competition, and operational autonomy into the public sector comes from the notion that private schools gain advantages from more efficient and responsive structures, policies, and procedures. The primary evidence of this private sector superiority is in the higher levels of achievement they garner on standardized tests.

As we have noted, this diagnosis and remedy advance from some fundamental assumptions about the relative importance and effectiveness of different organizations in the private and public sectors. And these assumptions undergird much of the thinking on public policy not only in the United States but in the wealthier market democracies as well as in developing countries throughout the world. Yet—assumptions aside—what do we really know about the relative performance of our schools? Many reform efforts are spurred on by the claim that certain types of schools are failing, but what does the evidence actually show? Are public schools inherently destined to fail?

The question of school achievement—indeed, the question of the state of American education—is, by its nature, a relative one. While critics and reformers have for years deplored the state of public schools, such condemnations often beg the comparative question: How are our schools performing compared to what? Which real or proposed alternatives offer appropriate models with which to contrast the performance of American schools? Critics get much mileage out of international comparisons to schools in other countries, or sometimes tacit contrasts to earlier generations of American education.[1] But it is important to consider what is actually being compared in such studies—whether, for instance, an elite group of students in one context is being held up against all students in another context.[2] In view of the widespread concern about the problems with American *public* schools, the most obvious point of reference for assessing their performance, especially in an age of vouchers, charter schools, and privatization, is to compare them to America's many private schools. The generally higher levels of achievement in private schools seem to suggest alternative approaches that could be directly employed or emulated to improve less effective public schools, as posited by market theorists.

The issue of the superior effectiveness of private schools has been well established by past generations of research. Beginning in the 1980s, in particular, much attention was given to the relative effects of school organizational type on academic achievement, much of it finding a beneficial "private school effect." Certainly, private schools tend to draw, on average, more advantaged families that can afford the added costs of tuition and transportation. And yet, since such schools were shown to achieve superior results with the disadvantaged students who typically frequent and are failed by public schools, there is a strong argument for policies that encourage students to leave government-run schools for schools in the private sector or to make public schools more autonomous and shift them into private or marketized institutional environments. Indeed, not only would this seem to be a more efficient and effective use of public resources in educating the public, but there is a serious equity concern about trapping poorer families in the public sector if it is chronically underperforming.

In the mid-1950s, several forces began to emerge that would later put this question squarely on the national agenda. On the intellectual front, Milton Friedman published a rather obscure and largely hypothetical essay in 1955 suggesting the use of vouchers for funding education instead of funding public schools.[3] His proposal was guided by the dual ideals of freedom of choice and economic efficiencies seen in the market, as they could then be applied to schooling.[4] At the same time, the U.S. Supreme Court's decision in *Brown v. Board of Education* to desegregate public schools led to a backlash, especially in southern states, where segregationists used "choice" and private academies to avoid integration—a trend that Friedman acknowledged in his essay. But Friedman and others—including some social liberals—also noted that choice had the potential to promote school integration, as students could attend schools outside their assigned, and often racially segregated, attendance area.

Meanwhile, Virgil Blum, a Catholic priest and professor in Milwaukee, was also proposing a similar choice system that would have provided government subsidies for Catholic schools—not unlike the arrangements in many Western democracies.[5] Of course, there had been a long history of tension in the United States over the idea of Catholic organizations running a separate system of education, with questions of Protestant control of the curriculum, religious prejudice, state funding, and church-state entanglements guiding much of these debates.[6] While Catholic schools during Blum's time were heading toward record enrollments, later declines in the 1980s and 1990s would make this a much more pressing issue, as many Catholic schools would struggle to attract tuition-paying students.[7]

As the political focus in U.S. policy debates turned to questions such as cycles of poverty, economic and educational opportunity, and school resources, the issue of school achievement in various types of schools assumed a more immediate tone. The challenge then was how best to use public resources to improve the educational opportunities for young people, and particularly for those disadvantaged students stuck in failing public schools. One seemingly obvious possibility would be to increase funding for schools serving poor students. Yet in a watershed study commissioned by the federal government to illuminate the impact of unequal school resources, sociologist James Coleman and colleagues examined the influence of various factors on schools, famously finding—much to everyone's surprise—that achievement gaps were much less a result of school inputs than of a student's family background and peers.[8]

This finding is probably one of the most monumental contributions of social science to policy debates in the last century, with the implication being that spending more money on public school programs would do little to address that achievement gap, which was largely a product of family background. Although some scholars at the time, and since, have questioned the methods, conclusions, and interpretations of what came to be known as the "Coleman Report," liberal and radical thinkers, frustrated with bureaucratic efforts at equity and the slow pace of progress toward equitable educational opportunity, looked to school choice and school autonomy as new ways to open up quality options for disadvantaged students.[9] Even as Coleman's report appeared to discount the differences that schools could make in improving educational opportunity, thinkers, including Coleman, came to endorse the idea of choice as a way to improve educational options for children. So, although initially rooted in hypothetical arguments, plans like Friedman's proposal for school vouchers caught the attention of policymakers because of the potential for either moving students to educational alternatives outside the traditional district-run sector or importing characteristics of choice and competition into the public education sector.

Such proposals cast questions of school sector in a new light. Prior to the emergence of choice between schools as a policy plan, parents typically used private schools for one of three reasons: (1) to teach or reinforce religious and cultural identity, in the case of Catholic and other church-affiliated schools; (2) to initiate their children into elite social networks, such as with elite prep schools; (3) or to keep their children from attending school with children from different social backgrounds, as with "white flight academies" in the South. Notably, achievement was usually not itself the major factor in such choices. But with the application of Friedman's economic logic to schooling, and the concern of equity-minded reformers for providing better educational opportunities for disadvantaged children, researchers began to focus attention on actual evidence on the relative performance of schools in public and private sectors. This research now goes back almost three decades but has become more pointed in recent years in its implications for education reform.

As noted, it is exceedingly clear that, on average, private schools have higher scoring students than do public schools. The task for researchers has been to distinguish to what extent the differences in scores reflect differences in the populations served in the different sectors or the possibility that private schools are, indeed, more effective than public schools in preparing students. Researchers were really able to get at this question in a comprehensive manner for the first time in the early 1980s, picking (and arguing) over a single, large study for the better part of a decade and coming to an apparent consensus on the issue in the mid-1980s and early 1990s.[10] In addition to the seminal work on achievement in public and private schools, two recent debates—on charter schools and voucher programs—have highlighted the question of the role of school organizational type in promoting academic achievement. Research reports on public and independent schools point to the presumed importance of public and private sectors for understanding the organizational behavior of schools and, ultimately, the propensity of different models of schooling to effect superior academic performance.

Discerning the Private School Effect

Charter schools and voucher programs are currently the most obvious manifestations of the assumption popular in policy-making circles regarding the superior performance of private, independent, and autonomous organizations, free from government administration and bureaucracy. In education, such assumptions are based in solid, well-respected research comparing schools in public and private sectors. A slew of influential studies emerged from the High School and Beyond (HSB) data set, a longitudinal study of over 58,000 students in the graduating classes of 1980 and 1982, attending approximately 1,000 public and private schools. Using these data, researchers examined student achievement—as measured by two one-hour, multiple choice exams—in different types of schools while accounting for differences in family background factors, as measured through surveys.

Having gained fame from his earlier study of equal educational opportunity in the 1960s, James Coleman and his colleagues first explored the HSB data, finding notable advantages in outcomes for students in the private sector. Even after controlling for the fact that private schools on average serve more affluent families, they found significant achievement advantages for private schools, indicating that the superior achievement was a result not of enrolling more affluent students but of private schools employing more effective organizational practices—what is known as the "private school effect."[11] The obvious implication was that private schools do a better job of educating the same students that are failing in many public schools, so policies should support the move of such students to the private sector.[12]

Subsequent, highly respected studies focused primarily on why such schools were more effective.[13] Researchers found the Catholic schools to be more effective for disadvantaged students because of the schools' unique social and academic organizational characteristics, communities based on shared values, a curriculum that engages students in core academic subjects, and distinctive forms of school governance.[14]

Then, in perhaps the most provocative work, political theorists John Chubb and Terry Moe used a follow-up survey of administrators and teachers drawn from a subsample of the HSB data to examine the achievement data of about 20,000 students from 400 schools.[15] Advancing from their background in public choice theory in their critique of public institutional environments, Chubb and Moe focused on pathologies inherent in the bureaucratic administration of the public sector. They argued that public schools were necessarily structured to be more susceptible to forces external to the educational enterprise in areas such as district oversight, collective bargaining arrangements, and political governance. These external influences were then associated with poorer academic environments and thus lower student achievement. They concluded that more effective schools have clear missions and more operational autonomy, with limited input from bureaucrats and special interests—in short, attributes associated with private schools. Having produced an acclaimed empirical justification, they proposed a plan to extend these attributes to schools in the public sector through a charter-style system that (1) expands the traditional notion of public schools to include new providers (including private schools); (2) presumes almost no interference from public authorities in the autonomy of schools; (3) depends on the idea of families choosing schools for their children; and (4) promotes the notion of competition between schools. Although their work has been contested, it has been extremely influential in policy circles.[16]

Since the heyday of public-private studies in the late 1980s and early 1990s, a general consensus has emerged among both researchers and policymakers that the private school effect most likely exists, especially for certain groups of students. Until recently, this claim has been only infrequently disrupted by the occasional study that further tests the existence of a private school effect. For instance, in examining 4,000 students in public, Catholic, and secular private schools in urban areas from the National Education Longitudinal Study of

1988 (NELS),[17] researchers found a positive effect for Catholic schools in mathematics, while secular private schools offered no advantage over public schools.[18] Other NELS research noted a moderate Catholic school effect on mathematics achievement for urban white students and larger gains for urban minority students, but no significant boost for suburban students.[19]

Yet the classic studies on public and private school effects on academic achievement are becoming quite dated. Students in the NELS studies graduated in 1992; students in HSB in 1980 and 1982—meaning they started school in the 1960s. In the meantime, substantial changes have continued to reshape private schools and the populations they serve. For instance, many urban Catholic schools—enrolling higher proportions of minority (and non-Catholic) students—are closing or in some cases converting to charter school status. And even as the Catholic school share of the private school market declines in favor of newer "conservative Christian" schools,[20] homeschooling increasingly draws students from both public and private sectors.[21] So schools are now operating in a different policy context. The HSB studies were written at a time when vouchers were essentially just an abstract idea. The NELS literature came to the fore when charter schools were just beginning their rapid proliferation and vouchers had not yet been ruled to be constitutional.

However, in recent years the conversation has shifted into a surrogate debate over policies supported by the idea of a private school effect. The apparent consensus on the existence of a private school effect has left the debate on public and private school achievement itself rather dormant. Researchers and policymakers have moved their focus to evidence of the private school effect in specific voucher programs that move children from public to private schools, as well as to charter schools, which are designed to emulate many of the presumably positive aspects of private schools. This focus highlights how policymakers' assumptions about the private (or autonomous) school effect are reshaping the education landscape in the United States. Voucher and charter school programs premised on the assumption of private or independent school effects are increasingly popular with state and federal policymakers, as well as with prominent private philanthropists. And major federal initiatives such as No Child Left Behind and Race to the Top endorse school choice and conversion to charter status as solutions for underperforming public schools, which are thought to be lacking internal incentives to succeed.

SCHOOL VOUCHER PROGRAMS

School vouchers give students the opportunity to leave public schools and attend private schools at reduced or no cost to the family.[22] One of the tenets of the thinking undergirding voucher plans holds that the relative autonomy and independence of schools in the private sector, combined with the possibility that discontented families can leave, creates the opportunities and competitive incentives for private schools to achieve superior levels of academic achievement; consequently, vouchers allow students otherwise trapped in the public schools the chance to learn more at these higher performing private schools. Starting in the early 1990s, policymakers in several states, as well as Congress, have embraced voucher programs, usually for students in large and failing inner-city school districts. The U.S. Supreme Court's 2002 ruling that voucher programs do not necessarily violate the Establishment Clause intensified interest in this strategy for reformers concerned about chronic failure in urban public schools.

In general, much of the research on voucher programs shows minimal or modest results at best, although many advocates argue that the voucher studies they conduct show strong evidence that the private school effect is a uniquely effective tool for improving the quality of education for disadvantaged students.[23] As with examinations of public and private school achievement, researchers have to take care that they are measuring the school's effect on achievement and not simply capturing differences in family background, particularly given that more affluent and assertive families may be more likely to send their children to private schools with or without a voucher. Efforts by some privatization advocates to set up small-scale, experimental-style studies that would negate any selection biases—that is, systematic differences between those choosing private schools and those remaining in public schools—have led to claims about significant learning gains for the students attending private schools in several cities. For instance, one such report found a substantial private school effect in terms of gains in mathematics and reading achievement for Milwaukee public school students who used vouchers to switch from public to private schools.[24] Similar reports on voucher programs in New York, Dayton, and the District of Columbia found significant gains for African American students using vouchers.[25] However, findings from these studies have been heavily criticized by other researchers.[26]

CHARTER SCHOOLS

While vouchers represent attempts to harness directly the private school effect by moving students to private schools, the charter school movement offers in some sense a more innovative strategy for accessing the private school effect by bringing to the public sector the more advantageous attributes associated with private schools. Although the charter school movement is diverse in its constituents and manifestations, all charter schools depend on the choices of families—that is, unlike with district-run public schools, families are not assigned to a charter school. Furthermore, advocates who pushed charter schools onto the national agenda explicitly linked charter schools to higher achievement, arguing that charter schools would, like private schools, use their greater autonomy and competitive incentives to find innovative ways of teaching and learning, resulting in greater academic outcomes.[27] For instance, freed from the regulations and restrictions imposed by collective bargaining agreements with teachers unions, charter schools would be responsible to the children who chose to enroll, rather than to groups of adults, such as teachers unions, organized to promote their own self-interests. Thus, charter schools are essentially autonomous schools that typically operate independently of local district bureaucracies and are therefore designed to harness and replicate the private school effect.

The question of achievement in charter schools, however, is inherently relative: How are charter schools performing compared with the regular public schools, for which they were supposed to offer an alternative? Yet simple, direct comparisons of achievement in charter and public schools—such as claims that charter schools "get better results"—fail to consider the fact that one type of school may be serving higher proportions of students who are disadvantaged, have special needs, or have other characteristics known to lead to lower school performance.[28] Indeed, it is likely that there are observable and unobservable differences in the populations served by charter and public schools, as evidenced by the facts that some families made the decision to enroll in a charter school and that charter schools are more concentrated in urban areas.

As with vouchers, actual studies of achievement in charter schools has been mixed, even though there appears to be a strong consensus in media and policy circles that these schools lead to greater gains in academic achievement. Studies of achievement in charter schools have highlighted how competing methodologies and various contexts across states may produce different results. For instance, while a few larger scale, multistate studies have found little effects from charter schools on academic achievement, some rigorous local-level studies have shown these schools to be boosting achievement for students.[29] A number of such reports have come from economist and market advocate Caroline Hoxby, who used randomization in finding that charter school status had a positive effect on academic achievement in her investigations of three charter schools in Chicago and charter schools in New York City, as well as in a matching study of the United States overall.[30] As with vouchers, these findings have been seriously disputed by other researchers,[31] yet policymakers are pursuing rapid expansion of these programs.[32]

Reexamining the Issue

Overall, based on the dramatic expansion of charters and the renewed interest from policymakers regarding vouchers, there appears to be some consensus—at least in policy-making circles as well as with some prominent researchers—on the existence and uses of the private school effect in voucher programs and what might be called by logical extension an independent or "autonomous school effect" with charter schools. So, in view of the apparent consensus on these organizational effects, it would appear that characteristics associated with private school organizations may be responsible for some significant advantages in academic outcomes at private and independent schools, at least as compared with public schools. In particular, reformers and researchers have highlighted attributes such as operational autonomy, cohesive community values, academic focus, and freedom from the bureaucratic imposition of external goals.[33]

In view of the popularity of reforms such as charter schools and vouchers with policymakers, we can identify guiding assumptions—

apparently drawn from the research—shaping the proliferation of policies premised on the private school effect. First, it would appear that there may be either a modestly or substantially beneficial private/independent school effect, at least for some students, with evidence of the inherent effectiveness of independent educational organizations ranging from negligible differences with achievement in public schools to significant and robust advantages for private schools.[34] Second, as some advocates have suggested, there is little evidence that these programs have a negative academic impact for the students who use them, although questions remain about the diminished peer effect for students remaining in district-run public schools.[35]

However, one assumption around these programs that deserves some attention is the importance of school sector for policymakers promoting choice of charter or private schools, and hence for researchers trying to understand relative gains in academic achievement from these types of programs. This is because policymakers assume that schools located in the private or independent sector have opportunities and incentives that cause them to produce greater gains in academic achievement than do public schools. Thus, this focus on public or private school sector has become the basis for diagnosing the problems with America's schools, as well as for prescribing the institutional remedies that are currently popular with market theorists, reformers, and policymakers—namely, moving education away from political and technocratic models toward market models of organization. Essentially, since schools in the independent/private sector are thought to be more effective because they are responsive to competitive incentives, it would seem quite sensible to either shift students into those sectors or create and scale up such competitive environments for the entire public school system.

But how much confidence should we have in the research base that is apparently motivating current efforts to use sector-based strategies to reform and reconfigure schools? Are the findings from those studies from the 1980s and 1990s still applicable in the current milieu of education in the twenty-first century? And do the apparently promising results from local studies reflect the potential of these policies to improve American education on a national level? Are superior outcomes in private and independent schools in some localities the result of organizational effectiveness in those sectors? Or do they reflect the fact that more advantaged families choose such schools? If the latter, then policies that seek to shift students or conditions from one sector to another may not have the intended effect and may in fact be counterproductive.

It makes sense, then, to determine whether academic outcomes in private and independent school sectors are, in fact, superior to those in public sector schools, as reformers expect. We know that the schools in these sectors tend to serve relatively different types of students, on average—different in many important and subtle respects that could corrupt attempts to measure how much of an impact the different schools have on a student's academic achievement. To detect the actual impacts of organizational factors, such as the private/independent status of different schools, we must choose the most appropriate analytical strategy from a small menu of options.

Perhaps most apparent, one highly regarded way of making sure that any gains are the result of schools and not home factors is randomization: an approach based on experimental models common in medical studies. This approach is appealing because researchers can create some type of experimental comparison, where students are randomly assigned to schools, including private and charter schools of choice. Randomization removes important influences that cannot be measured when studies try to control for various background factors thought to influence academic outcomes. It has been particularly popular with market advocates, who see it as the gold standard of research.[36] And, indeed, some randomized studies have tended to show advantageous academic effects from choice programs such as charter schools and voucher plans.[37] Consequently, this approach has enjoyed a privileged status in education research beginning with the G. W. Bush administration in terms of research support and credibility.

While this approach has some definite advantages and has become quite fashionable in some research circles, it also has several inherent drawbacks for understanding the actual organizational effects of different types of schools. First, randomized studies tend to be small and focused on specific communities. This may not be an issue when it comes to evaluating a program in a particular locality—for example, the performance of charter schools in New York City. But in terms of researching the effects of a given treatment in order to understand its potential to improve schools overall, questions of generalizability become crucial. For example, is there anything unique about charter schools in New York, or the context in that city or that state, that may impact the performance of charter schools there—for better or for worse—compared with how they might perform in other settings? Thus, efforts to make claims about, say, public and private school performance based only on voucher studies assume that these local studies are examining schools that are generalizable when they are not.[38] In fact, such studies compare a self-selected group of sought-after private schools willing to accept vouchers with an (unwilling) assortment of public schools included in the study simply because of the fact that they are bad enough that students want to leave them.

Furthermore, studies that rely on randomization to determine school effects start from the assumption that control and experimental groups are qualitatively similar—which they generally are at the start of the study. However, experience shows that substantial student attrition from schools over time seriously corrupts these studies. As voucher studies have demonstrated, significant numbers of lower performing students tend to drop out of the private schools, leaving more motivated voucher students in the study and thereby perverting the integrity of the treatment group.[39] Perhaps most importantly, the faith that randomization essentially washes away differences between compared groups means that researchers then ascribe any differences in achievement to school effects. But this is likely quite misguided. Students are often leaving more disadvantaged public schools for private schools with more affluent students. Thus, studies finding advantageous organizational effects in private and independent schools might actually be measuring a more beneficial peer effect in such schools; but the faith in randomization means that researchers often fail to measure the school-level demographics. Finally, unlike the medical model, students know whether they are assigned to the treatment or control group (placebos are not an option), and the fact that they have won or lost a lottery to a school they wish to attend might very well in itself have an impact on their subsequent school performance.

So randomization, although it offers some admirable and useful advantages, also suffers from some serious limitations in what it can tell us about the issue of public and private school performance. An alternative approach is to conduct an observational study. In that approach, instead of assigning students to a control or treatment group and relying on lotteries to diminish any differences between groups, such studies examine students in their environments and then use demographic data to control for measurable differences between groups. Such data can include detailed but representative information on student demographics, resources at home, and the peer effect at school. Collecting such data at the national level is done routinely by the National Center of Education Statistics (NCES). Observational data can result in much larger data sets that do not suffer from the generalizability problem plaguing studies relying on randomization. Observational data sets are often constructed to be nationally representative of different types of schools, for example.

As with randomization, there are limits to observational data. Researchers need to have reliable and comprehensive background data in order to control for nonschool factors that may impact student achievement. And researchers are inherently limited to controlling only for variables that can be measured and recorded. Although various surveys, interviews, assessments, and other instruments can produce a wide variety of relevant data, there often remain unobservable factors, such as the more subtle aspects of student or parent motivation, for example.

There are two types of observational data sets—cross-sectional and longitudinal. Cross-sectional data sets consist of data collected at one point in time. Hence, even large, nationally representative, education data sets that are cross-sectional (such as what we examine in the next chapter) can provide only a single snapshot of student achievement. Since such data sets lack information about student gains, caution is merited in drawing conclusions about the effects of schools in shaping student achievement over time. However, cross-sectional data are very commonly used by NCES, given that such data are the most straightforward and economical to collect. Hence, the size of cross-sectional data sets can be far greater than that of other data sets. And perhaps most importantly, cross-sectional data do not have the attrition issues that can corrupt the integrity of other data sets.

On the other hand, observational data can be collected over time. The HSB data set is probably the most famous example of this approach. Such studies are more expensive to administer, since researchers must track down students over the course of the study (sometimes several years) as they move or switch schools. Thus, attrition from the study can be a problem, and researchers have to consider how to deal with these "missing data." Nevertheless, longitudinal studies of students and schools have the advantage of measuring student growth from the point at which they enter the study while controlling for differences in the backgrounds of students attending different types of schools—and thus can offer a very good perspective on school effects. This is the approach we present in Chapter 5. And, unlike the HSB study, which dealt with secondary students in the early 1980s, we examine data across the early grades, since any initial differences at kindergarten between student groups are more likely to reflect differences in home advantages rather than school effects at the start.

As researchers began systematically studying the issue of relative school effects, starting with the arrival of the HSB data set, a number of foundational studies identified an organizational advantage for private schools. In fact, many pointed to their operational autonomy and market-style accountability to consumers—factors then emulated in charter school design. The next two chapters review both a cross-sectional analysis and a longitudinal analysis we conducted that call into question those findings. Using two different data sets, we find that although private school math scores are indeed higher than public school scores, this apparent private school advantage is due to the characteristics of the students they attract rather than to superior organizational effectiveness and, in fact, public schools are relatively effective. Since our initial analysis initiated a reexamination of the effects of different schools, a few other researchers have subsequently studied and debated this issue, using different data sets and methodological approaches—producing results that are aligned with what we have found.[40] However, we then go beyond these analyses to examine why we are seeing these patterns. That is, what factors explain the notable performance and effectiveness of public schools and the apparent diminishment of the vaunted private school effect? Our answer may surprise some. We find aspects of the market model for education to actually impede the academic effectiveness of schools. Specifically, while reformers laud the operational autonomy granted to independent schools,[41] the evidence analyzed in the following chapters actually shows that such autonomy is associated with less effective teaching, with schools using their freedom to hang onto outdated methods and to avoid staying current on the professional practices embraced by public schools. Said another way, instead of promoting instructional innovation, we find that private school autonomy can lead to curricular stagnation.

Social science research is often rightly accused of proving what we already know. The analyses that follow fall into that rarer category of studies that turn conventional wisdom on its head, showing that what was thought to be obviously true is not. Of course, this area of research has become highly politicized, with academic debates over appropriate analytical approaches often serving as a surrogate for deeper disputes over ideology and the appropriate role of governments and markets in education. As we will see in the concluding chapter, such conflict should be expected considering the vast amounts of resources at stake and the considerable amount of money and political pressure that are brought to bear through efforts to influence the common perceptions of the issues and the evidence.

4 *Achievement in Public, Charter, and Private Schools*

Common wisdom and common sense tell us that private schools are more effective than their public school counterparts. Private schools appear to produce more academically qualified students who seem to have a pipeline into better colleges and go on to more prestigious and profitable careers. And the superior academic results of private schools would seem to lend some credence to this popular conception.

Of course, the question is whether those superior student results are due to better private schools or to the fact that those schools tend to serve more academically advantaged families, that is, if differences in test scores between various school types—public schools, charter schools, or Catholic and other private schools—are primarily due to inherent differences in the effectiveness of these various school types or to differences in the student populations served by these different sectors. If it is the former, then policymakers should seek to further replicate private sector organizational models in the public sector, using approaches such as charter schools and vouchers to promote choice, organizational autonomy, and competition. But if it is the latter, then such structural changes are necessarily limited in their ability to address the roots of educational inequality and ineffectiveness in schooling.

As outlined previously, this is a particularly salient issue now. Earlier research on what we might call "school sector effects"—that is, the assumed institutional advantage that schools enjoy from being in the independent or private sector—indicated that private schools score higher even after adjusting for the fact that these schools tend to serve students with fewer "risk" factors such as special education needs or limited English proficiency (LEP). Much of the current generation of school reform is premised on assumptions regarding the superior organizational attributes of private schools—exemplified, for instance, in voucher and charter programs and in the choice provisions of the No Child Left Behind Act of 2001 and the Race to the Top policies of the Obama administration. Although assumptions about what is known as the "private school effect" have been commonplace for some time now, public and private school sectors have undergone significant changes in the last few decades—for instance, evangelical organizations are now educating many more students than they did a decade ago, while the Catholic school share of the private school sector has been seeing declines. Furthermore, generalized beliefs about school sector effects may miss important differences not only between, but also within, sectors.

While it is common knowledge that average achievement in private schools is higher than in public (and charter) schools, in this chapter we investigate this pattern further, determining whether the relationships between school type and academic achievement persist and particularly how they look across different types and subtypes of schools after accounting for differences in the populations they serve.

There are reasons to think that private schools—as well as charter schools, since they draw important characteristics from the private school sector—should produce better academic outcomes than public schools, even after adjusting for the demographic differences in the student populations that attend these schools. As prominent market theorists such as Chubb and Moe note,[1] schools such as private and charter schools are free of much of the bureaucracy that impedes the public schools, which are in the district-run public sector, and are able to avoid politicized debates around common controversies such as textbooks or abstinence education in focusing on a core academic purpose. Moreover, in the independent sector of private and charter schools, parents are best able to select a school based on its academic effectiveness and to choose an alternative option if that school does not meet their expectations, thereby creating competitive incentives that will force schools to improve. Therefore, we might expect that independent private and charter schools have inherent incentives to succeed. Furthermore, parents choosing private and charter schools, by virtue of making a choice, have demonstrated an admirable and useful dedication to their children's schooling—a factor associated with higher academic achievement that goes beyond typical indicators of a family's socioeconomic status (SES).

To test these assumptions, we examine evidence provided by a comprehensive and well-respected national dataset that is much larger than High School and Beyond (HSB). The National Assessment of Educational Progress (NAEP) is known as the nation's report card and has been called the gold standard by choice advocates because of its highly regarded measures of student achievement.[2] In addition, NAEP includes useful background information on students, their families, and their schools, which allows us to adjust for many out-of-school background factors known to influence student achievement and thereby distinguish the performance of different types of schools apart from the influence of the families they serve. And unlike HSB, which focused on secondary education, the NAEP data in question examined students in fourth and eighth grade, levels at which more students attend private schools.

Of course, consistent with common assumptions, the raw scores for private schools are higher than those for public schools, which are themselves similar to or higher than those for charter schools. But these patterns reflect how students perform, without accounting for the observable academic advantages and disadvantages they bring to school. This tells us nothing about actual school performance apart from those student background issues. So we employ an analytical strategy known as multilevel modeling that allows researchers to account for student influences at both the home and school level and thereby compare "apples to apples" when examining student achievement in various types of schools. Specifically, we can determine the degree to which gaps between different school types persist after adjusting for demographics at both the student and school level (including SES, race/ethnicity, gender, disability, LEP), as well as important additional variables such as school location.

In the following section, we offer a general description of the analyses conducted to compare different types of schools that serve different student populations. (For specific discussions of the variables and controls used, see Appendix A.) In examining this issue, we focus on student performance in mathematics. This focus allows us to further isolate school effects from family background factors, since mathematics is a subject that is learned primarily in school, as compared with other subjects, such as reading, which tend to be more heavily influenced by students' experiences at home.[3] The findings from this analysis include some consistent patterns that challenge much of the conventional wisdom on this topic. Specifically, when adjusting for differences in student populations, public school achievement is roughly equal to or higher than that of other school types. The chapter also illuminates some important differences in school performance within the independent school sectors.

The National Assessment of Educational Progress

One important advantage of the NAEP is that it offers detailed student, teacher, and administrator survey data regarding a variety of student and school characteristics. For this analysis, we used the 2003 NAEP administration, which for the first time presented the opportunity to examine public, private, and charter schools. Furthermore, compared with previous datasets used to study school sector and student achievement, this NAEP dataset was the first to aggregate large state samples up to the national level, resulting in record numbers of students and schools and allowing a more detailed comparison of various school types.

However, it is important to note that NAEP data are cross-sectional, not longitudinal. Longitudinal data have strengths when it comes to making claims about school effectiveness, because—as we show later—they allow us to consider initial achievement differences among students and thus examine student growth. However, longitudinal datasets are not without difficulties. The cost and complexity of following samples of students over time make it difficult to maintain the analytical integrity of those groups for comparison when students change schools or disappear from the experiment; hence, such studies tend to be much smaller in scope.[4] When using cross-sectional data, differences in participants' prior achievement are generally unknown.

In lieu of that information, the use of statistical models in cross-sectional studies of school performance allows researchers instead to account for the primary variables that are known to shape initial achievement differences, making it less likely that longitudinal data would tell a different story—something we test in our subsequent analysis. Thus, it is true, as some have observed, that cross-sectional data only offer a "snapshot" of achievement at a point in time and do not measure student growth over time. However, thanks to the large samples and extensive data on background factors known to influence achievement, the NAEP "snapshot" of achievement in different school sectors is a highly pixilated one.

NAEP SAMPLES

Over one-third of a million students were sampled for this NAEP dataset—far outstripping prior NAEP datasets (e.g., the 2000 NAEP included less than 50,000 students) and other datasets such as the 60,000 students in HSB, which was the basis for previous work on this issue. In view of the scope and richness of NAEP data, and given that there are no other nationally representative datasets that provide the numbers of schools and the detailed achievement/survey information that NAEP offers, this massive dataset offers some unique insights into the question of school sector superiority. For this administration, NAEP measured student performance in fourth and eighth grades only. The samples include 190,147 fourth graders and 153,189 eighth graders from representative samples of public and private schools (7,485 schools at grade 4 and 6,092 schools at grade 8). Tables 4.1 and 4.2 include average raw scores for the different types of schools, demonstrating—as expected—that all other types of schools, except charter schools, have higher raw academic achievement than public schools. These scores do not take the differences in student backgrounds into account, so they do not necessarily reflect differences in school effectiveness.

Although NAEP's main focus is academic achievement, the students, their teachers, and school administrators complete detailed questionnaires pertaining to a variety of factors, including students' attitudes and classroom experiences, teachers' educational backgrounds, and school climate. Students also report on their access to a variety of home resources, including a computer, atlas, encyclopedia, newspapers, magazines, and books. A "home resources" composite variable (with a scale of 0–6) was created from these six variables.

VARIABLES UTILIZED IN THE HIERARCHICAL LINEAR MODELING ANALYSIS

In this analysis, we use the student- and school-level variables from NAEP that have been found to correlate with mathematics achievement

Table 4.1: Sample sizes, achievement, student demographics, and school location by school type: Full grade 4 NAEP reporting sample (190,147 students from 7,485 schools)[a]

	Public (noncharter), $n = 182,328$ students, 6,797 schools	Catholic $n = 2,285$, students, 216 schools	Lutheran $n = 555$, students, 88 schools	Conservative Christian, $n = 651$ students, 78 schools	Other private, $n = 1,227$, students, 157 schools	Charter, $n = 3,101$, students, 149 schools
		Student factors (data analyzed at the student level)				
Mean student achievement (standard error):	234 (.3)	244 (.9)	245 (1.5)	240 (1.5)	248 (1.8)	228 (2.3)
Percent black	17	7	12	12	10	30
Percent Hispanic	19	12	3	8	3	20
Percent American Indian	1	0	0	0	0	1
Percent Asian	4	3	1	6	6	2
Percent LEP	10	1	1	0	0	8
Percent with IEPs	11	3	2	4	3	8
Percent free/reduced lunch	46	9	7	3	3	45
Home resources (of six items)	3.6	4.4	4.2	4.2	4.4	3.7

School factors (data analyzed at the school level)

School lunch (scale 1–6)[b]	4.1	2.1	1.9	1.6	1.6	4.2
Mean home resources	3.6	4.3	4.2	4.3	4.0	3.7
Percent minority	32	20	16	23	22	43
Percent LEP (scale 1–6)[b]	1.75	1.07	1.04	1.01	1.15	1.63
Percent large city	14	27	19	16	23	31
Percent rural/small town	39	16	22	26	17	23
Percent schools in Northeast	17	32	4	16	16	6
Percent schools in South	33	17	15	43	40	29
Percent schools in West	23	14	15	20	18	42
Percent schools in Midwest	27	37	66	21	26	23

[a] For Tables 4.1 and 4.2, sample sizes are the unweighted NAEP reporting samples, however, the means and percentages reported are for the samples that are weighted to represent U.S. students and schools.

[b] Scale was as follows: 1= 0%–5%; 2 = 6%–10%; 3 = 1%–25%; 4 = 26%–50%; 5 = 51%–75%; 6 = 76%–100%.

Table 4.2: Sample sizes, achievement, student demographics, and school location by school type: Full grade 8 NAEP reporting sample (153,189 students from 6,092 schools)[a]

	Public (noncharter), n = 146,512 students, 5,449 schools	Catholic, n = 2,463 students, 224 schools	Lutheran, n = 605 students, 96 schools	Conservative Christian, n = 659 students, 90 schools	Other private, n = 1,346 students, 148 schools	Charter, n = 1,604 students, 85 schools
Student factors (analyzed at the student level):						
Mean student achievement (standard error)	276 (.3)	289 (1.5)	296 (1.7)	286 (2.7)	298 (2.6)	271 (3.1)
Percent black	17	10	8	13	8	28
Percent Hispanic	15	12	5	4	4	19
Percent American Indian	1.2	.2	.5	.5	.5	2.6
Percent Asian	4	5	3	3	7	3
Percent LEP[b]	5	.4	1	.0	.2	6
Percent with IEPs[c]	11	3	2	2	3	11
Percent free/reduced lunch	38	15	11	.2	14	50
Home resources (of 6 items)	4.3	5.0	5.0	4.8	5.1	4.3
School factors (analyzed at the school level):						
School lunch (scale 1–6)[d]	4.0	2.3	1.7	1.4	1.8	4.1
Mean home resources	4.2	4.9	5.0	4.6	4.8	4.1
Percent minority	29	22	12	23	21	40
Percent LEP (scale 1–6)[d]	1.4	1.1	1.0	1.1	1.1	1.4
Percent large city	12	29	26	17	15	24
Percent rural/small town	51	10	21	28	32	30
Percent schools in Northeast	17	30	3	10	19	7
Percent schools in South	32	18	15	43	44	28
Percent schools in West	21	16	17	23	14	50
Percent schools in Midwest	30	36	65	25	24	15

[a] For Tables 4.1 and 4.2, sample sizes are the unweighted NAEP reporting samples, however, the means and percentages reported are for the samples that are weighted to represent U.S. students and schools.

[b] Limited English proficiency.

[c] Individualized Education Program, which is a mandated indicator for students with special needs.

[d] The scale was as follows: 1 = 0%–5%, 2 = 6%–10%, 3 = 11%–25%, 4 = 26%–50%, 5 = 51%–75%, 6 = 76%–100%.

and that could influence the relationship between school sector and achievement.[5] In selecting variables to include, the intent is to focus strictly on those that account for the differences in students/communities served by the school, as opposed to those factors that could be influenced by the school, such as the school discipline climate, teacher qualities, and even parent involvement. These other variables are analyzed in Chapter 6, which focuses on possible causes of the patterns identified in this chapter.

The variables used include the following: school type (public, charter, or private, including Catholic, Lutheran, conservative Christian,[6] etc.), student demographics, school demographics, and school location. See Appendix A for more details about the variables and analyses.

DATA ANALYSIS

In studies of students within schools, there is the conundrum of what counts as the "unit of analysis"—is it the individual students or is it the schools? Hierarchical linear modeling (HLM) resolves the dilemma by allowing researchers to examine students "nested" within schools and to include both student and school characteristics in their analyses.[7] Given its wide acceptance as the preferred method for analyzing large-scale school achievement data, we use HLM in our examinations of achievement by school type.

Results

DESCRIPTIVE COMPARISONS

As shown in Tables 4.1 and 4.2, at both the fourth and eighth grades, the mean mathematics achievement for charter school students is lower than that of other public school students, and the mean among public school students is lower than the means for private school students. However, as noted previously, schools differ in their student demographics and location—factors that we know can influence school achievement.

While private schools have the lowest percentages of minority students, charter schools have the highest. However, the percentages of students with LEP, an Individualized Education Program (IEP), and low SES backgrounds are roughly similar in charter and other public schools, indicating that the students in charter schools are in many ways comparable to those in other public schools on most demographic measures. But the proportions of such students on these measures are relatively low in private schools. Charter schools and some private schools are more likely to be located in larger cities, while public schools are disproportionately located in rural areas. Additionally, some school types are more concentrated in particular regions of the country. For example, conservative Christian schools are found disproportionately in the South, charter schools in the West, and Lutheran schools in the Midwest.[8]

These patterns highlight the question of whether the relatively high student achievement in private schools and relatively low achievement in charter schools is due simply to differences in demographics or location or if the achievement disparities persist after controlling for such differences. To consider this question, we analyze these data using multilevel, multivariate analyses that allow us to account for a number of factors outside of school type that influence achievement, thereby better isolating the influence of school type itself.

GRADE 4 RESULTS

At each grade level, five HLM models are used to examine achievement by school type. The HLM equations are included in Appendix A, along with raw, unweighted, descriptive statistics for the variables used in the HLM analyses (see Table A2). Table 4.3 presents the grade 4 HLM results. Standard errors are included for the intercept and school type coefficients, given that these coefficients are of primary interest in this study. Model 1, the traditional HLM null model, indicates that the school mathematics mean for all of the schools averaged 235.7 points. It also reveals that 29% of the variance in achievement is between schools and 71% of the variance involves students within schools.

Model 2 indicates that the mean math achievement for noncharter public schools is 234.2 points. In comparison, without adjusting for any demographic or other differences among schools, school achievement means are almost 10 points higher in Catholic schools, roughly 11 points higher in Lutheran and "other private" schools, about 4 points higher in conservative Christian schools, and 6 points lower in charter schools.

Table 4.3: School sector and demographic variables predicting fourth-grade NAEP mathematics achievement (166,736 students from 6,664 schools)

	Model 1: null model	Model 2: school sector only	Model 3: sector + student demographics	Model 4: sector + student and school demographics	Model 5: sector + demographics + location
			Fixed effects		
Intercept: school mean achievement[a]	235.7*** (0.3)	234.2*** (0.3)	247.4*** (0.3)	247.0*** (0.2)	247.4*** (0.4)
School level:					
Catholic[a]		9.5*** (1.1)	0.1 (0.9)	−7.0*** (0.9)	−7.2*** (0.9)
Lutheran[a]		10.7*** (1.9)	2.5 (1.4)	−4.1** (1.4)	−4.2** (1.4)
Conservative Christian[a,b]		4.2 (2.3)	−4.3* (1.8)	−11.3*** (1.8)	−11.9*** (1.8)
Other private[a,b]		11.0*** (2.1)	2.8 (1.7)	−4.6** (1.5)	−5.6*** (1.5)
Charter[a]		−6.1** (2.3)	−4.6** (1.7)	−4.7** (1.7)	−4.4** (1.6)
Percent lunch				−2.0***	−2.1***
Mean home resources				5.2***	5.2***
Percent minority				−1.1	−2.8**
Percent LEP				1.3***	1.7***
Large city					−0.2
Rural					−2.1***
Northeast					−0.6
South					2.7***
West					−2.4***
Student level:					
Black			−16.9***	−15.6***	−15.8***
Hispanic			−7.5***	−6.6***	−6.5***
American Indian			−5.8***	−4.6***	−4.2***
Asian			6.3***	6.4***	6.4***
Female			−4.4***	−4.4***	−4.4***
LEP			−11.5***	−11.3***	−11.3***
IEP			−20.8***	−20.9***	−20.9***
Lunch			−8.2***	−7.2***	−7.2***
Home resources			2.6***	2.4***	2.4***
			Random effects		
Intercept (variance between schools)	215.2	201.0	78.5	55.4	51.5
Level 1 (variance within schools)	515.1	515.1	421.1	420.9	421.0
Intraclass correlation (proportion of variance between schools)	.29	.28	.16	.12	.11

Table 4.3: *continued*

	Model 1: null model	Model 2: school sector only	Model 3: sector + student demographics	Model 4: sector + student and school demographics	Model 5: sector + demographics + location
Variance in achievement between schools explained (%)	NA	7	64	74	76
Variance in achievement within schools explained (%)	NA	0	18	18	18

Note: NA = not applicable.

[a]Coefficient and standard error.

[b]Participation rates did not meet National Center for Education Statistics reporting requirements. Results for these subsamples should be interpreted with caution.

*$p < .05$.

**$p < .01$.

***$p < .001$.

Model 3 adds student-level demographic variables, revealing that by adjusting for differences in individual students' backgrounds, the positive private school coefficients lose their significance. To help the reader interpret this more complex model, the intercept of 247.4 is the estimated mean achievement of a student who is a 0 on all of the binary predictors and at the mean of all of the continuous predictors. Said another way, 247.4 is the estimated achievement for a non-IEP, non-LEP white male student with average home resources who attends a typical public school. In a typical Catholic school, the predicted achievement of such a student would be a statistically insignificant 0.1 point higher. If the student is black[9] instead of white, the achievement would be an estimated 16.9 points lower within the same school, regardless of type (given that no interaction effects were found).

These results of Model 3 indicate that the differences in student background factors in the populations served by different schools essentially explain the superior test scores in private schools at the fourth grade level. In fact, in the case of conservative Christian schools, the coefficient becomes significantly negative, suggesting that any achievement advantage in those schools is primarily a product of the more affluent characteristics of the families they serve, and when those background advantages are considered, conservative Christian schools are, on average, significantly underperforming academically (however, readers should be cautioned because of the limits of the grade 4 conservative Christian and "other private" samples). With charter schools, there are relatively high concentrations of minority students at the fourth grade. When demographic factors are taken into account, their coefficient increased from –6.1 to –4.6, yet remained significantly negative relative to other public schools.

Model 4 adds school-level demographic measures, prompting the coefficients for all private school types to become significantly negative relative to public schools, ranging from –4.1 for Lutheran schools to –11.3 for conservative Christian schools. Again, more specifically, 247 is the estimated mean achievement for white, non-IEP, non-LEP, lunch-ineligible males with average home resources, in a public school of average minority, LEP, and SES populations. In a Catholic school of similar demographics, the estimated achievement of such a student would be 7 points lower, or 240.

The inclusion of school-level demographics in Model 4 explains an additional 10% of the variance between schools, suggesting that, in addition to students' own backgrounds, the demographic composition of schools has a substantive influence on achievement. This phenomenon is what is known as the "peer effect," where the demographics and aspirations of a given student's schoolmates can positively (or negatively) impact that student's own academic achievement.[10] Overall, the addition of student- and school-level demographics in Models 3 and 4 had a strong effect on the private school coefficients; the initial private school advantage was reversed after accounting for the higher proportions of advantaged students attending those schools.

Because the concentration of particular school types varied by U.S. locale, we include location variables in our final model. Model 5 adds school location (urban and rural) and U.S. region, yet the coefficients for the various school types are not markedly different from those in model 4.[11] After adjusting for demographics and location, achievement estimates were 7.2 points lower for Catholic schools, 4.2 points lower for Lutheran schools, 11.9 points lower for conservative Christian schools, 5.6 points lower for other private schools, and 4.4 points lower for charter schools.

Model 5 also highlights some important inequities that persist across all schools (again, race- and SES-related interactions with school type were examined but proved to be insignificant). Specifically, within schools, black students score an average of 15.8 points lower than their white schoolmates of similar SES, LEP, and disability status, while this gap is 6.5 points for Hispanic students and 4.2 points for American Indian students. Students of LEP score 11.3 points lower than similar, non-LEP students within the same school, and this difference is 20.9 points for students with IEPs. Students who qualify for free/reduced lunch score 7.2 points lower than their peers who are ineligible (but demographically similar in every other way), and for each of the six additional items students report having at home, the predicted achievement is 2.4 points higher, or nearly a 10-point gap between students with six items versus their demographically similar schoolmates who report having only two.[12] Also according to model 5, in addition to student-level demographics correlating significantly with achievement, school SES and percentage of minority and LEP students are significantly correlated with achievement.

These statistical models suggests that, despite what is assumed in sector-oriented reforms, school characteristics actually play a relatively small role in differentiating achievement. The addition of the school sector variables explains relatively little (7%) of the variation in achievement between schools. Yet adding the student-level demographics to the analysis explains an additional 57% of the variance between schools (64%, instead of 7% in model 2) and 18% of the variance within schools. The final model explains 76% of the variance between schools and 18% of the variance within schools, primarily owing to the demographic controls, as opposed to school sector or location variables.

GRADE 8 RESULTS

The same five HLM models were created for eighth grade, as presented in Table 4.4. Model 1, the null model, shows that the overall mean school achievement was 279.7 points.

Model 2 indicates that the eighth-grade school math achievement means for (noncharter) public schools averaged 275.5 points. In comparison, school achievement means were over 14 points higher in Catholic schools, 21 points higher in Lutheran, 14 points higher in

Table 4.4: School sector and demographic variables predicting eighth-grade NAEP mathematics achievement (131,497 students from 5,377 schools)

	Model 1: full model	Model 2: school sector only	Model 3: sector + student demographics	Model 4: sector + student and school demographics	Model 5: sector + demographics + location
			Fixed effects		
Intercept: school mean achievement[a]	279.7*** (0.6)	275.5*** (0.4)	290.5*** (0.4)	290.6*** (0.4)	291.9*** (0.7)
School level:					
Catholic[a]		14.3*** (1.5)	3.3** (1.2)	-3.0* (1.4)	-3.8** (1.4)
Lutheran[a]		21.2*** (2.7)	9.1*** (2.1)	1.8 (2.2)	1.0 (2.2)
Conservative Christian[a]		5.4 (3.3)	-4.1(2.7)	-10.4*** (2.7)	-10.6*** (2.7)
Other private[a,b]		14.3*** (3.7)	5.0 (2.5)	-2.0 (2.5)	-2.3 (2.6)
Charter[a,b]		0.9 (4.0)	1.8 (2.7)	2.4 (2.0)	2.4 (2.0)
Percent lunch				-1.9***	-1.8***
Mean home resources				4.5***	4.4***
Percent minority				-5.9***	-7.5***
Percent LEP				0.8	1.0
Large city					1.3
Rural					-1.5*
Northeast					-0.7
South					-0.4
West					-2.2*
Student level:					
Black			-21.7***	-19.6***	-19.7***
Hispanic			-10.9***	-9.3***	-9.3***
American Indian			-9.0***	-7.9***	-7.6***
Asian			6.9***	7.2***	7.3***
Female			-4.0***	-4.0***	-4.0***
LEP			-15.4***	-15.1***	-15.1***

Table **4.4**: *continued*

	Model 1: null model	Model 2: school sector only	Model 3: sector + student demographics	Model 4: sector + student and school demographics	Model 5: sector + demographics + location
IEP			−34.6***	−34.7***	−34.7***
Lunch			−7.8***	−7.0***	−7.0***
Home resources			4.6***	4.5***	4.5***
Random effects					
Intercept (variance between schools)	372.6	325.8	133.3	104.4	103.1
Level 1 (variance within schools)	627.5	627.8	476.1	476.2	476.3
Intraclass correlation (proportion of variance between schools)	.37	.34	.22	.18	.18
Variance in achievement between schools explained (%)	NA	13	64	72	72
Variance in achievement within schools explained (%)	NA	0	24	24	24

Note: NA = not applicable.

[a]Coefficient and standard error.

[b]Participation rates did not meet National Center for Education Statistics reporting requirements. Results for these subsamples should be interpreted with caution.

*$p < .05$.

**$p < .01$.

***$p < .001$.

"other private" schools, and more than 5 points higher in conservative Christian schools. Achievement in charter schools was roughly 1 point higher than in other public schools.

With the inclusion of student-level demographic variables, model 3 substantially reduces the positive private school coefficients, yet the Catholic and Lutheran coefficients remain significantly positive. Model 4 indicates that when both student and school demographic differences are controlled, public school means are significantly higher than those of Catholic and conservative Christian schools and statistically equal to means for the other schools. And finally, as seen in model 5, once school location is added, the results are similar to those of model 4.[13] Overall, the full model reveals that, when compared with public schools, the mean mathematics achievement of schools with similar demographics/location is a statistically significant 3.8 points lower for Catholic schools and a significant 10.6 points lower for conservative Christian schools. The remaining differences between public school means and those of others are not significant. It is worth noting that, unlike at grade 4, the coefficient for charter schools was positive (but statistically insignificant with $p = .22$), although readers should be cautious on account of the limits of the grade 8 charter school sample.

As in grade 4, model 5 also highlights important inequities that persist across all school types. Specifically, black students score an average of almost 20 points lower than their white schoolmates of similar SES, LEP, and disability status within the same school. This gap is roughly 9 points for Hispanic students and 8 points for American Indian students. Students of LEP score 15 points lower than similar students within the same school who are not LEP, and this difference is almost 35 points for students with IEPs. Regarding SES, for each of the six additional items students reported having at home, the mean achievement is 4.5 points higher. With the exception of school lunch (for which the coefficient is roughly −7 at both grades), each of these demographic coefficients is larger at grade 8 than at grade 4. Also according to model 5, the −7.5 coefficient for the percentage of minority students within a school is significant and greater in magnitude than the −2.8 coefficient at grade 4. Hence, race- and SES-related disparities tend to be larger at grade 8 than at grade 4, indicating that disparities widen as students progress through school. Furthermore, the impact of home advantages is magnified at grade 8 when compared with grade 4.

The final model explains 72% of the variance between schools and 24% of the variance within schools. As at grade 4, the majority of the variance explained is due to student- and school-level demographic factors. In fact, although school type appears to explain 7% and 13% of the variance in achievement between schools at grades 4 and 8, respectively, if we reorder the models and enter school type after demographic/location variables, school type—the key factor in market theory—accounts for just an additional 2% of the variance between schools at grade 4, and 1% at grade 8.

SUMMARY OF RESULTS

Figures 4.1 and 4.2 display the HLM results in a more visual way. In each bar graph the differences in school achievement are represented both before and after adjusting for demographic and location differences among schools, with public schools serving as the baseline. The bars show the HLM coefficients from model 2 (school sector only) and model 5 (with demographic and location controls), thereby displaying

Figure 4.1: Predicted differences between mean achievement in public schools and other types of schools, before and after adjusting for demographics/location and grade 4.

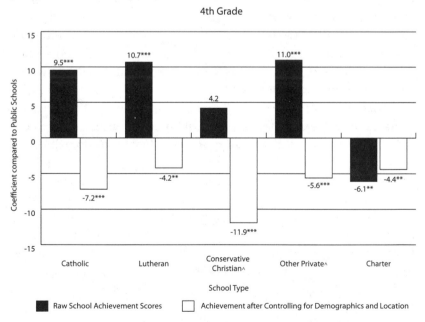

4th Grade

Coefficient compared to Public Schools

9.5*** 10.7*** 11.0***
4.2
-4.2**
-5.6*** -6.1** -4.4**
-7.2***
-11.9***

Catholic   Lutheran   Conservative Christian^   Other Private^   Charter

School Type

■ Raw School Achievement Scores   □ Achievement after Controlling for Demographics and Location

Figure 4.2: Predicted differences between mean achievement in public schools and other types of schools, before and after adjusting for demographics/location and grade 8.

8th Grade

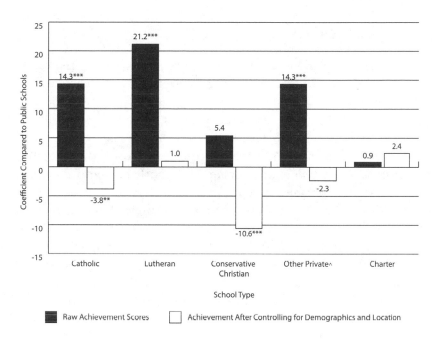

the predicted difference between the mean achievement of the five school types and that of public schools both before and after taking demographic factors into account. In contrast to the assumptions of public choice or market theory, the higher test scores of private and independent schools, which theorists argue is due to their more autonomous organizational status or their location in the private sector, is instead the result of the fact that they serve more affluent students. Those achievement advantages disappear once the private and independent schools' demographic advantages are factored into the mix. In fact, when the background advantages of their students are considered, most of these types of schools are actually underperforming relative to public schools. In terms of ways to interpret the disparities between school achievement means, a popular approach is to consider a 10–11 point disparity as very roughly representing a difference of one grade level. In that light, a difference of 5 or 10 points may seem substantial. In terms of effect size, a 10–11 point difference in school means represents a moderate to large effect of roughly .5–.7 when compared with the standard deviations in school achievement at grades 4 (14.7) and 8 (19.3).

Does School Sector Matter?

The results for both fourth and eighth grades consistently indicated that demographic differences between public and private schools more than account for the relatively high raw NAEP mathematics scores of private schools in these data. After adjusting for demographic differences, no charter or private school means are higher than public school means to any statistically significant degree[14]; moreover, particularly at grade 4, public schools actually score significantly higher than do private and charter schools.

While the current crop of reformers champion consumer-style choice across different types of schools and draw on models from the more competitive and autonomous private school sector, our analysis indicates that school sector does not matter all that much; it plays a relatively small role in predicting academic achievement, particularly when compared with other factors such as student demographics. The analysis points instead to notable differences within school sectors. Much of the research on private school effects has focused on the beneficial impact of Catholic schools. Yet these results show that means for both public and Lutheran schools tended to be higher than for Catholic schools after accounting for differences in student populations. Additionally, as the Catholic share of the private school sector has declined, conservative Christian schools have accelerated in growth. This is particularly interesting in view of our finding that conservative Christian schools are the lowest performing school type at both grades, raising intriguing questions about market theorists' assumptions regarding rational consumers seeking the highest quality academic options for their children.[15]

This analysis of nationally representative achievement data seems to suggest that, in many ways, public schools are doing relatively well, at least compared with private schools. These findings appear to challenge the notion that the private sector necessarily produces better results in areas such as education. Furthermore, the data here suggest significant reasons to be suspicious of claims of general failure in the public schools and raise substantial questions regarding a basic premise of the current generation of school reform.

Still, there are limitations to this type of analysis that need to be considered. The remarkable size and representative nature of the NAEP samples and the general consistency and robustness of the results at grades 4 and 8 lend support for the reliability of this analysis. However, any analysis of NAEP has limits. The most important limitation of these data lies in the fact that NAEP data are cross-sectional and therefore do not allow for examinations of individual student growth in achievement over time.

In response to our analysis, some market advocates hypothesized (without supporting evidence) that students who are lower achieving than others in their demographic peer group are more likely to enroll in private or charter schools.[16] Given that the coefficients favoring public schools were less striking in grade 8 than in grade 4, such proponents infer from these data the possibility of a long-term, positive effect of being in private or charter schools.[17] This question is best addressed with longitudinal data to measure school effectiveness over time, which is what we do in the next chapter.

5 *The Effectiveness of Public and Private Schools*

The large, nationally representative National Assessment of Educational Progress (NAEP) dataset indicates that, after accounting for the greater advantages of students served in private schools, public school fourth and eighth graders' mathematics achievement is higher, on average, than that of students in private schools. While this finding is intriguing, it is not clear how illuminating it may actually be. These cross-sectional data do not necessarily help us understand the effects of different schools on achievement. We cannot conclude from these data that schools are responsible for the differences in achievement since other factors not measured in the data could also be at play. It is at least theoretically possible that the results reflect a selection bias of more able students being placed in public schools, with students in need of more help being placed in private schools. In order to determine whether or not these types of scenarios are at play, we need to measure the academic growth of students in different schools over time.

As we have noted, these initial findings were rather accidental, and other tools can be effectively employed to determine whether these findings hold true with alternative analytical approaches and data. In this chapter, we examine a longitudinal dataset to offer an analysis of student growth in the different types of schools. This is a particularly useful approach for three related reasons. First, it tells us whether students in a particular type of school start their school careers at a level that is academically above, similar to, or beneath their peers in other types of schools. Second, we can measure how much achievement growth is then evident in each type of school. And thus, third, by also accounting for other factors that can influence achievement, we can then determine the relative effectiveness of each type of school in boosting student achievement—a clear advance from the analysis in the previous chapter. Drawing on nationally representative data from the Early Childhood Longitudinal Study, Kindergarten Class of 1998–99 (ECLS-K), the results of the analysis are quite illuminating and informative regarding the relative effectiveness of public and private schools.

Refocusing the Issue

In view of policy debates about the relative strengths of both charter schools and private schools funded by voucher programs, the NAEP results are both surprising and provocative. However, the policy concern with increasing achievement—and particularly with the chronic achievement gap between affluent and disadvantaged students—requires evidence on what types of schools are best (and least) able to address those issues. Policymakers have been embracing private-style models to increase achievement, particularly for poor and minority students. While analysis of the NAEP data might suggest that such approaches are somewhat unfounded or misguided, those data do not allow us to say with certainty that any one type of school boosts student achievement more than others.

Since policymakers want to use schools to address the achievement gap, the real question for policymakers and researchers is how much different types of schools, such as private and charter schools, can add to the academic achievement of students, especially those who might otherwise be trapped in failing public schools. This concern raises the question as to whether the unexpected achievement advantages for public schools evident in the NAEP data would hold also for data that follow student growth over time. Said another way: Was the surprising performance of public school students caused by their public schools? This is an important consideration, because the question of the different effects of different schools is at the heart of the issue—a very contentious issue—on policy options and school reform.

Most observers might assume that students starting their school careers in private schools would be entering school with more developed academic skills than their public school counterparts. After all, we know that, on average, they are more likely to come from more socioeconomically advantaged families, with more educated parents, more educational resources in the home, and fewer disabilities—factors associated with academic attitudes and skills. Thus, all things being equal, it would seem that students who enter kindergarten in private schools would be more able to do some basic math and reading, for instance, and would also have the advantage of coming from families that care enough about education to pay out-of-pocket for what they believe is a superior educational experience for their children.

But that might not necessarily be the case. It may seem strange, but it could be the case that parents send their better performing children to public schools and their siblings who are struggling to private schools, where they might get more help in catching up to their peers. In fact, this is exactly the claim of Greg Forster of the Friedman Foundation, who, in trying to challenge our NAEP findings, wrote, "A much more likely explanation for the . . . results is that when students enter private schools, they tend to have test scores a little lower than other students of their race and socioeconomic status."[1]

And indeed, while that may be an odd claim that could be easily investigated (as we do in this chapter), this does highlight a weakness of NAEP's cross-sectional structure and points to the imperative to examine how students fare over time in various schools in order to determine which schools are more effective in boosting student achievement.

STUDYING PRIVATE AND PUBLIC SCHOOL EFFECTIVENESS

In this longitudinal analysis, we examine the ECLS-K database to address two issues: (1) whether public school students enter their school careers ahead of their peers in private schools, as market theorists such as those at the Friedman Foundation have suggested; and (2) the relative academic effectiveness of different types of schools.

Since the NAEP analysis indicates that fourth and eighth graders in public schools score at a level at least equal to that of demographically similar students in private schools, it is essential that we determine how public and private school student achievement compares in early kindergarten, which can be accomplished with ECLS-K. Then we need to measure how much those students learn as they progress through their academic careers in the different types of schools. We focus in particular on Catholic schools, as the largest school type within the private school category and the single school type most likely to embrace voucher programs.[2] We cannot include in our analysis an examination of charter schools, as they are not sufficiently represented in the

ECLS-K data set for the purposes of making substantial claims of their effects. As with the NAEP analysis, we examine achievement in mathematics, since, as one market advocate noted, "Math tests are thought to be especially good indicators of school effectiveness, because math, unlike reading and language skills, is learned mainly in school."[3]

ECLS-K is a database administered by the federal government's National Center for Education Statistics (NCES). It contains data from a nationally representative sample of more than 21,000 students in both public and private schools. It includes both background and achievement data for the stratified random sample of students who started kindergarten in 1998. The data set provides a measure of initial achievement for these students based upon assessments administered during the fall of kindergarten. Then follow-up administrations of this cohort of students provide longitudinal data on their achievement gains as they progress through school.

Thus, this data set embodies two major advantages. First, there are rich data for each student. ECLS-K includes individual data on students, as well as data on their classrooms, teachers, and schools, which are useful when considering differences not only in student outcomes but in the processes through which students are educated. These data were collected through multiple methods, including comprehensive surveys of teachers and administrators, surveys and interviews of parents, observations conducted by trained researchers, and data from the students. Parents were asked a wide range of questions about their families and homes, including questions about socioeconomic issues such as occupation, income, and home resources. Trained researchers conducted math (and reading) assessments of students in individualized settings.

Second, ECLS-K assessments were developed with notable care. Experts constructed individual items, drawing on specialists in assessment, curriculum, and content areas, as well as national and state standards. Mathematics assessment items gauge an extensive array of content, ranging from basic counting and place value to fractions, geometry, and measurement. Like NAEP, the assessments are highly respected. Items were first tested in the field, and their construct validity was affirmed by measuring the correlation of students on the various items with their performance on existing assessments.[4]

As with NAEP, ECLS-K contains data on students nested within schools. Therefore, we again use multilevel models to analyze the data on student and family background factors, school type, and academic achievement. Because these are longitudinal data, students can be expected to change schools and even sectors as the study proceeds. This raises some issues that need to be addressed. For one, it should be expected that some students will "disappear" from the data. That is, as time goes on, they will have moved to new residences or otherwise dropped out of the data collection, despite reasonable efforts by researchers to locate them for subsequent rounds. While this can be problematic, there are ways of dealing with these missing data issues, which we describe later.

Furthermore, it should be expected that there will be a number of students who remain in the study but change not only schools but school sectors as they proceed through their education. This has the potential of confounding our efforts to determine how much any one type of school adds value to a student's learning. Because we are interested in the effects of different types of schools, we track students who stayed in the same school sector over the course of this study, even if they changed schools within that sector (but only within a single sector).

Because of the expense of tracking students over time, the ECLS-K sample is considerably smaller than the NAEP sample, involving 9,791 students in 1,531 public and private schools (1,273 and 258, respectively). With hierarchical linear modeling (HLM), we can "adjust" or account for differences in the demographic composition of public and private schools at both the school and the student level. This means, for instance, that we can consider the socioeconomic status (SES) of an individual student and then also control for the SES of the other students at his/her school. This is a key capability, because—unlike much of the work on vouchers—it allows us to account for the peer effect, thereby determining the degree to which any achievement advantages are due not to a superior academic program but to being in an environment with other students who have better resourced, more educated parents.

For the ECLS-K analysis, we use the following demographic variables at the student level:

- An SES composite provided by ECLS-K, based on parents' education, occupation, and income
- Race
- Whether a language other than English is spoken at home[5]

Table 5.1: Demographics of the ECLS-K study sample by school type

	Public, $n = 7{,}951$ students	Catholic, $n = 1{,}185$ students	Other private, $n = 655$ students
Mean SES	−0.11	0.44	0.63
Black, %	13.0	4	6
Latina/o, %	21	15	9
Asian, %	5	6	5
Non-English at home, %	14	8	4
Female, %	50	51	53
Disability, %	39	35	33

- Gender
- Parent-reported disability status of the student[6]
- Age of student when starting kindergarten

And we use the following school-level variables:

- The SES of a school (the average SES of the students sampled from a school, using the student SES variable)
- The percentage of white and Asian students at a school, as reported by the principal
- Whether a school is located in an urban or rural area
- The region of a school (West, South, Northeast, or Midwest)

In Table 5.1, demographic variables are displayed by school type. These data provide compelling evidence that, when compared with private schools, public schools serve a substantially higher proportion of low-SES and minority students, as well as more students who have disabilities or do not speak English at home. For example, public school students are more than one half of a standard deviation lower than Catholic schools in terms of SES, and there are more than three times as many black students in public schools than in Catholic schools.

Next we conduct two HLM analyses. First we consider initial school achievement at the start of students' academic careers. This allows us to consider alternate explanations for the NAEP results and gives us a baseline for understanding students' subsequent academic growth. Second, we examine those academic gains over time in the different schools.

INITIAL ACADEMIC STANDING

In view of the theoretical possibility raised by market advocates at the Friedman Foundation that children in private schools performed beneath their demographically comparable peers in the NAEP analysis because parents tend to send their lower performing kids to private schools,[7] we conduct HLM analyses using students' initial performance (as assessed in the fall of their kindergarten year) as the outcome, with the student and school demographic variables described above as the predictors. If, as the Friedman Foundation asserts, initial achievement is lower in private schools, then this would explain away the NAEP results and may indicate that parents recognize that private schools are more effective vehicles for raising achievement for their children, and especially for their less academically able children. It may thus be an indirect indication of the relative effectiveness of private schools and provide further support for the idea of providing vouchers for families to send children to private schools.

However, if initial achievement is in fact higher in private schools, then that would mean that parents are not sending their lower performing children to private schools, as Forster claims, but instead that private schools are attracting more academically prepared students from the start. This would indicate that public schools' notable performance on NAEP is not simply a matter of serving easier-to-educate students and that something else must be happening within public and private schools to explain the results.

In examining the actual ECLS-K data, the raw scores are higher for private schools, as we might expect and as we saw with the initial NAEP scores. It is already well-known that these schools tend to serve populations with fewer risk factors than in public schools—factors known to depress achievement scores regardless of the effectiveness of the school that serves them. However, as we noted in the previous chapter, the real question is the degree to which those achievement patterns persist after we account for differences in student background factors that are known to influence achievement. Those results are presented in Figure 5.1.

In order to understand the results of this analysis of ECLS-K data, it is useful to know that the standard deviation is about 6 points for students in kindergarten (and about 17 points for students in fifth grade, indicating a narrower range of scores when students start school).

Figure 5.1: ECLS-K kindergarten mathematics achievement after adjusting for demographics.

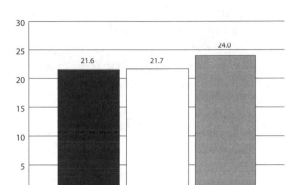

This means that a difference of 2 to 3 points in the average scores for different schools would be considered a relatively small effect size at fifth grade but a more substantial, medium-size effect in kindergarten. Alternatively, readers might consider that student growth is approximately 15 points a year on average from the start of kindergarten through the end of fifth grade. In that sense, a 2- to 3-point difference would correspond to a couple of months of academic growth.

As Figure 5.1 indicates, the HLM analysis demonstrates that initial achievement in public and Catholic schools is virtually even after controlling for background factors. Students in public schools began school with average scores of 21.6, while comparable Catholic school students averaged 21.7. Yet initial academic achievement in other private schools was substantially higher—at 24 points, approximately 2 to 3 months ahead of other students when they start school.[8] Since this is initial academic achievement, it does not measure academic gains that any school or school type produces but instead reflects the academic ability of the students whom different schools attract when those students start their school careers. Since these differences cannot be attributed to the schools, they must instead be a result of non-school factors such as family influences, including a commitment to education (demonstrated by the fact that some families are willing to provide transportation and tuition in pursuit of what they see as a better education).

Furthermore, these initial results completely negate the hypothesis that public schools' superior NAEP scores are due to parents sending their lower scoring students to private schools. Not only is this untrue, since no school type scored lower than public schools in initial academic achievement, but the opposite is true, particularly in the case of non-Catholic private schools. That is, as many people already know, parents of more academically advanced students are more likely to send their children to these private schools, thereby giving those schools an immediate boost at the start.

ACADEMIC GROWTH IN PUBLIC AND PRIVATE SCHOOLS

Of course, the real issue is not simply which schools or sectors attract the more academically able students, but which schools produce greater gains in achievement for the students who attend them. Thus, for the second stage of the ECLS-K analysis, we use those students' achievement scores from the fifth grade as the outcome, while controlling for those same demographic variables, as well as their prior, initial achievement in kindergarten.[9] If achievement gains are greater in private schools than in demographically comparable public schools, then this outcome—reflecting common wisdom on the topic—would justify interventions such as vouchers for private schools, where students could get exposure to more effective educational processes. (Although charter schools are not tested in this analysis owing to being underrepresented in the sample, greater private school achievement gains would suggest that charter school reforms that try to emulate private school structures and processes are likely a fruitful policy strategy.)

However, if achievement growth is no different in different types of schools, then the relationship assumed by reformers and market theorists between school sector and achievement is weak and not a useful approach to improving educational opportunities for students. Moreover, if achievement growth in public schools is greater than in other school types—that is, if public schools can catch up to or surpass achievement in private schools as the students in the sample progress—then this suggests that public schools are actually more effective than private schools at promoting student achievement.

Figure 5.2 presents fifth-grade mathematics achievement in the three main school types after accounting for background factors and initial school achievement. A fascinating result emerges. Mathematics

Figure 5.2: ECLS-K fifth-grade mathematics achievement after adjusting for demographics and kindergarten scores.

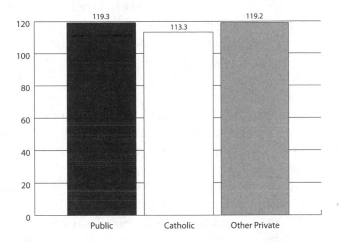

achievement gains for students in public schools outpace those of the other school types over the course of the study. While in terms of initial achievement, public school students began their schooling slightly behind their Catholic school counterparts, and significantly behind those students in other private schools, the academic growth for students in public schools outpaces that of students in Catholic and other private schools, so that by fifth grade they have essentially caught up with their private school peers and are a statistically significant 6 points ahead of Catholic school students. That is, public school students gained almost a half-year more of learning than demographically comparable students in Catholic schools—the schools most likely to enroll public school students with vouchers.

These results could be looked at in two somewhat contradictory ways, both of which still undermine the assumptions of market theory. First, overall, between-sector differences are relatively small. As we have seen before with the NAEP analysis, nonschool background factors are still the primary influential force in the academic prospects for students. While all of the variables in this analysis combined accounted for 62% of the between-school differences in achievement, school type or sector itself explained only 5% of the differences. Nonschool demographic factors explain a substantially larger share. This is important because recent waves of reformers focus their efforts on changing school-level factors. And market theorists in particular put primary emphasis on assumed differences in school sectors, when those are, in fact, relatively minor considerations.

At the same time, a rather remarkable pattern is evident in the data. After controlling for demographic background issues in order to isolate school effects, students in public schools start out scoring the lowest of all groups when they enter kindergarten, but they learn at least as much as "other private" school students during elementary school, and their gains substantially outpace those of Catholic school students. Inasmuch as there is a school sector effect, it favors public schools, not private schools. The superior academic gains in public schools over Catholic and other private schools not only confirm but significantly advance the findings from the NAEP data because they speak directly to the causal effectiveness of public schools. Said another way, the vaunted "private school effect" found in past research, while it may exist for some students, is now significantly overshadowed by a public school effect that is evident in the two most prominent national data sets.

A New View on Public and Private Schools Effects

The ECLS-K data present compelling evidence that public schools are more effective than Catholic schools and are at least as effective as other private schools in raising student achievement. This analysis is particularly compelling because it considers students' academic achievement at the start of their school careers and then examines their subsequent academic growth over time in different school sectors. The findings are a strong indication that the results of the broader NAEP analysis of school performance in different types of schools are an accurate reflection of actual school effects, despite the limitations of those cross-sectional data.

Still, as with any large-scale data set, there are limits to the ECLS-K data. The most glaring issue for both data sets is that they can capture only observable factors such as SES and achievement variables and are unable to control for "unobservable" issues such as parent commitment to education and student initiative—issues that are at least theoretically held constant in randomized studies.[10] However, if anything, this limitation presents relative school performance and achievement in ways that artificially depress public school outcomes compared with private and charter school results. That is, while public and private school students in the NAEP and ECLS-K studies were essentially equalized in terms of measurable demographic differences, we could not account for hidden factors that cause one parent to select and pay tuition to a private school while another, demographically similar parent does not. Arguably, students whose parents choose private and charter schools for them have the hidden advantage that their families have demonstrated a real commitment to education in terms of investing time, money, and effort for their child's schooling. We cannot measure nor statistically control for this commitment, so our NAEP and ECLS-K results, if anything, overestimate private and charter school performance.

Yet, in all of the policy and research debates about reforming public schools to adopt more private models, it is easy to forget that a typical student in a math class probably cares very little about the school's governing structure. And parents are often interested in other factors such as convenience, proximity, safety, and who else enrolls when they decide on a school. But from a public policy perspective, where expenditures and academic outcomes matter, the type of school can be very important.[11] While differences between school sectors in this regard are not nearly as great as market theorists have suggested, they are, in fact, the opposite of what those reformers have assumed and argued. The evidence is rather compelling that, at least on a national scale, the independent school sectors are not necessarily more effective than public schools. In fact, the reverse appears to be true in these data. Thus, the notably pervasive policies and reforms that are based on the misguided assumption of market theory and that are popular with policymakers need to be questioned.

Privatization proponents and choice advocates will no doubt attack findings such as these that do not align with their agenda (as, no doubt, would choice opponents if our results were different). In view of the evidence challenging their agenda, they will assert that the promise of better outcomes predicted by market theory is no longer paramount as long as parents are happy in their choice of schools (ignoring the need for better educational options); they will contend that the focus on overall averages obscures variations within school sectors that include some outstanding private and independent schools—ignoring the premise that their autonomy is expected to make the independent sector itself more effective.

They will also claim that private and charter schools play an important role in American education, since parents choose these schools for multiple reasons beyond academic achievement. We agree that this is true. But it is also true that assertions about superior academic effectiveness in the independent sector should not play the pivotal role in these arguments. Hopes that moving students to the independent sectors will increase achievement may be valid in individual cases, but policies to encourage such shifts on a mass scale are based on an illusion. Since we initially produced these findings, other independent and respected researchers, using other approaches, assumptions, and specifications, have found similar patterns—although they have not pursued the issue of why these patterns are becoming apparent, as we do in the following chapter. For instance, after we released our NAEP results, researchers at ETS produced reports for the NCES studying performance of public schools relative to charter and private schools while controlling for differences in student populations.[12] That work extended the analysis to include mathematics as well as reading and essentially affirmed our findings on the notable performance of public schools. Indeed, even a methodologically flawed attack from voucher proponents came to similar conclusions on charter schools.[13] Later, in the wake of our initial results on ECLS-K,[14] researchers at Stanford University using the same data found no private school effect in reading or mathematics but a public school effect in mathematics.[15] Similarly, research out of the University of Notre Dame on student gains at the start of their school careers found a slight advantage for public schools.[16] Thus, while the findings presented in this book may appear to be surprising, counterintuitive, or even outlandish to some, they are increasingly in good company.

Indeed, this analysis contributes to a growing understanding, based in the empirical evidence rather than ideological expectations, that questions earlier assumptions about the private school effect. Previous thinking on this issue drew on studies of students who began school in the 1960s, while more recent cross-sectional and now longitudinal data indicate something quite different. Rather than drawing only on a single methodological approach or a single data set, our findings offer

very similar results from different data sets, presenting a robust rein-
terpretation of the issue.

SCHOOL DIFFERENCES UNDERLYING
ACHIEVEMENT PATTERNS

The evidence we have presented to this point focuses largely on schools
as generic "machines," which can be evaluated by their output. This approach is typical in much of the research on this topic, where schools
are treated as a "black box"—there are inputs, then some magical, but
obscure, processes occur before we see the finished products. For example, voucher advocates have claimed to find significant achievement
results for students who transfer to private schools but have generally
not demonstrated what specific attributes or processes of those schools
may lead to their purported performance advantages. It is assumed
that different inputs and outcomes can be weighed in order to identify
the best box, but there is no understanding of the inner process that
produces the results, which is necessary for replication or scaling up
effective practices. Market theorists argue that those specific processes
(on which they are agnostic) are of minor importance to the external
incentives that are placed onto the black box of schooling.

However, as we have demonstrated, schools susceptible to the external incentives that market theorists endorse are not outperforming
the schools they deride. So it is important to get past market theorists' assumption that organizational structure trumps specific school
practices such as curricular and pedagogical issues and to consider the
specific attributes that help explain the perhaps surprising patterns we
are seeing in school performance and effectiveness.

6 *Understanding Patterns of School Performance*

WITH CORINNA CRANE, PH.D.

The studies presented in the previous chapters provide compelling evidence from two nationally representative data sets that the common wisdom on private school superiority is incorrect and that policies based on those common assumptions are misguided. Despite independent schools' greater autonomy, which market theorists claim is key to school effectiveness, public schools are often outperforming and outgaining these private and charter schools, suggesting serious limitations in the efforts to improve schools through private sector–based reforms. Thus far, we have uncovered consistent patterns of public and private school achievement in both cross-sectional and longitudinal data, but we have not yet explored the reasons for these patterns. Yet this can be a particularly intriguing exercise in view of the fact that the patterns seem to go against the popular theoretical perspective currently dominating policy making, with its focus on organizational effects, choice, and competition. Just as the overall achievement patterns challenge some of the dominant thinking in policy circles, so too do some of the findings that we present here on the factors actually linked to higher achievement.

In this chapter we outline our analyses of the two data sets regarding the different factors that could account for the notably positive effects of enrolling a child in a public school. Some of the factors that policymakers and market theorists celebrate turn out to have little impact on student achievement, while other factors that they dismiss are actually useful predictors of school success. Still other achievement-related factors that are thought to differ substantially by school sector actually do not once school demographics are considered.

Theory on School Sector Causes of Achievement Differences

Public choice and market theorists have argued that specific attributes of schools are tied to a school's location in the public, district-run sector or in the independent, charter, and private sectors. For example, Chubb and Moe famously found that a school's governance structure—and particularly the autonomous, independent nature of private schools— is positively associated with more effective educational practices, as evidenced by superior outcomes.[1] Charter schools advance from this premise, and there is some descriptive evidence to support the contention that there are substantive differences in the organizational and educational practices in different sectors. For instance, research in Ohio found differences in the instructional practices at public, private, and independent schools.[2] However, as Benveniste, Carnoy, and Rothstein noted in their study of a small but diverse set of schools in California, those differences may be greater within each sector rather than between the different sectors.[3] Yet these two studies were not able to link any detected differences in school factors to student learning. The questions then arise as to the extent to which those differences might be apparent in wider, nationally representative samples of different school types and how much they might explain distinct patterns in the effectiveness of the various types of schools.

If there are substantive differences in the internal practices of public and private schools, such as in the areas of curriculum or staffing, for instance, such differences could offer more grounded and useful explanations for the variations in outcomes between schools than do more general, theoretical arguments advanced by market advocates. Or school practices might prove to be irrelevant in shaping achievement patterns by sector, despite assumptions about their importance. It is important, however, to recall that demographic differences between the populations served in different schools are a—if not the—major predictive variable for explaining the variance in academic outcomes across schools. While both recent and classic research has found a limited impact on achievement from school factors, and greater differences within than between the various school sectors, policymakers have been particularly enamored with the idea of boosting outcomes through school sector–oriented strategies.[4] That is, they hope to improve instruction and other school processes within public schools by forcing them to act more like private or charter schools.[5]

Here we consider the different internal factors that may influence achievement and determine how they are concentrated in specific school sectors. As we show, there are particular practices and school climate factors that explain achievement patterns in schools. Some of these factors fly in the face of market theory and current policy approaches to improving the nation's schools.

In exploring these factors, we again draw on evidence from both the sizable National Assessment of Educational Progress (NAEP) and the longitudinal Early Childhood Longitudinal Study, Kindergarten Class of 1998–99 (ECLS-K) data sets. As we have shown earlier, there are clear advantages to the longitudinal data in ECLS-K for identifying causal mechanisms that influence school effectiveness. However, the notably comprehensive NAEP data set has proven to be remarkably accurate in our initial analyses of achievement by school sector, producing findings that were confirmed in the ECLS-K work. Given the enormous samples and relevant school- and teacher-level variables available in NAEP, and given the longitudinal strengths of ECLS-K, we again draw on both forms of data as we explore the reasons schools differ in their ability to accelerate student growth.

NAEP AND ECLS-K EXAMINATIONS

Our approach to analyzing potential causes of achievement differences by sector was generally similar within each of the two data sets, but availability of particular variables differed by data set. Additionally, in the ECLS analysis, we did more work up front to screen out factors that appear to differ by sector but that no longer do once demographic differences are considered.

NAEP Variables and Analyses

Again, we used the NAEP data set, containing information on over 340,000 fourth and eighth grade students from nationally representative samples of public and private schools. A wide variety of demographic, school climate, and instruction-related variables were included in a series of twelve multilevel models (with students at level 1 and school at level 2) to determine the extent to which school sector–related achievement differences persisted after we included particular variables. Entering variables in sequence in this way allows us to examine the effect of specific clusters of variables on the coefficients for each school type, thereby revealing the extent to which each cluster might explain achievement differences by school type.

In the NAEP analysis, in addition to school demographics and location, we examined class size, school climate (teacher morale, student conflicts, parent involvement, student attendance), teacher education (certification, new teachers, professional development), time spent on math, teaching methods (curricular emphases, multiple choice test use, calculator use), and students' beliefs about math (i.e., whether math is simply fact memorization and whether there is only one way to solve math problems), and attitudes toward math (students' agreement with the statement "I like math"). The specific variables available differed slightly between grades 4 and 8, but most variables were examined at both grades. See Tables 6.1 and 6.2 for descriptive data on the variables by school type. See Appendix A for more details on the NAEP samples, variables, and methods used in these analyses.

ECLS-K Variables and Analyses

As described in Chapter 5, ECLS-K offers advantages for analyzing achievement in public and private schools, including longitudinal data and a wide variety of survey data collected from administrators, teachers, and parents. However, its sample of students and schools, although still nationally representative and large by most standards, is substantially smaller than NAEP samples, making it impossible to focus on a variety of specific public and private school types. Hence, our analysis of ECLS-K focuses on comparisons of public and Catholic schools only, the two most prevalent school types in the data set and the two most analyzed in prior literature.[6]

In Chapter 5, we discussed differences in ECLS-K mathematics gains by sector between kindergarten and grade 5. However, to look more closely at possible reasons public school gains are larger than those in Catholic schools, we zero in on the grade span in which disparities in math gains are largest—that is, between grades 1 and 3.[7] Given that there are no grade 2 data included in ECLS-K, we examine potential achievement-related factors in grade 3, using grade 1 achievement data as a baseline to allow an analysis of contributors to gains made from spring of grade 1 to spring of grade 3.

Students, classrooms, and schools that are not public or Catholic

Table 6.1: Potential achievement-related factors by school type: Full grade 4 NAEP reporting sample (190,147 students from 7,485 Schools)

	Public (noncharter), n = 182,328 students, 6,797 schools	Catholic, n = 2,285 students, 216 schools	Lutheran, n = 555 students, 88 schools	Conservative Christian, n = 651 students, 78 schools	Other private, n = 1,227 students, 157 schools	Charter, n = 3,101 students, 149 schools
Student factors:						
Days absent last month[a]	1.9	1.8	1.7	1.8	1.8	1.9
Talk about studies at home[b]	3.4	3.5	3.5	3.4	3.6	3.5
Traditional math beliefs[c]	1.9	1.8	1.8	1.9	1.7	1.9
Percent do not like math[d]	16	16	19	22	20	19
Percent like math[d]	47	43	39	39	39	44
School factors:						
School enrollment[e]	2.3	1.5	1.1	1.3	1.3	1.7
Class size[f]	3.5	3.2	2.0	1.8	1.8	3.2
Teacher morale (z-scale)	-0.2	0.5	0.4	0.4	0.5	0.1
School conflict (z-scale)	0.2	-0.4	-0.5	-0.3	-0.4	0.0
Parents involved (z-scale)	-0.2	0.6	0.0	0.2	0.3	0.0
Parents volunteer (z-scale)	-0.1	0.4	0.0	0.1	0.0	0.5
Percent certified teachers	89	75	72	44	64	62

Percent new teachers	20	23	10	26	23	38
Professional development (0–12 types)	3.2	2.3	1.8	2.2	2.4	3.3
Time on math[g]	3.2	3.7	3.5	3.4	3.5	3.2
Emphasis on geometry, measurement, data, algebra[h]	8.6	7.6	7.5	7.8	7.9	8.6
Emphasis on number/operations[i]	2.9	2.9	2.9	2.9	3.0	2.8
Multiple choice[j]	0.9	0.7	0.6	0.8	0.5	0.8
Calculators[k]	1.6	1.2	1.0	0.6	1.1	1.2

Note: Sample sizes reflect unweighted NAEP reporting samples; however, means and percentages are for the samples weighted to represent U.S. students and schools.

[a] 1 = 0 Days; 2 = 1–2 days; 3 = 3–4 days; 4 = 5–10 days; 5 = more than 10 days.

[b] 1 = Never or hardly ever; 2 = 1–2 times a month; 3 = once a week; 4 = 2–3 times a week; 5 = every day.

[c] Mean of two variables on 1–3 scale: 1 = not like me; 2 = little like me; 3 = a lot like me.

[d] 1 = 0%–5%; 2 = 6%–10%; 3 = 11%–25%; 4 = 26%–50%; 5 = 51%–75%; 6 = 76%–100%.

[e] 1 = 1–299; 2 = 300–499; 3 = 500–699; 4 = 700 or more.

[f] 1 = 0–15; 2 = 16–18; 3 = 19–20; 4 = 21–25; 5 = 26 or more.

[g] 1 = Less than 1 hour; 2 = at least 1 hour; 3 = at least 2 hours; 4 = 3 hours or more.

[h] Sum of four variables on 1–3 scale: 1 = little/no emphasis; 2 = moderate emphasis; 3 = heavy emphasis.

[i] 1 = Little/no emphasis; 2 = moderate emphasis; 3 = heavy emphasis.

[j] 0 = Less than twice per year; 1 = 1–2 times per month; 2 = 1–2 times per week.

[k] 0 = No instruction in or student access to calculators; 1 = either instruction in or student access to calculators; 2 = both instruction in and access to calculators.

Table 6.2: Potential achievement-related factors by school type: Full grade 8 NAEP reporting sample (153,189 students from 6,092 schools)

	Public (noncharter) (n = 146,512 students, 5,449 schools)	Catholic (n = 2,463 students, 224 schools)	Lutheran (n = 605 students, 96 schools)	Conservative Christian (n = 659 students, 90 schools)	Other private (n = 1,346 students, 148 schools)	Charter (n = 1,604 students, 85 schools)
Student factors:						
Days absent last month[a]	1.9	1.8	1.8	1.8	1.8	1.9
Talk about studies at home[b]	3.0	3.1	3.2	3.0	3.4	3.1
Traditional math beliefs[c]	2.5	2.2	2.3	2.4	2.2	2.5
Likes math[d]	3.2	3.3	3.1	2.9	3.3	3.3
School factors:						
School enrollment[e]	2.4	1.4	1.1	1.2	1.3	1.5
Teacher morale (z-scale)	-0.3	0.5	0.5	0.5	0.5	0.3
School conflict (z-scale)	0.3	-0.5	-0.5	-0.4	-0.5	-0.1
Drugs/alcohol (z-scale)	0.3	-0.6	-0.6	-0.5	-0.3	-0.3
Parents involved (z-scale)	-0.4	0.8	0.3	0.3	0.4	0.1
Parents volunteer (z-scale)	-0.3	0.8	0.2	0.5	0.2	0.5
Percent certified teachers	75	63	54	41	46	47
Math majors[f]	1.1	0.7	0.6	0.8	0.8	0.8
Percent new teachers	23	23	20	33	21	42
Professional development (0–12 types)	5.4	4.8	3.0	3.3	3.7	5.6
Time on math[g]	3.7	3.8	3.5	3.6	3.6	3.6
Calculators[h]	2.6	2.5	2.7	2.4	2.3	2.4

Note: Sample sizes reflect unweighted NAEP reporting samples; however, the means and percentages reported are for the samples weighted to represent U.S. students and schools.

[a] 1 = 0 Days; 2 = 1–2 days; 3 = 3–4 days; 4 = 5–10 days; 5 = more than 10 days.

[b] 1 = Never or hardly ever; 2 = 1–2 times a month; 3 = once a week; 4 = 2–3 times a week; 5 = every day.

[c] Mean of two variables on 1–5 scale: 1 = strongly disagree; 2 = disagree; 3 = undecided; 4 = agree; 5 = strongly agree.

[d] 1 = Strongly disagree; 2 = disagree; 3 = undecided; 4 = agree; 5 = strongly agree.

[e] 1 = 1–399; 2 = 400–599; 3 = 600–799; 4 = 800–999; 5 = 1,000 or more.

[f] 0 = No math/math education major or minor; 1 = math/math education minor; 2 = math/math education major.

[g] 1 = Less than 1 hour; 2 = at least 1 hour; 3 = at least 2 hours; 4 = 3 hours or more.

[h] Mean of three variables on 1–4 scale: 1 = never or hardly ever; 2 = 1–2 times a month; 3 = 1–2 times a week; 4 almost every day.

were removed from the analysis, and only students who were in the same school sector in first and third grade are included. The final sample included 11,860 students, 4,911 classrooms, and 1,972 schools, including 172 Catholic and 1,800 public.[8] We draw from ECLS-K questionnaire data collected from students, teachers, and administrators, focusing on the items that past research suggests might differ by school sector and be related to student achievement. In order to further reduce the number of variables in the final analysis as well as avoid issues of multicollinearity, we created composite variables when there were clusters of related variables. (More details about the samples, variables, and analysis methods are included in Appendix B.)

We go a step further in our ECLS-K analysis than in our prior NAEP analyses by examining—up front—which variables differed by school type both before and after controlling for school demographics. Specifically, to determine whether public and Catholic school personnel differed in their responses to relevant survey questions, we compare the raw means by school sector using basic t-tests. The results of these analyses give a snapshot of what, on average, public or Catholic school teachers and administrators report on these variables. However, the raw differences found could be due more to the demographic composition of the students in those schools than to the school sector itself. Therefore, in addition to t-tests, binary logistic regressions are used to determine whether the variables differed by sector after controlling for demographics. The results for the school- and classroom-level variables are presented in Tables 6.3 and 6.4 and are discussed in more detail below.

After identifying the ECLS-K variables that persistently differed by school type, we used a series of three-level models (students, classrooms, and schools) to determine which of those variables might help explain the public-Catholic school disparity in mathematics gains between first and third grades. As variables pertaining to school and class climate, building characteristics, curriculum and teaching practices, parental involvement, professional development, and teacher characteristics were added, we monitored the effect of these factors on the Catholic school estimate, thereby shedding light on possible explanations for the difference in math test score gains. The dependent variable for this portion of the study was the third grade mathematics t-score, with a control included for first grade spring mathematics test

Table 6.3: ECLS-K school-level descriptive statistics, *t*-test results, and logistic regression results: Catholic (*n* = 172) and public (*n* = 1,800)

Variable	Sector	Descriptive statistics		T-test results (Catholic-public):	Logistic regression results (accounting for demographics)		
		Mean	Standard deviation	*t*-value	B	Standard error	Wald
School descriptors and demographics:							
Midsize city location[a]	Public	0.21	0.41	0.41	0.61**	0.22	7.40
	Catholic	0.23	0.42				
Large suburb location[a]	Public	0.29	0.46	0.87	−0.83***	0.19	18.37
	Catholic	0.33	0.47				
Midsize suburb location[a]	Public	0.08	0.28	−1.76	−0.40	0.37	1.13
	Catholic	0.05	0.22				
Small or large town location[a]	Public	0.06	0.25	1.02	0.91**	0.34	7.21
	Catholic	0.09	0.28				
Rural location[a]	Public	0.10	0.30	−2.41*	−0.64	0.37	2.99
	Catholic	0.05	0.22				
Small school (< 150 students)[b]	Public	0.03	0.17	2.16*	1.56***	0.38	16.54
	Catholic	0.08	0.27				
Large school (750 students or more)[b]	Public	0.19	0.39	−7.78***	−1.41***	0.38	13.63
	Catholic	0.05	0.21				
Percent free/reduced-price lunch eligible student	Public	0.46	0.28	−21.05***	Included as control		
	Catholic	0.10	0.21				
Percent of average daily attendance[c]	Public	4.26	0.95	3.66***	0.12	0.09	2.03
	Catholic	4.63	1.27				
Building characteristics:							
School's percent capacity[d]	Public	−0.08	0.19	−3.12**	−1.92**	0.59	10.81
	Catholic	−0.15	0.26				

Classrooms meet needs[e]	Public	0.60	0.43	4.21***	0.39	0.21	3.40
	Catholic	0.74	0.41				
School climate:							
Security composite[f]	Public	0.11	0.26	−3.29**	0.77	0.48	2.55
	Catholic	0.06	0.18				
School climate composite[g]	Public	3.71	0.37	1.78	−0.23	0.28	0.68
	Catholic	3.76	0.32				
Neighborhood climate composite[h]	Public	3.23	0.50	−0.68	−1.15***	0.26	20.42
	Catholic	3.21	0.40				

Note: School sector was recoded as a binary variable with Catholic = 1 and public = 0.

[a] Binary variables with large city as the default omitted category: 1 = yes; 2 = no.

[b] 1 = Yes; 2 = no.

[c] 1 = <90%; 2 = 90% to <92%; 3 = 92% to <94%; 4 = 94% to <96%; 5 = 96 to <98%; 6=98% to 100%.

[d] Calculated by subtracting the principal-reported number of students the school can accommodate from the number enrolled and dividing this by the number the school can accommodate.

[e] 0 = Not always adequate, 1 = Always adequate.

[f] Composite of two measures—bars on windows/doors and presence of security guards. 0 = neither security measure, .5 = 1 security measure, 1 = 2 security measures.

[g] Composite of outside observers' ratings regarding the presence of decorated hallways, attentive teachers, personable principal, helpful staff, order in hallways, and order in classrooms. Scale of 0 (low) to 4 (high).

[h] Based on observers' ratings of the absence of litter or trash near the school, graffiti near the school, boarded-up buildings near the school, and people congregating near the school, as well as principal-reported ratings of the extent to which substance abuse, gangs, unkempt areas, heavy traffic, violent crime, and general crime are a problem in the area. Scale of 0 (low) to 4 (high).

*p < .05.

**p < .01.

***p < .001.

Table 6.4: Class-level descriptive statistics, *T*-test results, and logistic regression results: Catholic (*n* = 267) and Public (*n* = 4,365)

Variable	Sector	Descriptive Statistics		T-test Results (Catholic-Public):	Logistic Regression Results (Accounting for demographics)		
		Mean	Standard deviation	t-value	B	Standard error	Wald
Parental involvement:							
Percent of parents who attend conferences[a]	Public	4.27	0.90	8.69***	−0.09	0.11	0.65
	Catholic	4.67	0.71				
At least one parent volunteers regularly[b]	Public	0.80	0.35	11.90***	0.40	0.39	1.03
	Catholic	0.95	0.20				
Percent of parents who attend other school activities[a]	Public	3.33	0.98	14.45***	0.32***	0.08	16.66
	Catholic	4.21	0.92				
Parents support school staff[c]	Public	0.69	0.40	10.19***	0.42	0.24	3.06
	Catholic	0.88	0.30				
Climate[d]:							
Administrator support composite	Public	3.91	0.76	4.93***	0.30**	0.10	9.15
	Catholic	4.14	0.67				
Student misbehavior composite	Public	2.31	0.78	−12.49***	−0.32**	0.11	8.66
	Catholic	1.86	0.57				
Teacher satisfaction composite	Public	4.23	0.58	7.51***	0.65***	0.14	22.02
	Catholic	4.50	0.51				
Staff support composite	Public	4.18	0.55	5.75***	0.38**	0.14	• 7.68
	Catholic	4.38	0.49				
Professional development: time in math workshop[e]	Public	1.47	0.97	−7.09***	−0.40***	0.07	29.56
	Catholic	1.04	0.94				
Teacher autonomy[d]:							
Paperwork interferes with teaching	Public	3.45	0.94	−14.95***	−0.77***	0.07	107.69
	Catholic	2.58	0.85				
How much teacher controls curriculum	Public	4.16	0.82	11.42***	0.67***	0.11	35.40
	Catholic	4.60	0.61				
Job security is based on state/local tests	Public	2.31	0.95	−9.78***	−0.40***	0.09	21.06
	Catholic	1.73	0.81				
Teacher characteristics:							
Bachelor's degree or less[f]	Public	0.25	0.37	5.33***	1.33***	0.16	66.40
	Catholic	0.40	0.46				

Beyond master's degree[f]	Public	0.08	0.23	−5.65***	−1.65**	0.48	11.85
	Catholic	0.03	0.15				
Temporary or alternative certification[f]	Public	0.09	0.24	2.75**	0.66**	0.23	8.56
	Catholic	0.14	0.32				
No certification[f]	Public	0.03	0.00	3.95***	5.06***	0.78	41.88
	Catholic	0.08	0.01				
3 Years' teaching experience or less[f]	Public	0.15	0.31	1.13	0.33	0.20	2.65
	Catholic	0.18	0.36				
25+ Years' teaching experience[f]	Public	0.22	0.36	−0.34	−0.08	0.18	0.19
	Catholic	0.22	0.38				
Curriculum and instruction:							
Total class enrollment	Public	20.84	3.25	6.16***	0.07***	0.02	12.99
	Catholic	22.92	5.53				
Desks facing front[f]	Public	0.17	0.32	8.38***	1.56***	0.17	88.48
	Catholic	0.40	0.45				
Number of computers per child[g]	Public	0.15	0.13	−6.80***	−6.34***	1.04	37.23
	Catholic	0.10	0.11				
Never or hardly ever use calculators[h]	Public	0.44	0.43	7.63***	1.29***	0.16	67.54
	Catholic	0.65	0.44				
Traditional composite[i]	Public	3.10	0.44	5.20***	0.91***	0.17	27.63
	Catholic	3.24	0.37				
Reform composite[i]	Public	2.70	0.49	−5.84***	−0.90***	0.14	44.88
	Catholic	2.50	0.54				

Note: School sector was recoded as a binary variable with Catholic = 1 and public = 0.

[a] 1 = None; 2 = 1%–25%; 3 = 26%–50%; 4 = 51%–75%; 5 = 76%–100%.

[b] 1 = Regularly; 0 = none.

[c] 1 = Agree or strongly agree; 0 = neither agree nor disagree, disagree, and strongly disagree.

[d] The climate and teacher autonomy variables are on the following scale: 1 = strongly disagree; 2 = disagree; 3 = undecided; 4 = agree; 5 = strongly agree.

[e] 0 Hours; 2 = 1–3 hours; 3 = 4–8 hours; 4 = 9 or more hours.

[f] 1 = Yes; 0 = no.

[g] Teacher-reported number of computers in the classroom that the children are allowed to use divided by the total class enrollment.

[h] Based on a 4-point scale: 1 = never or hardly ever; 2 = once or twice a month; 3 = once or twice a week; 4 = almost every day.

[i] Mean of variables on a 4-point scale: 1 = never or hardly ever; 2 = once or twice a month; 3 = once or twice a week; 4 = almost every day.

*p < .05.

**p < .01.

***p < .001.

scores. Interaction terms of race/ethnicity and socioeconomic status (SES) by sector were also included to examine whether there were significant differential effects.

Owing to the detailed nature of the NAEP and ECLS-K analyses, we leave more detailed tables of results for Appendices A and B. Highlights of the descriptive statistics and the multilevel analyses are discussed below.

Factors Shaping Achievement in Public and Private Schools

In the following sections, we briefly review key literature on school factors that have been found to both vary by school sector and predict student achievement, including school size, class size, school climate, teacher qualifications, and instructional practices. For each factor, we then draw from our NAEP and ECLS-K analyses, as appropriate (given the variables in question) to examine relationships among the factor, school sector, and student achievement. In the concluding section of this chapter, we summarize the findings and draw conclusions about which variables help explain public-private school differences in mathematics gains during elementary school.

SCHOOL SIZE

There are reasons to think that the size of a school can impact its academic performance. A half-century ago reformers argued for larger, more comprehensive schools that could offer more services and a broader curriculum and be more cost-efficient due to economies of scale.[9] On the other hand, more recent reform forces, including the Gates Foundation, have pushed for smaller schools, believing that the more manageable size and intimate environment can have benefits.[10] Indeed, several studies have found a connection between smaller school size and higher academic performance, with the size influencing the climate of the school through issues such as lower absenteeism, class participation, and a nurturing environment.[11] Especially with regard to minority students in public schools, Finn and Voelkl linked smaller school size to greater student engagement in terms of class participation, completing schoolwork on time, and joining extracurricular activities.[12] Others suggest that it is not simply the case that increasing school size diminishes school effects or achievement, since there may be optimal sizes depending on context.[13]

The Impact of School Size, Sector, and Achievement

From our NAEP and ECLS-K descriptive analyses, we see a strong pattern of public schools being larger than private schools. For example, in the ECLS-K data, 8% of Catholic schools enroll less than 150 children, compared with 3% of public elementary schools; while almost one in five public elementary schools serve more than 750 students, compared with one in 20 Catholic schools (see *t*-test results in Table 6.4). Moreover, this difference remains highly significant even after controlling for school demographics in the ECLS-K data (see logistic regression results in Table 6.3).

In our NAEP analyses of factors influencing achievement, we included school size in its original ordinal scale and found no relationship between this variable and achievement at grade 4 but a marginally positive relationship at grade 8 (see Tables A9 and A10). We attended to this variable with more care in the ECLS-K analyses by creating a set of binary variables that would allow us to see whether small schools or large schools have higher achievement than midsized schools. The findings suggest that large elementary schools have significantly lower achievement than midsized schools (see Table B2). Overall, the addition of school size variables did little to shed light on the achievement patterns by sector.[14]

CLASS SIZE

The classic research on the relationship between class size and achievement dates back to the studies of Tennessee's Project STAR (Student/ Teacher Achievement Ratio) experiment from the 1980s. While most evaluations of this large-scale, randomized effort found that students in smaller classes significantly outgained the control groups in achievement in the early grades,[15] some economists have criticized those findings, or have come to different conclusions, which have themselves then been challenged.[16] While there is by no means a strong consensus, many objective observers would agree that smaller class size, while expensive, is probably positively related to higher achievement, especially at the early grades, although the degree to which those effects are sustained over time is not clear.

The Impact of Class Size, Sector, and Achievement

The fourth grade NAEP data indicate that public schools have slightly larger class sizes than Catholic and charter schools and substantially larger classes than Lutheran, conservative Christian, and other private schools. Yet in the ECLS-K data, grade 3 teachers in Catholic schools reported average class enrollments of 22.92 students, compared with 20.84 in public schools, a significant difference that persisted even after controlling for school demographics. The much larger NAEP samples probably provide a more accurate picture of school characteristics such as class size, but the general message across the two samples is that the class enrollments of public and Catholic elementary schools are not terribly different, on average.

Additionally, the NAEP and ECLS-K evidence regarding the effects of smaller class sizes is rather inconsistent. Analyses of the NAEP data suggest that smaller class size is, in fact, positively correlated with higher academic achievement, even after accounting for other factors known to influence achievement. Since the private schools sampled tended to have smaller classes for their students, smaller class sizes seemed to actually provide a boost to private school scores. However, in our analysis of first through third grade gains in ECLS-K, we found no significant relationship between class size and math achievement gains. This discrepancy could be due to the grade level examined, differences in the NAEP and ECLS-K samples and models, the lack of variation in class size in the samples, or other issues. Moreover, it is possible that smaller class sizes are more important for teaching other subjects, such as reading. Overall, the issue of class size does little to help us understand why public school students outscore their private school counterparts during elementary school.

SCHOOL CLIMATE AND COMMUNITY

Going back at least to the High School and Beyond studies, researchers have recognized the importance of issues associated with a school's climate.[17] For instance, researchers have highlighted the shared sense of community in Catholic schools—an environment linked to higher academic achievement. Other studies have focused on the shared relationships and values found in Catholic schools, which have been associated with a positive learning environment.[18] For example, in a comprehensive analysis of public schools in Chicago, Bryk and Schneider identified a strong link between social relationships between parents and educators and improved math scores,[19] and others have noted a connection between school employees' trust in parents and improved academic achievement.[20]

Of course, related to climate and trust is parental involvement, which is also known to be positively linked to academic achievement. Researchers have noted a causal link between strengthened school-family relationships for disadvantaged children and increased academic outcomes.[21] For instance, studies of the famous Comer School Development Program highlight benefits for students, as well as for parents and schools, when parents are involved with their children's education, including for low-income families.[22] But the type of involvement might be critical. While parental involvement may be tied to better outcomes, an analysis of NELS data indicated that parent volunteering at a school was unrelated to math achievement.[23] On the other hand, Lee and Bowen found that, after considering several different types of parental involvement, only within-school parent involvement, such as attending parent-teacher conferences and volunteering, were significantly linked with achievement.[24]

Prior research has found notable school sector differences in school climate and parental involvement. Teachers in private schools have reported more autonomy in their work, freedom from paperwork, more support from their principals, and a greater sense of community at their schools.[25]

Teachers in Catholic schools enjoyed more parental support because of their trust in the teaching staff.[26] Private school parents tend to be more involved in their children's education than are parents of public school students.[27] For instance, Catholic school parents have been shown to be more likely to know their children's friends, volunteer at school, and participate in parent-teacher organizations.[28] In contrast, public schools appear to have an environment that is less conducive to learning. For instance, teachers in public high schools were more likely to report that students faced obstacles, including poverty, chemical abuse, threats, and crime.[29] Public school teachers were more likely to report examples of absenteeism, disrespect, and fighting among students at their schools.[30]

However, the school climate and parental involvement found in private schools may have more to do with the high-SES families participating in those schools than with something specific to the schools' culture.[31] Our data actually support this hypothesis.

The Impact of School Climate, Sector, and Achievement

The raw NAEP data for fourth and eighth grades do indeed confirm that teacher morale, school climate, and parental involvement tend to be higher in various forms of private schools than in public schools (see Tables A7 and A8). The eighth grade NAEP data also indicate that student drug and alcohol use are a greater problem in public than in private schools. Similarly, in the raw ECLS data for grade 3, Catholic school teachers report significantly greater administrator and staff support, greater curricular autonomy and less paperwork, fewer security measures at their schools (such as window bars and security guards), and better student attendance and behavior (see Tables 6.3 and 6.4). Public school teachers were more likely to report that their job security depended on students' test performance.

Catholic school teachers also reported greater parent involvement on several measures, including the degree to which parents attend conferences, volunteer regularly, attend other school activities, and support school staff. For example, while 95% of Catholic school teachers reported that at least one parent volunteers regularly, only 80% of public school teachers reported this. Also, 88% of Catholic school teachers agreed or strongly agreed that parents support school staff while only 69% of public school teachers felt this way. Furthermore, while 74% of Catholic school teachers reported that their classroom needs are met, only 60% of public school teachers reported this.

However, although Catholic school teachers reported more positive school climates, there was no difference in the raw school climate rating as scored by outside observers. Moreover, we found through our logistic regression analysis that many key differences in the ECLS-K school climate and parental involvement measures are due to the SES of those who attend the schools rather than the nature of the schools themselves. That is, after controlling for SES, there were no longer any differences between public and Catholic schools in terms of parents attending conferences, volunteering, and supporting school staff, as well as no differences in student attendance, classroom needs being met, and security measures (see Tables 6.3 and 6.4). Still, some differences did persist, including enhanced parental attendance at nonconference activities, administrative and staff support, teacher autonomy, less paperwork, fewer testing pressures, and better student behavior in Catholic schools.

In our analyses, we examine whether any of these variables actually relate to achievement and if they tend to provide an advantage to one school type or another. In our analysis of the NAEP data, school climate variables had a mixed relationship with student achievement across sectors. First, although student attendance and routine parent involvement (i.e., participation in parent-teacher conferences, open houses, PTA) were highly significant predictors of achievement at grades 4 and 8, parents volunteering in the schools was not. Teacher morale was positively associated with achievement, while conflicts were negatively associated, however, these relationships were only significant at grade 4. At grade 8, drugs/alcohol was not related to achievement. The climate variables correlating positively with achievement tended to be those that were more prevalent in private schools. Hence, we would typically expect to see substantial decreases in the coefficients of the private schools when these variables that provide advantages to them were added to the models (see Model 6 in Tables A9 and A10). However, the pattern was not clearly evident, consistent with our ECLS-K findings that sector differences in many key school climate factors are due primarily to the high-SES demographics of those schools.

In the ECLS-K analyses, we included those variables that differed by school type after controlling for SES. Again, these included administrator support, staff support, teacher satisfaction, classroom needs met, parental attendance of other school activities, student behavior, teacher satisfaction, paperwork interference, teacher autonomy, and job security relying on testing. Strikingly, there were no significant relationships between any of these variables and achievement gains between first and third grade, once demographics and other key factors were included in the models (see Appendix B, Tables B2–B4). Hence, despite prior literature linking Catholic schools with enhanced climate and achievement, the NAEP and ECLS-K analyses indicate that the school climate/involvement measures that matter most are more related to SES than to school sector, and consequently, school climate and parental involvement do little to help us understand differences in public-private school achievement.

TEACHER CERTIFICATION AND PROFESSIONAL DEVELOPMENT

There has been considerable debate about the importance of teacher certification in enhancing classroom effectiveness. Especially in the No Child Left Behind era, with the concern for a highly qualified teaching force and the rise of alternatives to traditional teacher training such as Teach For America, policymakers and reformers have shown an interest in what factors contribute to effective teaching and, presumably, greater student growth. In view of the typical model of teacher preparation—university-based programs leading to state-level certification as a teacher—and the widespread (if unproven) sense that the teaching force is underperforming, teacher training and certification have come under intense scrutiny and attack as an ossified system that may really add no value to a teacher's effectiveness.

Indeed, some critics see traditional teacher training and certification as a manifestation of the monopoly that the public education "establishment" has over public resources and institutions intended for public schooling.[32] They see virtually no evidence to support the almost exclusive claim exercised by traditional training programs over entry to the profession[33] and point to the apparent success of alternative routes to the classroom in producing better student outcomes. As such, this logic points to more flexible or even marketized systems where entry to teaching is opened up to those with specific abilities in particular subject areas, even—and, for some critics, especially—if they have no training in education theory and pedagogical techniques.[34]

However, some research has shown a positive effect from teacher training and certification programs on student achievement. Perhaps most famously, Linda Darling-Hammond has identified a beneficial impact from teacher qualifications such as college major and teaching credentials, on the one hand, and academic achievement on the other.[35] Other prominent researchers have also noted such connections.[36] For example, while it has been critiqued by market advocates,[37] a review of some sixty research studies concluded that there is a significant relationship between school inputs such as teacher qualifications and student academic outcomes.[38]

Similarly, there are mixed views on the benefits of various forms of professional development. Yet most of the studies of this phenomenon examine the impact on teacher learning, rather than on students' academic achievement. (Part of the reason for this is that it is often difficult to isolate teacher professional development as a causal factor for student achievement, given the fact that professional development opportunities are often offered as part of wider reform efforts.[39]) Yet, at least in mathematics, there is some evidence indicating that teacher professional development can improve student outcomes when that additional teacher training centers on students' mathematical thinking and on the mathematics teachers teach.[40]

The Impact of Teacher Education, Sector, and Achievement

Since private and most charter schools are free from any requirement to hire certified teachers, there are fewer such teachers in those schools. For example, according to the fourth grade NAEP data, while 89% of public school teachers are certified (in some manner), these percentages are 75% for Catholic schools, 62% for charters schools, and only 44% for conservative Christian schools. NAEP eighth grade data show similar trends, as well as a greater tendency for teachers in public schools to hold a minor or major in mathematics (see Tables 6.1 and 6.2).

The ECLS-K data suggest similar certification patterns for public and Catholic third grade teachers, with 3% of public school and 8% of Catholic school teachers holding no certification at all and another 9% of public and 14% of Catholic school teachers holding temporary or alternative certification. More generally, Catholic school teachers tend to have less education overall, with 40% of Catholic school teachers holding a bachelor's degree or less, compared with only 25% of public school teachers. And both ECLS-K and NAEP data indicate that public school teachers participate in more professional development than do private school teachers, although the quality and scope of those workshops is not evident from the data available (see Tables 6.3 and 6.4).

These patterns persist after controlling for school demographics. Considering the achievement differences favoring public schools that we noted in the previous chapters, the obvious question then is whether differences in teacher education and certification in the various schools might, in fact, help explain those achievement differences.

The short answer appears to be "yes," particularly for teacher certification. Contrary to some of the current arguments against the importance of teacher certification, both NAEP and ECLS-K data indicate that having a teacher with a certificate is actually a positive predictor of higher student achievement. And since certificates are much more prevalent in public schools and more of a rarity for teachers in private and charter schools, this fact helps explain why students in public schools outperform their peers in demographically comparable charter and private schools.

Given that the teacher background variables are the first variables encountered in this chapter that appear to help explain achievement patterns by school type, here we offer additional help to readers interested in understanding the relationships conveyed in the hierarchical linear modeling tables. Further discussion is found in the appendices. In Tables A9 and A10, Model 7 adds teacher background variables, including certification, whether teachers majored or minored in mathematics (grade 8 only), whether teachers were new, and the number of different professional development activities in which teachers participated. Of these variables, only the employment of certified teachers was a significant, positive predictor of achievement at both grades 4 and 8.

As a specific example of the meaning of the 2.3-point coefficient (2.9 at grade 8) reported for "certified teachers" in Model 7, schools in which 80% of assessed fourth graders had certified teachers scored an average of .23 points higher than schools with only 70% of students with certified teachers. Although this appears to be a small effect, relationships identified here between student achievement and the teacher-reported data, in particular, are likely conservative estimates of the relationships that exist and would be identified by using more sensitive measures over time. Still, it is important to note the strikingly consistent pattern in that all of the private and charter school coefficients increased between .5 and 1.3 points from Model 6 to Model 7, with the largest increases occurring for the conservative Christian schools at both fourth and eighth grades. For example, at grade 4 the conservative Christian coefficient increased from −11.6 to −10.3, indicating that the addition of teacher education variables to the model explained more than 10% of the advantage that public school students seem to have over conservative Christian students, with a very similar pattern holding for Catholic and other forms of private schools at both grades 4 and 8.

Consistent with the NAEP results, as we look across the ECLS-K models in Tables B2–B4, we see only two major jumps in the Catholic school coefficient after basic demographics are added. The baseline Catholic school coefficient is −2.81 in Model 6, which contains school- and classroom-level demographics but no other explanatory variables. We see this increase to −2.62 with the inclusion of instructional practices in Model 6, conveying that roughly 7% of the disadvantage of being in a Catholic school is explained. Then we see only slight changes to the Catholic school coefficient in all additional models except for the change from Model 9 to 10, when teacher education variables are added which cause the Catholic school coefficient to increase from −2.54 to −2.27 (or an 11% reduction in the remaining Catholic student achievement deficit).

It is worth noting that, according to the NAEP data, a mathematics major or minor at grade 8 is not a predictor of student achievement. This is interesting in view of critiques of teacher training programs that contend that such programs rely too much on theory-based courses, to the detriment of the teacher's opportunity to learn more in his or her subject area.

Professional development for those teachers already working in schools was a mixed predictor of student achievement. Although this NAEP variable was not significant at grade 8, at grade 4 it was a positive predictor of achievement that was ultimately "washed out" with the addition of instructional practices/emphasis variables, suggesting that the reason that professional development predicted achievement was because it enhanced teachers' instruction. In the ECLS models, we added workshop attendance to the models after instructional factors were already included and so the lack of significance of that variable is not surprising. However, in a follow-up analysis, we found that mathematics teacher workshops did indeed predict broader mathematical emphases among teachers, which, in turn, predicted achievement (as will be discussed further below).

INSTRUCTIONAL PRACTICES

While there has been much discussion of teacher qualifications, the issue only takes into account very blunt measures of inputs in terms of teachers' levels of training. But what a teacher actually does in the classroom would seem to be an even more essential consideration (which can and should be examined relative to his or her level of training and, ultimately, the students' academic outcomes).

In fact, at about the same time that the school choice and charter school movements started to advance, the United States also started to adopt substantial changes to curriculum and instruction in several areas, especially mathematics. Starting in 1989, and over the subsequent two decades, the National Council of Teachers of Mathematics (NCTM), in conjunction with states and the federal government, began to move away from a focus on rote memorization and procedures and started to push for the centrality of students' mathematical reasoning.[41] The general approach emphasizes a wider range of tools such as the use of mathematical manipulatives and calculators, along with more meaningful assessment and broader curricular goals emphasizing measurement, data analysis, geometry, algebra, and probability, in addition to the traditional emphasis on number and operations.

Of course, with such a wide-scale move toward substantive change, the obvious question is whether such changes succeeded in improving students' math learning. But, as with any complex reform effort, it becomes difficult to isolate the impact of a particular curriculum or form of instruction. Available evidence that compares students receiving reform-oriented curricula and pedagogies shows them outscoring control groups.[42] However, other observers have noted stagnant achievement levels on the long-term trend NAEP mathematics data,[43] reminding us that the results of impact studies depend upon the outcome measure used.

Several other studies have found a positive relationship between reform-oriented instructional measures and student achievement on the Main NAEP test. For instance, researchers using earlier NAEP data concluded that teachers who emphasize reasoning, collaborative problem solving, and nonnumber mathematics strands have students who score higher, even after demographics are considered.[44] This reform-oriented bump is also evident at the student level. When students adhere to traditional mathematical attitudes that run counter to the NCTM reforms—for instance, when they agree that "Learning mathematics is mostly memorizing facts" and "There is only one way to solve a math problem"—NAEP scores are persistently lower.[45] However, given NAEP's cross-sectional nature, reverse causality is possible with these correlations—that is, perhaps students who are already high achieving are more likely to receive reform-oriented instruction.

Common wisdom holds that parents often flee public schools for more "tried-and-true" traditional approaches to curriculum and instruction in private schools, and several studies are consistent with this view. While some studies have found inconsistent patterns,[46] most have found that private school teachers tend to use more traditional instructional methods than do public school teachers.[47] Even Bryk, Lee, and Holland, who found advantages for Catholic schools, observed that instruction in the Catholic high schools they visited was largely textbook and lecture driven and noted that efforts were needed to improve teachers' pedagogical skill.[48] However, as noted previously, Catholic school teachers are more likely to report enjoying greater autonomy in terms of pedagogical goals, control of curriculum, and freedom from testing pressures.[49]

The Impact of Instructional Practices, Sector, and Achievement

Our findings with the raw NAEP and ECLS-K data are consistent with those of other researchers—namely, we find that the instructional practices reported by public school teachers tend to be more aligned with current mathematics education reforms than those practices employed by private school teachers. According to the grade 4 NAEP data, public school teachers report a greater emphasis on nonnumber mathematics strands (geometry, measurement, data analysis/probability, and algebra) and allowing students greater access to calculators as part of mathematics instruction (see Table 6.1).[50]

Consistent with NAEP, the ECLS-K data indicate that Catholic school classrooms are more traditional on average, with desks in rows facing the front (40% of Catholic school classrooms compared with 17% of public schools) and less technology (one computer for every ten students in Catholic schools, versus one for every seven students in public schools). Indeed, two-thirds of Catholic school teachers said that they "never" or "hardly ever" allow their students to use calculators, compared with 44% of public school teachers (see Table 6.4).

The ECLS-K teacher survey also included eleven questions about teachers' mathematics instructional practices. These items logically cluster into two categories: traditional teaching practices and reform-oriented practices; and owing to concerns about multicollinearity, we created two corresponding composite variables by averaging the items (see Appendix B for more information). The reform-oriented practices variables included how often students in the class use measuring instruments, use manipulatives, solve problems in small groups, write about how they solved a math problem, talk to the class about mathematics work, work on math projects, discuss solutions to math problems with other students, and work on math problems that reflect real life situations. The traditional practices composite included how often children in the class use a math textbook, work on math worksheets, and take math tests. As shown in Table 6.4, public school teachers scored significantly higher on the reform composite and lower on the traditional composite, and these patterns persisted after controlling for demographics.

The question then is how much these instructional practices actually predict achievement gains. According to the NAEP data, a teacher's tendency to emphasize nonnumber mathematics strands and to include at least some emphasis on calculators in mathematics instruction is a statistically significant predictor of better student achievement. Similarly, the degree to which students report beliefs about mathematics that align with, and are probably a result of, reform-oriented instruction is also a positive predictor of academic success at both grades 4 and 8.[51] As discussed further in Appendix A, we see consistent increases in the private school coefficients as reform-oriented teaching practices, student beliefs, and "I like math" are added to the models, indicating that achievement gaps by sector narrow after equating these factors. In other words, reform-oriented practices and dispositions are measurably more common in public schools than in demographically similar private and charter elementary schools, and these aspects seem to contribute to the superior mathematics performance of public schools. However the cross-sectional nature of NAEP means that we need to be cautious in drawing conclusions from these data alone, as it is possible that students who are already higher achieving tend to have teachers who use reform-oriented instructional practices. Hence, it is important to examine whether patterns in the ECLS-K data are similar.

Indeed, the patterns do hold as we look at factors predicting student growth between first and third grades in ECLS-K. Third grade teachers who reported using more reform-oriented practices had students with higher mathematics test score gains after controlling for demographics and prior test scores (as discussed further in Appendix B in conjunction with Table B3). It is worth noting that the traditional practices composite was not related to achievement gains, nor were the technology-related variables.

In an extended analysis in Appendix B, we also find that public and Catholic school teachers report an equal emphasis on number and operations in their mathematics curriculum but that public school teachers report a greater emphasis on NCTM's four nonnumber strands— geometry, measurement, statistics/probability, and algebra/patterns (see Table B6).[52] Moreover, we find that teachers' attendance at mathematics workshops—more common among public school teachers— predicts a heavier emphasis on these nonnumber mathematics strands (see Table B7). This nonnumber curricular focus is a consistent, positive predictor of achievement and appears to explain a portion of the public school advantage in early mathematics gains (see Table B8).

Overall, the ECLS-K third grade data indicate that reform-oriented teaching practices and curricular emphases are more prevalent in public school classrooms and are also positively correlated with mathematics test score gains. Hence, disparities in curriculum and instruction seem to explain a portion of the Catholic school disadvantage in elementary grades.

EQUITY AND SCHOOL SECTOR

It is important to note that across all of the models, large race- and SES-related inequities persisted and that demographic variables together with prior achievement (which is heavily correlated with demographic factors) accounted for the vast majority of the variation in achievement among students, classrooms, and schools in our models. Given past findings that disadvantaged students, in particular, benefit from attending Catholic schools,[53] we examined interactions between student SES and race/ethnicity with the ECLS-K third grade data, with first grade achievement again serving as the baseline (see Table B5).

None of the interaction terms for race and SES by sector were significant. The SES interaction term was very close to 0, indicating that neither sector is better or worse at teaching math to students of low or high SES. Still, the sample size for Catholic school students in several of the racial categories was very small, making it difficult to draw firm conclusions about the lack of such effects. Other researchers using the same database have also failed to find evidence of differential effects by school sector.[54] See Appendix B for more information on this analysis.

Potential Explanations for the "Public School Advantage"

In our comprehensive analyses of two large-scale, nationally representative data sets, we have uncovered notable evidence that the private or independent school advantage in academic achievement is a reflection of the more advantaged students who attend them than of any superior organizational effectiveness of private or independent schools. Indeed, instead of a private school advantage, we have found substantial (albeit unexpected) evidence of a significant public school advantage. In fact, while there are considerable difficulties in measuring demographic differences between schools, and whole sectors of schools, these difficulties would generally obscure factors that would tend to favor private school students. For example, "unobservable" factors such as parent initiative are likely higher in private schools—since parents had to make greater efforts to enroll their children in such schools—but cannot be captured by our data. However, such hidden factors would generally tend to boost private school achievement to a greater degree. In that sense it is somewhat surprising that those hidden advantages are not boosting private school achievement even more, suggesting that public schools are successfully adopting measures that overcome such factors.

Our initial study using the immense NAEP data set uncovered two key findings. First, some important aspects of school climate that predicted achievement were, indeed, more prevalent in private schools, but that prevalence was due to the high-SES nature of the families served rather than to the school organizational structure. Second, the only NAEP variables we found that both predicted achievement and were more prevalent in public schools were teacher certification, reform-oriented instructional practices, and student beliefs that are consistent with reform-oriented practices (see Table 6.5).

Given our lingering questions about whether these patterns would hold up in a longitudinal analyses with a different data set, we examined the ECLS-K data, focusing on the grade span in which the public school advantage increased the most over the data set's K–8 span—that

Table 6.5: Summary of relationships among predictors, sector, and achievement

	NAEP Analysis	ECLS-K analysis (Catholic vs. public only)
Consistent, significant predictors of achievement:		
Raised private/charter school coefficients (so more prevalent in public schools and **could explain greater public school gains**)	· Teacher certification · Reform-oriented instruction (nonnumber emphasis, calculator use) · Students' reform-oriented beliefs · Students liking mathematics	· Teacher certification · Reform-oriented instruction (mathematical discussion, writing, and problem solving, emphasis on nonnumber curricular strands)
Mixed/null effect on private/charter school coefficients (so no consistent disparity by school type after controlling for demographics)	· Some school climate measures (parent involvement, student attendance)	*NA—in the ECLS-K analysis, given that we screened out variables that did not differ between public and Catholic schools after controlling for SES, no variables that correlated with achievement could have a null effect on public or Catholic school coefficients.*
Lowered most private/charter school coefficients (so more prevalent in private/charter schools)	· Smaller class size (available at grade 4 only)	
Mixed or marginally significant predictors of achievement	· School size (slightly positively associated) · Some school climate measures (teacher morale, conflicts, parent volunteers, talk at home) · Time for professional development	· School size (midsized elementary schools appear most beneficial)
Not significant predictors of achievement	· Time on math · Drugs/alcohol · Teachers have math major/minor (grade 8 only) · New teachers · Use of multiple choice tests	· School climate measures[a] · Time for professional development · Teacher holds graduate degree · Traditional instructional emphases (including focus on number and operations) · Computers, calculator use · Class size

[a] Most measures of parent involvement—attending conferences, volunteering regularly, and supporting school staff—no longer differed by school sector after we controlled for SES and were therefore not included in the ECLS-K HLM models. The remaining variables—administrative/staff support, parent involvement, student behavior, teacher satisfaction, teacher autonomy—were unrelated to achievement gains in the ECLS-K models.

is during first through third grades. In examining third grade teacher and school characteristics to see what might explain the greater public school math gains, we considered dozens of potential factors. Despite the substantial differences in the variables available, the samples involved, the data set's design, and our specific methods of analysis, we found remarkably consistent results.[55]

As with NAEP, in ECLS-K we again found that that many positive aspects of school climate were more prevalent in Catholic schools, such as student attendance, lack of security measures employed, and most forms of parent involvement. However, many of these differences washed out when we compared demographically similar public and Catholic schools. The school climate variables that did persist in differing by sector did not ultimately correlate with larger academic gains. Ultimately, just as with NAEP, the only factors that help us understand why public school students outperform their Catholic counterparts are teacher certification and curricular and instructional practices that are driven by reforms advocated by the professional association for the mathematics education discipline.[56]

Hence, the results from our analyses suggest that public school students are outpacing Catholic school students, at least in earlier grades, in part because of a closer match between public schools teachers' curricular emphases and the skills emphasized in current, professionally driven reforms, which tend to be the ones measured in assessments such as "the nation's report card," that is, the NAEP. Teachers who report focusing more on the nonnumber mathematics strands (as public school teachers do) have students with greater test score gains. Catholic schoolteachers more often focus on traditional, number-/computation-focused instruction, while public school teachers focus more on reasoning, communicating, and the broader mathematical emphases endorsed in the NCTM *Principles and Standards*.[57]

Public school teachers are also more likely than their Catholic school counterparts to be part of teacher education experiences that immerse them in the latest professional expertise about mathematics teaching and learning. Despite the possible benefits of private school teachers having the freedom to choose what they will teach and how they will teach it, our results suggest that teachers who are free to do as they please within their school walls might hold onto outdated curricula and methods of instruction, even while the goals and methods promoted in the larger field of education (as reflected in NAEP, ECLS-K, and other assessments) continue to evolve. Hence, school reforms that allow or even encourage schools to ignore existing professional expertise in curriculum, instruction, and teacher education could have unintended, detrimental consequences.

7 Reconsidering Choice, Competition, and Autonomy as the Remedy in American Education

There is an old joke about an economist walking across a college campus with a student. When the student notices a five-dollar bill on the ground, the economist is dismissive: "It can't be a five dollar bill. If it were, someone would have picked it up."[1]

While not exactly a rib splitter, this joke illustrates the inherent, if underappreciated, limitations of assumption-driven disciplines such as economics in understanding the world.[2] Too often, people not only interpret evidence through ideological assumptions but ignore facts that fall outside of, or run counter to, those assumptions. Particularly in areas such as market theory, surrogate evidence on the quality of organizational options based on presumptions of how rationally self-interested individuals would act is often privileged over actual evidence of how organizations are really performing. That is, ideological assumptions often trump empirical evidence.

Such is the case with education. If families—and especially parents with defined preferences for better schooling—are avoiding public schools and are instead competing to get their children into private and charter schools, often paying substantial amounts of their family income toward tuition or other costs, then this must indicate that such independent schools are better, according to this narrow economic logic. Indeed, such a conclusion is constantly affirmed in the media and in reports from countless think tanks and blogs. Yet as the data presented in this book indicate, those behaviors are not an accurate reflection of the reality of school effectiveness. So why would people pay for a product or service when a superior product or service is available for free? Such was the perplexity expressed by one prominent economist when faced with unexpected patterns such as these:

> This result is quite surprising, because it appears to violate simple price theory. Public schools are free; [independent] schools often charge substantial tuition, making them noticeably more expensive than the alternatives. Yet some percentage of parents systematically chooses [independent] schools despite high cost and mediocre performance. Is this real?[3]

According to this logic, public schools are known to be inferior because people are willing to pay for an alternative; if they had real value, we could tell because people would embrace them . . . just like they would have embraced the wayward greenback.

Yet the evidence presented here on mathematics achievement in nationally representative samples of elementary schools suggests otherwise. Despite what many reformers, policymakers, media elites, and even parents may believe, public schools are, on average, actually providing a relatively effective educational service relative to schools in the independent sector. In fact, the limitations of our data, if anything, likely underemphasize the notable performance of public schools, given that factors not measured in our data sets would favor private, independent schools—public schools are doing something right that overcomes these factors. While this challenges the very basis of the current movement to remake public education based on choice, competition, and autonomy, our analyses indicate that public schools are enjoying an advantage in academic effectiveness because they are aligned with a more professional model of teaching and learning. Meanwhile, attributes such as operational autonomy championed by market theory or, as it is increasingly a belief system rather than a policy theory, we might use the term "marketism"—may actually be hindering or even diverting schools in the independent sector from higher achievement as they use their freedom in embracing stagnant, less effective curricular practices.

Leaving aside the question of whether parents in general really are the rational consumers that marketists believe them to be, or if they have access to useable information on school quality, it is important to note that there are many different reasons families may wish to choose a private school—just as there are many purposes for schools. Certainly, our data are national in scope and therefore may not be very helpful for parents considering different options in their local neighborhood. We are dealing with averages, and there are certainly many instances where the local private or charter school offers better academic options for particular children. Besides, although rational-choice assumptions suggest otherwise, academic achievement might not be the most important consideration for families.

Obviously, some parents will prioritize safety in looking for alternatives for their children. Many parents consider extracurricular options or perceived pedagogical fit with their children's preferences. As the results on conservative Christian schools indicate, for many families, finding a school that reinforces their values may be more important than finding one that adds more academic value to a child's learning. Some children enroll in schools that their friends are attending or where other families look like they do.

Indeed, if parents are rational consumers seeking to maximize their children's learning and later earning potential, then there is actually a reason—although not necessarily a laudable one—for them to choose schools on the basis of the social profiles of the other students in the schools. While the organizational effectiveness of a school may not be perceptible to observers such as prospective families, the socioeconomic composition of a school is readily apparent and does have a significant impact on a child's learning through the peer effect.

That is, average raw achievement and most school climate measures are, indeed, higher in private schools—although, as we show, this is due to the demographics of the schools and not the school type. Of course, when we account for these enrollment differences in order to isolate school effects, it is clear that private and independent schools are not necessarily more effective. In fact, the instruction in public schools is actually more aligned with current assessments and the latest research on what works—factors that some schools use their autonomy to avoid. Hence, the fact that climate and achievement appear "better" in private schools does not mean that instruction is actually better in those schools.

However, there are other factors besides instruction that impact student achievement. A child's peers in school can also have a substantial effect, and, indeed, our data show that a less-advantaged peer group is negatively associated with growth for students in that school. Thus, if a parent is comparing a typical public school and a typical private school, then on average achievement and climate are better in that private school because of the higher socioeconomic status (SES) of the clientele they serve. Regardless of school type, having a child in a school with students from more affluent families with higher academic aspirations can have a beneficial impact on that child. Yet, choices based on such criteria can also lead to greater social sorting. Since we know that higher SES students are disproportionately enrolled in private and independent schools, there is a perhaps perverse incentive for parents to rationally pursue this option for their own children. That is, it is not because private/independent schools are better, but because they attract what are perceived to be "better" students, that they may represent an appealing option for parents. Of course, if more families without the socioeconomic advantages enroll in a private school—say, through a voucher program—to capitalize on that beneficial peer effect, the effect is diminished.

Hence, while many parents may see individual reasons to secure a spot in a private school for their children, as a general policy measure reflected in myriad reform proposals and programs, such moves are inherently flawed, according to these data. As policymakers increasingly seek to shift students en masse from public to private or independent schools, or to privatize public schools, our analyses and the analyses of others indicate that such efforts can create a less effective (and more socially segregated) system of schooling.[4]

The Failures of Marketism for Education

Given that individual parents make choices between particular local schools on the basis of their own values and preferences, the issues raised in our analyses are clearly more pertinent to policymaking than to individual parents selecting schools for their children. In recent years, both Republican and Democratic policymakers have publicly embraced similar goals for education, including increased achievement especially in math and science, providing equal educational opportunity for all students and narrowing the gap in achievement outcomes between groups. To achieve these goals, they have largely adopted policies that promote consumer choice, school autonomy, competition between schools, standardized outcome metrics, school-level accountability, and private provision—all essential elements of market theory.

But the market theory of education might not offer the best route to the goals set out for public education. As we have seen, the marketist theory is based on assumptions—drawn from a perspective on the public and private sectors—that are not supported by the evidence presented here on the relative effectiveness of different school sectors or by evidence about how schools actually work. While market theory assumes that the less regulated, more autonomous sectors will naturally engender more effective organizations, the data do not bear out that claim. Although marketists believe that choice will open up opportunities for disadvantaged children, the data show that private and independent schools underenroll such students.[5] Contrary to previous claims, disadvantaged and minority students who are in most such schools are, on average, no better served than they are in public schools, diminishing hope that private sector–based strategies have much potential to reduce achievement gaps between groups.

Indeed, the primary assumption of market theory—that differences between public and private/independent sectors are the crucial factor for school effectiveness—is essentially disproved by these data. Once we account for the SES differences between the populations of students served in the different sectors, it is clear that the variables that differ between sectors are not significant predictors of achievement. For each variable that predicted achievement, there were no significant differences in their frequency between sectors, with the notable exceptions of teacher certification and reform-oriented instruction—both of which are, interestingly enough, more prevalent in the public school sector and thus help explain the larger academic gains in public schools. Yet both of these factors are neglected and even dismissed by marketists.

The continued popularity of marketist reforms inspired by market theory, despite not only the dearth of data supporting these policies but the emerging evidence challenging them, offers a classic example of policymakers elevating means over the ends, an ideological strategy over the actual evidence, and a policy goal over the actual purpose of the institution. But while market theory focuses on how markets should work in education, there is a paucity of evidence supporting the marketist belief regarding how the private and independent sectors actually perform. The extended infatuation with vouchers for private schools, for instance, or the nationwide effort to expand charter schools, regardless of the thin empirical basis for these policies, speaks to the power of this belief to guide policy. Such initiatives continue to gain ground despite the fact that published, peer-reviewed studies consistently fail to find persuasive evidence that these programs are effective at achieving their promised goals.

Understanding the Continued Appeal of Marketism

The lack of compelling evidence in education to support market theory highlights the question as to why policymakers have been consistently enamored with elements of the theory for schools. Not just in the United States, but in countries around the globe, public officials and funding agencies have adopted education policies that emphasize competition, choice, autonomy, and privatization of both provision and the purposes of schooling. While the policy specifics can vary substantially between countries, much of the research from developed, market economies as far afield as Chile, New Zealand, Sweden, England, and Wales illuminates many of the serious problems with a market approach to schooling in areas like equity, access, segregation, and effectiveness.[6] In the United States, despite optimistic claims for the potential of market mechanisms to improve schooling for all, the evidence undergirding these policies is generally underwhelming and, as with the data presented in this book, often challenges the premise of those policies. But despite substantial data questioning the effectiveness of these reforms, policymakers continue to pursue these approaches for both empirical and political reasons.

EMPIRICAL CONFUSION

The empirical basis for market theory comes from the apparent consensus from earlier research, which has a lasting, if dated, legacy in policy discussions. Drawing from well-respected studies in the 1980s and 1990s, as well as some more controversial and recent research, the continued impression in many policy-making circles is that the research community has provided an established, even monolithic evaluation of the relative positive impact of the purported independent or private school effect.

In fact, these studies were challenged from the start regarding the strength of their conclusions in view of problems with their methods.[7] For instance, the early work from Coleman and colleagues on High School and Beyond was monumental in its findings of a private school effect[8] but, among its other flaws, did not use longitudinal data.[9] The subsequent work from Chubb and Moe, hailed by marketists then and since as empirical justification for expanding charter schools and voucher programs, was criticized by researchers familiar with their data and methods for putting allegiance to public choice theory over appropriate analysis of the data, demonstrating that "their conclusions . . . are not supported by the evidence."[10]

Despite their flaws, this wave of research findings set the tone and presumptions for policy assumptions for the decades that have followed. Policymakers have advanced major reform movements such as charter schools, voucher programs, No Child Left Behind, and Race to the Top, all of which reflect the assumptions and findings of these earlier studies. So how do we account for the substantial differences in the findings of that research compared with our more recent results? Certainly, some of the reasons have to do with the changing times. Studies using the High School and Beyond data examined Catholic schools, for example, as they were at the tail end of their pinnacle of popularity, serving a more homogenous population. Since then, for instance, many of the urban Catholic schools serving coherent parishes have declined. Catholic families have moved to the suburbs, urban Catholic schools have enrolled more non-Catholic and minority students, and their teaching pool has shifted further away from a reliance on religious orders. At the same time, conservative Christian schools have emerged as the fastest growing subsector, economic variations have influenced families' decisions to pay for a private school, and charter schools have arrived in many areas to provide competition not just with public schools but with private schools as well.

Another factor to keep in mind is that those earlier studies generally focused on students in secondary schools, while our data deal with students in the elementary grades. As students get older and college looms nearer, parental expectations, family support for studying, and students' perceived pressure to earn high grades—factors more prevalent in more affluent families and for families using private schools— become more important, and yet these factors are difficult to measure and thus difficult to adjust for statistically. Given that homework and other out-of-school influences are minimized at the earliest grades, it makes sense to look at those early elementary grades when comparing the relative effects of different school types.

Our findings point to another explanation that can shed some light on why more recent results tell a different story than the research legacy that policymakers embrace. In the late 1980s, the professional organization for American mathematics teachers, the National Council of Teachers of Mathematics (NCTM), promoted standards advocating a heavier emphasis on reasoning and problem solving and a greater balance among five strands of mathematics (number, measurement, geometry, statistics/probability, and algebra). Their recommendations for improving mathematics instruction were based on professional diagnoses of how students learn and what they would need to learn for the emerging economic conditions. This approach was backed by curriculum-development efforts funded by the National Science Foundation. Starting in 1990 the Main NAEP was designed to reflect NCTM's mathematics curriculum standards, as was the later ECLS-K assessment.

As our results indicate, these reforms have been adopted with greater enthusiasm in the public school sector, often at the technocratic direction of those centralized bureaucracies so despised in market theory. As these reforms gained traction in classrooms, all groups began making slow but steady gains—a phenomenon seen in NAEP mathematics scores throughout the past twenty years, unlike in other subject areas, including reading, in which no such comprehensive reforms occurred. In other words, when schools aligned their mathematics curriculum and instruction to the advice of experts with professional insights and to the national assessments based on that expertise, scores rose. Although the curriculum and instruction in private schools might have prepared students for the more basic skills needed in earlier times, this traditional approach does not serve their students well on today's mathematics assessments, which are geared toward a more analytical, knowledge-driven, problem-based economic imperative. As the Common Core State Standards are implemented across subject areas in the coming years, we could see an increase in the public school effect across subject areas, given that public schools are held accountable for helping their students reach those standards.

POLITICAL IMPERATIVES

If the empirical evidence is now showing that public schools really are doing better, then why are policymakers still so enamored with the independent/private sector as a market model for public education, particularly when that more autonomous, market-based sector has fallen behind in adopting more state-of-the-art curriculum and instructional methods advocated by researchers, professional organizations, and government agencies? Why are they so determined to draw on models from underperforming sectors to remake public education?

Thus, a second area to consider in addressing this disconnect involves the political forces created by the current policy climate that drive marketism. For the past several decades, often at the behest of multilateral finance agencies, countries around the globe have adopted market-based policies in many areas, including industrial organization, telecommunications, transportation, and public and social services.[11] Particularly in English-speaking market democracies, policy elites in both ruling and opposition parties have been embracing independent (nongovernment) and private sector-based strategies to address intractable social problems that liberal governments had been unable to solve through welfare state approaches in the postwar era.[12] This sea change was partly due to the prominence of key political players like Margaret Thatcher and Ronald Reagan, who built their political careers railing against the welfare state, and then Bill Clinton and Tony Blair, who endorsed mixed-market, public-private partnerships as an alternative to traditional state-run enterprises. But influential thinkers outside of government were notably persuasive in establishing the theoretical legitimacy of the move towards private/independent provision of social services. Certainly, Milton Friedman at the University of Chicago, as well as Friedrich Hayek (also later at Chicago), and Ludwig von Mises of the Austrian School had a profound influence on policymakers, both directly and through their intellectual influence on public choice theory (including market theory) and managerialism or New Public Management, and indirectly, by nurturing a generation of policy scholars who would propagate their ideas.

But none of these thinkers would have had the impact they did without the institutional advocacy and support provided by some leading philanthropies, foundations, and think tanks. In this regard, the work of such organizations in advancing market-oriented education policies is rather illustrative—particularly when they support those policies in deed, if not in name. Certainly, probusiness, free enterprise–oriented organizations have been promoting market models for education for decades. In the United States, conservative think tanks like the Heritage Foundation, the American Enterprise Institute, and the libertarian Cato Institute, with agendas around a broad range of issues, have been joined by more cause-specific organizations such as the Friedman Foundation for Educational Choice in advancing market solutions to problems in education. When the traditionally centrist Brookings Institution began producing pieces favorable to private/independent models, as with Chubb and Moe's seminal 1990 work, the agenda really moved into the political mainstream. Now advocacy groups such as Democrats for Education Reform, Students First, and the Alliance for School Choice actively promote evidence that they see as favorable to private and independent models of schooling.

Many such advocacy organizations have found generous patrons in a set of philanthropic funders that promote an agenda quite favorable to market-style approaches, including the Gates Foundation, the Walton Family Foundation, and the Broad Foundation.[13] Together with select advocacy groups, such funders have been instrumental in shaping the policy climate around education issues by providing political and financial support for pilot programs, stipulating particular policies for grantee districts, and underwriting researchers and research organizations that are more predisposed toward their agenda.[14] Indeed, while advocacy groups sometimes use remarkably poor research in arguing for (or countering) market models for schooling,[15] or spin credible studies to fit their agenda,[16] these major funding agencies have also directed strategic support to individuals and units at respected institutions, such as the Program on Education Policy and Governance (PEPG) at Harvard or the Hoover Institution at Stanford. In this way, they are able to capitalize on recognizable institutional brands in adding legitimacy to their policy claims, regardless of whether or not the rigor of research coming from these institutions merits the weight that is given to the studies in media and policy-making circles.

Research on charter schools and voucher programs for private schools illustrates these efforts. Large funders like the Walton Family Foundation (of Wal-Mart) have been—according to one market theorist—"instrumental in getting the [programs] passed. . . . They were then instrumental in providing political air cover for the program. They found and supported researchers to document it, and they helped promote it nationally."[17] Not only do they fund pilot programs and individual researchers, but they also underwrite efforts to create institutional alternatives to advance their agenda. While groups have traditionally done this through the quasi-lobbying think tank sector, market advocates have increasingly seeded and sustained academic units that provide an added veneer of objectivity to the empirical claims supporting their political agenda. These university-based groups, in turn, having quite often declined or failed to pass their promarket research findings through established, peer-reviewed academic journals, instead create alternative venues for publishing and promoting their work—a strategy not unlike what is employed by corporate-funded deniers of climate change.[18] Consequently, there are notable academic resources now leveraged in support of the political push for marketism in education.

Two academic entities aptly illustrate these patterns. The Walton Family Foundation provides funding to the PEPG at Harvard, which is run by a stable of provoucher scholars and public figures on its board. Similarly, the Walton Family Foundation was instrumental in creating the Department of Education Reform at the University of Arkansas, which is led by a PEPG associate and staffed with provoucher theorists and researchers.[19] The faculty at these two academic units have challenged the mixed findings from the official evaluations of voucher programs, performing secondary analyses in order to find a positive private school effect in programs in Milwaukee and Cleveland as well as producing positive findings in other cities.[20] While their controversial reports are launched with substantial promotional efforts (e.g., press releases, op-eds) and tend to garner considerable media attention, the methods they use to produce these findings on achievement have been challenged by respected researchers, and the reports typically do not pass through the peer-review process into scholarly journals.[21] Consequently, these Walton-funded entities have created their own "peer-reviewed" outlets staffed by voucher advocates to promote their agendas, including a highly visible magazine produced at the pro-privatization Hoover Institution at Stanford University.

These are just two instances among several from the public education sector as it is increasingly inundated with private-interest money.[22] Considering the substantial tax revenue committed to public education, it should come as no surprise that private foundations, philanthropies, think tanks, and advocacy groups representing a privatization agenda will create units in academia to advance their agenda—as do teachers unions and other interest groups. As on other complex issues such as global warming, they can provide the weight and credibility of an institutional brand that appears to provide some certainty and reliability in fields clouded by arcane methods, ideological squabbles, and conflicting findings.[23] But, as Oreskes and Conway have shown on other issues such as climate change or cigarettes, such groups often serve the primary purpose of muddying the waters for the broader public, particularly when a consensus is emerging among researchers that undercuts the agenda of their funders.[24]

Such is the case with the relative impact, or lack thereof, of the private/independent school sector on student achievement. Many policymakers are enthralled by the theoretical idea of market-oriented provision of education but want empirical evidence to provide political cover for that position. However, since we started working on this topic, a number of other independent researchers have found that the private or independent sectors are not superior to, and in some cases, are outpaced by, public schools for promoting growth in student learning. Yet, inasmuch as we see the beginnings of a consensus emerging on this issue, a familiar pattern begins to appear. As independent studies are published finding negligible evidence of a private/independent school effect,[25] academics or researchers associated with these advocacy organizations hurry to release a counterstudy—or even just a press release or "memo"—under a recognizable institutional brand in order to undercut those findings.[26] Yet these studies are often produced by academics with no experience with the data and methods, and although they serve the purpose of garnering attention for their perspective and raising questions in a media obsessed with presenting both sides, they are almost never peer reviewed—a key quality control measure particularly in areas demanding a level of technical sophistication and expertise.[27]

Alternatively, in lieu of publishing new research to counter a new study, some advocacy groups simply refer back to older reports from these quasi-think tanks, no matter how irrelevant, in order to muddy the waters. For example, in response to research indicating that private schools were not outperforming public schools, a policy analyst at the Heritage Foundation produced no new evidence or analyses that could rebut those findings but instead pointed to previous studies produced by voucher advocates that claim to show that students receiving vouchers learned more in private schools.[28] Of course, the issue is not whether or not a voucher student can select a better school, or whether certain private schools in a given community are superior, but whether private schools in general are more effective than demographically

similar public schools—the crucial question for policymakers interested in private sector remedies, but something that the studies cited
by the Heritage Foundation cannot and do not address. Yet, through
these types of efforts, interest groups and advocates such as these are
able to introduce significant confusion and doubt around rigorous research without referring to relevant or credible counterevidence. In so
doing, they provide the facade of empirical support for political efforts
to promote market theory in education.

Beyond Marketism for Education

Two decades ago, as charter schools and voucher programs were moving from idea to implementation, public choice theorists John Chubb
and Terry Moe famously analyzed federal data from the early 1980s,
producing findings of a private or independent school effect while
laying out what became the most influential empirical support for a
market theory of education. Claiming that "choice is a panacea" for the
problems facing America's schools,[29] they argued for the superiority of
private, independent schools, contending that since more autonomous
schools are more effective, choice is a preferred policy option, largely
because of the consequent competition between schools as they pursue ways to attract students.

However, the largest, most comprehensive data sets do not support
that widespread view. In fact, the evidence presented here shows what
a few have long suspected, but many do not want to admit, regarding the present patterns in America's schools. Indeed, while not widely
known, a growing body of evidence suggests that private, autonomous,
choice-based schools are not necessarily more innovative or academically effective but instead often perform at lower levels even as they
attract more able students.[30] In this, the largest data set ever analyzed
for these issues in the United States, public school students actually
outperformed their demographic peers in most types of private and
independent schools in a subject most closely tied to school effects.
Further analyses indicate that academic growth is greater for students
in public schools than for those in private schools.

Yet the continued expansion of publicly subsidized independent
school programs such as charter and voucher plans raises questions
both about policymakers' interest in empirical evidence despite rhe-

torical allegiance to the notion of "what works" and evidence-based decision making and about the usefulness of market theory for guiding the reform efforts around public schooling. As noted in the previous section, there are reasons why policymakers continue to pursue market-based school reforms, despite the questionable nature of evidence supporting those moves. However, the research discussed in this book raises serious questions about the potential for education policies based on market logic to address or alleviate the problems in education.

While markets certainly have their place in life, being excellent systems for the efficient production and distribution of so many goods and services, why has the evidence been so thin in support of a market theory of education? In order to answer that, we must consider the specific assumptions of market theory as they relate to the idea of public education. Three main assumptions of market theory deserve particular scrutiny in view of the evidence presented in this book: (1) the failure of public sector institutions, (2) the centrality of consumer choice, and (3) the importance of competition between autonomous entities as the primary source of innovation and improvement.

Assumption 1: Public Sector Failure

First, market theory and its public-choice precursor are premised on the idea of the failure of the public sector relative to the performance of the private sector (or the potential performance of private sector organizations if they are allowed to perform functions monopolized by the government). In contrast to the old idea of market failures around certain issues, these ideological perspectives hold that private production and provision are necessarily superior whenever possible, and see pathological failure ingrained in the very structures of the institutions of public education. That is, returning to our initial framework of competing models for public education, they indicate a strong allegiance to the conception of schooling as a business, with the idea of democratic/political control and the notion of technocratic governance of schooling both extremely distasteful.

While a simplistic look at the evidence suggests that private school students indeed score higher, closer scrutiny of the evidence rather conclusively demonstrates that this is not because public schools are failing but because they serve less advantaged students. In fact, public schools in this study actually add more value to their students' learning. This pattern runs counter to the usual narrative that government endeavors fail and that the private sector does a better job. But, despite the popular narrative, it is not unheard of for the public sector to offer a superior service or perform a function for less cost. Health insurance and environmental protection serve as examples where efficiency and effectiveness advantages are seen in the public and technocratic models—areas where providers are expected to embrace professional norms, yet to be responsive to societal needs regardless of economic advantage.

Assumption 2: The Centrality of Consumer Choice

In responding to what it sees as the inherent pathologies of government enterprises—or what it casts as government "monopolies"—market theory for education follows public-choice thinking in elevating the importance of consumer-style choice for organizing the production and distribution of educational services. Families' right to choose the type of education their children receive is thought to be important not simply as a moral right (which is irrelevant in this line of thinking) but as the guiding force that shapes the range of options that should be available. This recasts the beneficiaries of public education from the wider community to a focus on more immediate choosers of various education service options. This approach has an attractive logic to it. As in other consumer markets, individual customers are more likely than a faceless bureaucrat to know the particular needs and preferences of their own children. People more directly affected by the quality of a service are most likely to express preferences regarding the level of quality and more likely to demand improvements. The notion that "the customer is always right" is a compelling claim that is central to market models in consumer goods and services.

While this logic works in many areas of our lives, the theory becomes problematic in education as soon as it runs into the real world of evidence. Fundamental to the theory is that parents are wise and informed consumers acting on behalf of their children, and many are.[31] However, much evidence suggests that many parents do not have access to useful information on school options (a pattern that schools in competitive climates can and do use; see below) and that such information—and the tendency to use it—is unequally distributed, with children most in need of better quality options least likely to have parents willing or able to effectively advocate for their children.[32] Moreover, although market theory and parents' self-reported preferences suggest that they will seek out higher performing schools, our data along with other research indicate that parents often pursue demonstrably inferior schools[33]—for instance, the fastest growing segment of the private school sector, conservative Christian schools, is also the lowest performing, and many low-performing charter schools have waiting lists of families hoping to enroll.

There are several possible reasons for this. For example, parents can prioritize other factors such as proximity or the institutional reputation of a school (even if that reputation is undeserved); others consider where their child's friends are enrolling, or the sports or extracurricular programs, or the safety or values of a school—things more immediate than children's standardized test score gains and therefore often a focus of school marketing efforts.[34] Indeed, some simply seek any alternative to a run-down or poorly run neighborhood public school. But while all of these reasons are understandable, parents' tendency to look at nonacademic factors also highlights the limitations of market theory's focus on parent choice as the primary driver of quality improvement in education. In fact, many schools seem to recognize these tendencies and divert school resources away from the instructional improvements assumed by market theory and instead focus on advertising and other promotional efforts.[35]

Assumption 3: Competition between Autonomous Organizations Spurs Improvement

Market theory positions competition as the primary mechanism through which choice produces better schools. It contends that this happens because giving schools greater operational autonomy is essential for allowing schools to innovate and effectively respond to local conditions and consumer preferences in competing for the choices of students. According to this perspective, as consumers are encouraged to exercise choice between providers, schools have to compete to outperform each other; greater flexibility to do so allows them to innovate, improve, and thereby drive improvements across the system.

Again, this is a neat and appealing argument, and one that reflects the logic of markets for many consumer goods and services. Market theorists have been quite vocal in asserting the centrality of such competition for improving education.[36] The work they cite to support this typically distinguishes the level of competition as an input and then compares academic outcomes, under the assumption that improvements in outcomes reflect some unnamed variations within the "black box" of schooling. For instance, using this approach, some have pointed to a rise in students' test scores for public schools subjected to competition as proof that competitive threats force schools to be more effective, as they presumably then place more emphasis on efforts to improve student achievement.[37]

However, much of this work using the black-box approach, while it garners considerable attention and admiration from market advocates, has been challenged by other scholars who have not been able to replicate the findings or who have noted substantial problems with the methods.[38] While there is an attractive element to the simple assumption about the power of competition, more nuanced research that looks inside the black box of schools indicates that schools do not necessarily respond to competition in ways market theorists predict—that is, by using what autonomy they enjoy to innovate in finding more effective ways of educating students. Indeed, research on school competition does not provide strong support for the notion that greater competition leads to better outcomes and suggests instead that there may be detrimental impacts from competition on how school operate.[39]

Indeed, some studies look beyond simple inputs-outcomes metrics and instead examine actual changes in the processes, such as in resource allocation, in schools subjected to competitive pressures. Their findings challenge the market theory contention that competition will necessarily improve outcomes for all. For instance, when researchers in different countries actually examined what happens in schools subjected to competition, the evidence does not support the market logic that schools simply shift their attention to efforts at increasing achievement.[40] While competition puts pressure on district budgets, it does not seem to induce the reallocation of resources predicted by market theorists—a crucial step toward better academic outcomes in that logic. Instead of working to become more effective, schools in competition with each other often focus on other strategies, such as marketing and excluding costly and difficult-to-educate students.[41]

Why? Our data point to market theory's elevation of market logic in education, particularly in how nonmarket organizations such as schools respond when immersed in the competitive market environment prescribed by the theory. Market-oriented reformers call for fixing public schools by treating them more like businesses, granting them greater autonomy, and forcing them to compete for students. Market advocates see school autonomy—as opposed to the American tradition of (noncompetitive) district autonomy—as an essential factor because it allows school leaders to innovate and respond effectively to local conditions without being hamstrung by a central bureaucracy. Of course, we expect businesses to compete by using their autonomy to offer consumers better products or services, and market theory predicts schools will do so by innovating to improve productivity, which will be evidenced by higher test scores. Yet our findings in this volume cast serious doubt on the assumption that schools in the private or independent sector—schools that must directly compete for students— produce better outcomes. In fact, the dual remedies of autonomy and competition are fraught with their own difficulties when applied to the real world of education. According to our data, not only might autonomy and competition not work as well as reformers have promised, but they may make matters worse.

For instance, as shown in Chapter 6, Catholic schools enjoy greater autonomy, but the specific variables related to autonomy in schools— for instance, teacher control over curriculum, the degree of burdensome paperwork that interferes with teaching, and whether job security was tied to tests—are not related to increased student achievement. This is because such schools too often do not use that autonomy to employ innovative or cutting-edge instruction, instead adhering to traditional instructional methods and an outdated, narrow mathematics curriculum. That is, the more market-driven independent school sector appears to be using its greater autonomy to avoid proven curricular reforms drawn from professional insights on teaching and learning, leading to curricular stagnation.

In fact, instead of innovating to produce greater academic outcomes, schools competing with each other may be using their autonomy to compete in areas outside of instructional efficiency, such as marketing to attract "better" students.[42] Thus, recent evidence suggests that school choice systems may be leading to higher levels of segregation, not simply because parents choose schools where students reflect their own children's social characteristics, but because schools recognize this tendency and use their autonomy to adopt marketing and enrollment policies that exacerbate such trends.[43] Although it presents a tidy portrait of how schools can streamline their functions in focusing on consumers, market theory misses the fact that the multiple responsibilities placed on public schools as institutions created to serve common, nonmarket goals often require that they be shielded from the competitive pressures of the market. Autonomy combined with competition may drive improvements in the business world. But in education, market-style autonomy without professional training and insights can allow or—particularly when combined with competitive incentives—even encourage schools to avoid doing the right thing.

Thus, while private and independent schools are structured to respond directly to competition because of their higher levels of autonomy, there may be perverse incentives that cause them to use that autonomy in ways not directly related to innovating to improve academic effectiveness but through easier, less risky strategies such as marketing and student exclusion. Public schools, on the other hand, have generally been more shielded from competition in order to pursue goals that are neglected by market forces. Perhaps unexpectedly for market advocates, they are relatively effective with the students they serve, possibly because they are better able to focus on a professional ethos of student learning. However, that ethos may be threatened as competitive incentives are imposed on public schools and they must adopt market-style strategies in order to compete with charter and private schools for students.

Schooling, Markets, and Society

Markets are an integral and essential element of life in a developed society. They serve as an unsurpassed mechanism for achieving the efficient distribution of resources into productive endeavors. Under the right conditions, markets are an amazing source of innovation and affluence. They can liberate the creative and entrepreneurial tendencies associated with the unrivaled affluence of modern societies, freeing individuals to pursue their needs and wants and allowing others to find ways of meeting those demands and then benefit from their efforts to do so—thereby encouraging competition to find ways of satisfying people's preferences. As an organizing principle in education, markets are appealing in their elegant simplicity, their focus on consumers' choices, and the fact that they have the potential to improve options without onerous micromanaging, burdensome regulations or additional expenses.

Of course, there are also problems with markets. The proper functioning of a market depends on a number of assumptions that are not always operational, including sufficient demand for a private good or service, informed consumers, an institutional environment where producers and consumers are reasonably free and secure to pursue their own interests, and a sufficient level of competition between providers seeking to meet demand. Yet sometimes these preconditions are not in play, and given certain conditions, markets can misfire horribly. Even when they are working well, markets can lead to inequitable outcomes, since those with resources are better positioned to use markets to increase their advantages and pass them on to their children. Nevertheless, humans have yet to create any other single mechanism that has such power to create wealth.

Still, markets must be regarded as just that—an extremely useful but often problematic mechanism. They are not by themselves the universal model for all of human existence. However, market advocates, or marketists, are increasingly expanding the purview of markets into areas previously seen as inappropriate for market organization—ignoring or denying the limitations of markets while seeing the proliferation of markets as an end in itself. In recent years, we have seen the further penetration of business style institutional models into areas such as genetic ownership, drinking water, corrections, social services, and, of course, public schooling. While there is nothing inherently right or wrong about that marketization of many given endeavors—after all, it is important to consider which organizational model is better suited for achieving particular goals—there is a problem with a headlong rush towards market models for virtually all endeavors, especially when we disregard the evidence on the effectiveness, or lack thereof, of markets for meeting those goals. It is important to remember the difference between a society with markets as an essential but not singular tool and a "market society" where the importance of almost all goods, services, relationships, and efforts is measured, organized, and produced only for their economic value.[44]

Thus, efforts to test market models for public education are worth-while enterprises insofar as they can be shown to advance socially desirable goals for schools and not harm students in the process. Markets can be useful in many other areas of life. Yet universal education embodies goals that resist the simplistic imposition of market models for the organization and distribution of schooling for meeting those goals.

Appendix A: Details about National Assessment of Educational Progress (NAEP) Data and Analyses

The 2003 Main NAEP restricted-access data were used for this study. The NAEP mathematics assessment is based on a combination of multiple choice, short answer, and extended constructed response items from the five areas of mathematics recognized by the National Council of Teachers of Mathematics:[1] number, geometry, measurement, algebra, and statistics/probability. Despite NAEP's primary focus on achievement, the sampled students, their teachers, and school administrators complete detailed questionnaires pertaining to a variety of school climate– and instruction-related aspects. The 2003 Main NAEP mathematics samples were much larger than previous NAEP samples, as they encompassed "State NAEP" samples for the first time.

NAEP Samples and Missing Data

The full NAEP samples contained 190,147 students from 7,485 schools at grade 4 and 153,189 students from 6,092 schools at grade 8. The full NAEP samples were used for descriptive comparisons by school type. However, there were some missing data that reduced the samples used in the (hierarchical linear modeling) HLM analyses.

NAEP ACHIEVEMENT ANALYSIS (CHAPTER 4)

The HLM samples used to examine achievement by school type contained 166,736 students across 6,664 schools at grade 4 and 131,497 students across 5,377 schools at grade 8. Missing data impacted the samples for conservative Christian and "other private" schools (73%–79% of schools included in the HLM analysis) more than the samples for the

Table A1: Comparison of sample sizes, student demographics, school achievement, and school location: Full NAEP sample and HLM achievement analysis sample (Chapter 4)

	Grade 4		Grade 8	
	Full sample	HLM sample (% of full sample)	Full sample	HLM sample (% of full sample)
TOTAL NO. OF STUDENTS:	190,147	166,736 (88)	153,189	131,497 (86)
Percent female	49	49	50	50
Percent black	18	18	17	17
Percent Hispanic	13	13	11	11
Percent American Indian	2	2	2	2
Percent Asian	4	4	4	4
Percent white	62	63	66	66
Percent LEP	7	7	4	4
Percent with IEPs	12	11	11	11
Percent free/reduced-price lunch	42	45	36	37
Mean no. of home resources (out of 6 items)	3.7	3.7	4.3	4.3
TOTAL NO. OF SCHOOLS:	7,485	6,664 (89)	6,092	5,377 (88)
Catholic	216	180 (83)	224	203 (91)
Lutheran	88	73 (83)	96	79 (82)
Conservative Christian	78	57 (73)	90	70 (78)
Other private	157	124 (79)	148	114 (77)
Charter	149	126 (85)	85	72 (85)
Public	6,797	6,104 (90)	5,449	4,839 (89)
Mean school achievement	235.3	235.7	279.3	279.7
School lunch (1–6 scale)[a]	4.0	4.0	3.8	3.8
Mean number of home resources	3.7	3.7	4.4	4.4
Percent minority	30	29	27	27
LEP (1–6 scale)[a]	1.6	1.6	1.4	1.4
Percent large city	17	18	15	15
Percent rural	41	41	43	43
Percent Northeast	18	18	17	17
Percent South	31	31	31	32
Percent West	26	24	24	23
Percent Midwest	25	27	28	28

Note: Mean school achievement is the intercept of the base model in each case (i.e., weighted school means). The other percentages are the raw, unweighted descriptive statistics for each set of data.

[a] 1 = 0%–5%; 2 = 6%–10%; 3 = 11%–25%; 4 = 26%–50%; 5 = 51%–75%; 6 = 76%–100%.

Table A2: Raw, unweighted descriptive statistics for NAEP variables used in the HLM achievement analysis (Chapter 4)

	Grade 4 (166,736 students, 6,664 schools)				Grade 8 (131,497 students, 5,377 schools)			
	Minimum	Maximum	M	SD	Minimum	Maximum	M	SD
Student level:								
Plausible value 1	97.53	332.82	233.62	28.31	114.17	415.14	276.68	35.70
Plausible value 2	109.04	339.29	233.65	28.29	109.76	414.25	276.72	35.66
Plausible value 3	99.31	337.54	233.64	28.25	97.43	400.27	276.74	35.73
Plausible value 4	98.53	336.78	233.71	28.23	110.77	400.08	276.69	35.72
Plausible value 5	106.96	341.66	233.67	28.23	107.41	411.10	276.66	35.67
Black	0.00	1.00	0.18	0.39	0.00	1.00	0.17	0.37
Hispanic	0.00	1.00	0.13	0.33	0.00	1.00	0.11	0.31
Indian	0.00	1.00	0.02	0.13	0.00	1.00	0.02	0.13
Asian	0.00	1.00	0.04	0.20	0.00	1.00	0.04	0.20
Female	0.00	1.00	0.49	0.50	0.00	1.00	0.50	0.50
LEP	0.00	1.00	0.07	0.25	0.00	1.00	0.04	0.19
IEP	0.00	1.00	0.11	0.32	0.00	1.00	0.11	0.31
Lunch	0.00	1.00	0.45	0.50	0.00	1.00	0.37	0.48
Home resources	0.00	6.00	3.69	1.48	0.00	6.00	4.33	1.42
School level:								
Catholic	0.00	1.00	0.03	0.16	0.00	1.00	0.04	0.19
Lutheran	0.00	1.00	0.01	0.10	0.00	1.00	0.01	0.12
Conservative Christian	0.00	1.00	0.01	0.09	0.00	1.00	0.01	0.11
Other private	0.00	1.00	0.02	0.14	0.00	1.00	0.02	0.14
Charter	0.00	1.00	0.02	0.14	0.00	1.00	0.01	0.12
Percent lunch	1.00	6.00	4.02	1.55	1.00	6.00	3.76	1.53
Home resources	0.00	6.00	3.72	0.66	0.00	6.00	4.35	0.64
Percent minority	0.00	1.00	0.29	0.33	0.00	1.00	0.27	0.31
Percent LEP	1.00	6.00	1.61	1.20	1.00	6.00	1.39	0.92
Large city	0.00	1.00	0.18	0.38	0.00	1.00	0.15	0.36
Rural	0.00	1.00	0.41	0.49	0.00	1.00	0.43	0.50
Northeast	0.00	1.00	0.18	0.38	0.00	1.00	0.17	0.38
South	0.00	1.00	0.31	0.46	0.00	1.00	0.32	0.47
West	0.00	1.00	0.24	0.43	0.00	1.00	0.23	0.42

remaining school types (82%–91%). However, the demographics of the reduced HLM samples were remarkably similar to the demographics of the entire data set, and in our varied analyses we saw no indication that missing data biased the study's results.[2] See Tables A1–A4 for detailed descriptive statistics regarding the samples used in the achievement

Table A3: NAEP sample sizes, achievement, student demographics, and school location by school type: Grade 4 HLM achievement analysis sample (166,736 students from 6,664 schools)

	Public (noncharter), n = 160,403 students, 6,104 schools	Catholic, n = 1,802 students, 180 schools	Lutheran, n = 474 students, 73 schools	Conservative Christian, n = 500 students, 57 schools	Other private, n = 913 students, 124 schools	Charter, n = 2,644 students, 126 schools
Student factors[a]:						
Mean student achievement (standard error)	234 (0.3)	245 (1.0)	246 (1.6)	240 (1.5)	250 (2.0)	228 (2.8)
Percent black	17	6	12	9	9	31
Percent Hispanic	18	11	3	10	4	21
Percent American Indian	1	0	0	0	0	1
Percent Asian	4	3	1	6	5	2
Percent female	49	49	55	52	45	53
Percent LEP	9	1	1	0	1	9
Percent with IEPs	11	4	2	4	3	8
Percent free/ reduced-price lunch	45	9	8	3	4	47
Mean number of home resources (of six items)	3.6	4.5	4.3	4.3	4.5	3.7
School factors[b]:						
School lunch (1–6 scale)[c]	4.1	2.0	1.8	1.4	1.5	4.2
Mean number of home resources	3.6	4.4	4.2	4.3	4.2	3.7
Percent minority	31	19	18	18	20	45
Percent LEP (1–6 scale)[c]	1.8	1.1	1.0	1.0	1.2	1.7
Percent large city	14	28	20	15	21	37
Percent rural/small town	38	12	21	28	12	17
Percent schools in Northeast	17	32	3	17	14	5
Percent schools in South	33	18	16	41	45	.29
Percent schools in West	22	14	15	19	20	41
Percent schools in Midwest	28	36	66	23	21	25

Note: Sample sizes reflect the unweighted National Assessment of Educational Progress reporting samples; however, the means and percentages reported are for the samples weighted to represent U.S. students and schools.
[a] Data analyzed at the student level.
[b] Data analyzed at the school level.
[c] 1 = 0%–5%; 2 = 6%–10%; 3 = 11%–25%; 4 = 26%–50%; 5 = 51%–75%; 6 = 76%–100%.

Table A4: NAEP sample sizes, achievement, student demographics, and school location by school type: Grade 8 HLM achievement analysis sample (131,497 students from 5,377 schools)

	Public (noncharter), n – 126,041 students, 4,839 schools	Catholic, n – 2,074 students, 203 schools	Lutheran, n – 470 students, 79 schools	Conservative Christian, n – 518 students, 70 schools	Other private, n = 1,097 students, 114 schools	Charter, n = 1,297 students, 72 schools
Student factors[a]:						
Mean student achievement (standard error)	276 (0.4)	290 (1.5)	297 (2.1)	287 (2.3)	300 (2.9)	272 (3.8)
Percent black	17	9	8	11	8	30
Percent Hispanic	15	11	6	4	4	19
Percent American Indian	1	0	1	0	1	3
Percent Asian	4	4	3	3	7	3
Percent female	50	53	52	51	49	53
Percent LEP	5	1	0	0	0	6
Percent with IEPs	11	3	2	2	2	11
Percent free/ reduced-price lunch	37	14	10	0	12	49
Mean number of home resources (of six items)	4.3	5.0	5.0	4.8	5.1	4.3
School factors[b]:						
School lunch (1–6 scale)[c]	4.0	2.3	1.7	1.2	1.6	4.0
Mean number of home resources	4.2	4.2	5.0	4.4	4.9	4.2
Percent minority	28	22	12	17	23	39
Percent LEP (1–6 scale)[c]	1.4	1.1	1.0	1.0	1.1	1.2
Percent large city	12	30	25	11	18	25
Percent rural/small town	51	11	20	26	22	25
Percent schools in Northeast	17	30	4	10	19	9
Percent schools in South	33	20	14	49	41	31
Percent schools in West	20	15	19	20	13	44
Percent schools in Midwest	30	35	63	21	27	16

Note: Sample sizes reflect the unweighted National Assessment of Educational Progress reporting samples; however, the means and percentages reported are for the samples weighted to represent U.S. students and schools.

[a] Data analyzed at the student level.

[b] Data analyzed at the school level.

[c] 1 = 0%–5%; 2 = 6%–10%; 3 = 11%–25%; 4 = 26%–50%; 5 = 51%–75%; 6 = 76%–100%.

analyses (discussed in Chapter 4), including comparisons between the HLM and full NAEP samples.

NAEP ANALYSES OF ACHIEVEMENT-RELATED FACTORS (CHAPTER 6)

The full NAEP samples were used in descriptive comparisons of potential achievement-related factors by school type (see Tables 6.1 and 6.2). Due to missing data, the samples used in the HLM analyses contained 157,161 students from 6,288 schools at grade 4 and 119,364 students from 4,870 schools at grade 8. Again the demographics of the reduced HLM samples were similar to the demographics of the entire NAEP data set, diminishing concerns that missing data biased the study's results. For example, the percentages of black and Hispanic students in the full NAEP and HLM samples were identical at grade 4 and differed by only 1 percentage point at grade 8 (see Table A5). Missing data affected the samples for the smaller, conservative Christian and other private samples (66%–71% of schools included in the HLM analysis) somewhat more than the samples for other school types (72%–85%). For a more detailed analysis, we compared descriptive statistics for all variables by school type in the full samples (Tables 1 and 2 in Chapter 4) versus the HLM samples (Tables A7 and A8). Again, statistics were generally similar, with the most substantial difference occurring within the fourth grade conservative Christian school HLM sample, which appeared in some ways to contain more advantaged students than the full sample (e.g., the HLM fourth grade sample of conservative Christian schools was 8% black, compared with 12% in the full sample of these schools). However, most other demographic differences between the HLM and full samples of various school types were small, typically varying by less than a few percentage points. Tables A5–A8 contain detailed descriptive statistics for the HLM samples used in the analyses reported in Chapter 6.

A NOTE ABOUT SCHOOL PARTICIPATION RATES

Although the National Center for Education Statistics (NCES) strives to ensure that NAEP has representative samples for overall categories across sectors, variations within those samples mean that some subcategories may not be completely representative. For instance, there

Table A5: Comparison of sample sizes, student demographics, school achievement, and school location: Full NAEP sample and HLM sample

	Grade 4		Grade 8	
	Full sample	HLM sample (percent of full sample)	Full sample	HLM sample (percent of full sample)
TOTAL NO. OF STUDENTS:	190,147	157,161 (83)	153,189	119,364 (78)
Percent female	49	49	50	50
Percent black	18	18	17	16
Percent Hispanic	13	13	11	10
Percent American Indian	2	2	2	2
Percent Asian	4	4	4	4
Percent white	62	64	66	68
Percent LEP	7	7	4	4
Percent with IEPs	12	11	11	11
Percent free/reduced-price lunch	45	44	37	36
Mean number of home resources (out of six items)	3.7	3.7	4.3	4.3
Days absent last month	1.9	1.9	1.9	1.9
Talk about studies at home	3.4	3.4	3.0	3.0
Traditional math beliefs	1.9	1.9	2.4	2.4
Does not like math	16	16		
Likes math	46	47	3.2	3.2
TOTAL NUMBER OF SCHOOLS:	7,485	6,288 (84)	6,092	4,870 (80)
Catholic	216	170 (79)	224	179 (80)
Lutheran	88	69 (78)	96	71 (74)
Conservative Christian	78	55 (71)	90	59 (66)
Other private	157	112 (71)	148	97 (66)
Charter	149	114 (77)	85	61 (72)
Public	6,797	5,768 (85)	5,449	4,403 (81)
Mean school achievement	235.3	235.9	279.3	280.3
School lunch (1–6 scale)[a]	4.0	4.0	3.8	3.7
Mean number of home resources	3.7	3.7	4.4	4.4
Percent minority	30	29	27	27
LEP (1–6 scale)	1.6	1.6	1.4	1.4
Percent large city	17	17	15	14
Percent rural	41	41	43	42
Percent Northeast	18	18	17	17
Percent South	31	31	31	33
Percent West	26	24	24	22
Percent Midwest	26	27	27	28
School enrollment	2.2	2.2	2.6	2.7
Class size	3.4	3.4		
Teacher morale	−0.1	−0.1	−0.3	−0.4
School conflict	0.1	0.1	0.3	0.3
Drugs/alcohol			0.3	0.3

Table A5: *continued*

	Grade 4		Grade 8	
	Full sample	HLM sample (percent of full sample)	Full sample	HLM sample (percent of full sample)
Parents involved	−0.1	−0.1	−0.2	−0.2
Parents volunteer	−0.0	−0.0	−0.2	−0.2
Percent certified teachers	88	90	75	82
Math major			1.1	1.1
Percent new teachers	20	20	24	26
Professional development	3.1	3.2	5.5	5.6
Time on math	3.2	3.2	3.7	3.7
Emphasis on geometry, measurement, data, algebra	8.4	8.4		
Emphasis on number/operations	2.9	2.9		
Multiple choice	0.8	0.8		
Calculators	1.6	1.6	2.6	2.6

Note: Mean school achievement is the intercept of the base model in each case (i.e., weighted school means). The other percentages are the raw, unweighted descriptive statistics for each set of data.
[a] 1 = 0%–5%; 2 = 6%–10%; 3 = 11%–25%; 4 = 26%–50%; 5 = 51%–75%; 6 = 76%–100%.

were relatively low numbers of Lutheran and conservative Christian schools at both grades as well as of charter schools at grade 8. Also, the participation rates of conservative Christian schools did not meet NCES reporting standards in grade 4, and these rates were not met for charter schools in grade 8 or for other private schools in grades 4 or 8. A 70% participation rate (before alternate schools are substituted) is required to meet NCES reporting standards. However, the consistency of the patterns of results across grades 4 and 8, along with NCES's procedures for replacing schools that refuse to be part of the NAEP sample, diminish concerns about sample limitations. Moreover, the design of NAEP's school weight reduces potential bias resulting from school nonresponse. We decided to include all of the data in our analyses to provide as much information as possible on patterns in public, charter, and private school achievement.

Addressing NAEP Data Complexities

Any statistical analysis of NAEP data is complicated by two methodological challenges: (1) NAEP's multistage cluster sampling design and

Table A6: Raw, unweighted descriptive statistics for NAEP variables used in the HLM analysis

	Grade 4 (157,161 students, 6,288 schools)				Grade 8 (119,364 students, 4,870 schools)			
	Minimum	Maximum	Mean	Standard deviation	Minimum	Maximum	Mean	Standard deviation
Student level:								
Plausible value 1	99.32	332.82	234.01	28.22	118.66	415.14	277.50	35.25
Plausible value 2	110.74	339.29	234.04	28.20	119.72	414.25	277.54	35.23
Plausible value 3	99.31	337.54	234.03	28.17	97.43	400.27	277.58	35.28
Plausible value 4	98.53	336.78	234.10	28.14	118.13	399.86	277.50	35.27
Plausible value 5	106.96	341.66	234.06	28.15	107.41	411.10	277.48	35.22
Black	0.00	1.00	0.18	0.33	0.00	1.00	0.16	0.37
Hispanic	0.00	1.00	0.13	0.33	0.00	1.00	0.10	0.30
Indian	0.00	1.00	0.02	0.13	0.00	1.00	0.02	0.13
Asian	0.00	1.00	0.04	0.20	0.00	1.00	0.04	0.20
Female	0.00	1.00	0.50	0.50	0.00	1.00	0.50	0.50
LEP	0.00	1.00	0.07	0.25	0.00	1.00	0.04	0.19
IEP	0.00	1.00	0.11	0.32	0.00	1.00	0.11	0.31
Lunch	0.00	1.00	0.44	0.50	0.00	1.00	0.36	0.48
Home resources	0.00	6.00	3.70	1.47	0.00	6.00	4.34	1.41
Days absent last month	1.00	5.00	1.87	1.04	1.00	5.00	1.91	1.01
Talk about studies at home	1.00	5.00	3.44	1.55	1.00	5.00	2.96	1.45
Traditional math beliefs	1.00	3.00	1.90	0.60	1.00	3.00	2.43	0.84
Does not like math	0.00	1.00	0.16	0.37				
Likes math	0.00	1.00	0.47	0.50	1.00	5.00	3.18	1.28

Table A6: *continued*

| | Grade 4 (157,161 students, 6,288 schools) | | | | | Grade 8 (119,364 students, 4,870 schools) | | | |
	Minimum	Maximum	Mean	Standard deviation		Minimum	Maximum	Mean	Standard deviation
School level:									
Catholic	0.00	1.00	0.03	0.16		0.00	1.00	0.04	0.19
Lutheran	0.00	1.00	0.01	0.10		0.00	1.00	0.01	0.12
Conservative Christian	0.00	1.00	0.01	0.09		0.00	1.00	0.01	0.11
Other private	0.00	1.00	0.02	0.13		0.00	1.00	0.02	0.14
Charter	0.00	1.00	0.02	0.13		0.00	1.00	0.01	0.11
Percent lunch	1.00	6.00	4.00	1.55		1.00	6.00	3.75	1.52
Home resources	0.00	6.00	3.72	0.66		0.00	6.00	4.36	0.63
Percent minority	0.00	1.00	0.29	0.33		0.00	1.00	0.26	0.31
Percent LEP	1.00	6.00	1.62	1.20		1.00	6.00	1.38	0.90
Large city	0.00	1.00	0.17	0.38		0.00	1.00	0.14	0.35
Rural	0.00	1.00	0.41	0.49		0.00	1.00	0.42	0.49
Northeast	0.00	1.00	0.18	0.38		0.00	1.00	0.17	0.38
South	0.00	1.00	0.31	0.46		0.00	1.00	0.33	0.47

West	0.00	1.00	0.24	0.43	0.00	1.00	0.22	0.42
School enrollment	1.00	4.00	2.22	1.05	1.00	5.00	2.70	1.45
Class size	1.00	5.00	3.44	1.21				
Teacher morale	-6.47	0.89	-0.13	1.03	-5.64	0.96	-0.35	1.07
School conflict	-1.13	6.18	0.11	1.03	-1.24	6.31	0.34	1.07
Drugs/alcohol					-0.68	4.36	0.26	1.00
Parents involved	-3.59	1.60	-0.11	0.97	-2.76	1.79	-0.24	0.91
Parents volunteer	-2.08	2.37	-0.02	0.99	-1.56	2.54	-0.17	0.89
Percent certified Teachers	0.00	1.00	0.90	0.22	0.00	1.00	0.82	0.28
Math majors					0.00	2.00	1.13	0.66
Percent new teachers	0.00	1.00	0.20	0.28	0.00	1.00	0.26	0.33
Professional development	0.00	12.00	3.21	2.04	0.00	12.00	5.56	2.27
Time on math	1.00	4.00	3.24	1.00	1.00	4.00	3.72	0.78
Emphasis on geometry, measurement, data, algebra	4.00	12.00	8.39	1.31				
Emphasis on number/ operations	1.00	3.00	2.87	0.25				
Multiple choice	0.00	2.00	0.78	0.57				
Calculators	0.00	2.00	1.56	0.61	1.00	3.67	2.26	0.62

Table A7: NAEP sample sizes, achievement, student demographics, and school location by school type: Grade 4 HLM sample (157,161 students from 6,288 schools)

	Public (noncharter), n = 151,296 students, 5,768 schools	Catholic, n = 1,662 students, 170 schools	Lutheran, n = 442 students, 69 schools	Conservative Christian, n = 472 students, 55 schools	Other private, n = 830 students, 112 schools	Charter, n = 2,459 students, 114 schools
Student factors:						
Mean student achievement	235	245	246	241	249	228
Percent black	17	6	13	8	9	32
Percent Hispanic	18	11	2	9	3	20
Percent American Indian	1	0	0	0	0	1
Percent Asian	4	3	1	6	5	2
Percent female	49	48	55	53	45	53
Percent LEP	9	1	1	0	0	9
Percent with IEPs	11	4	2	4	3	9
Percent free/reduced-price lunch	44	8	8	3	4	47
Mean number of home resources (of six items)	3.7	4.5	4.3	4.3	4.6	3.7
Days absent last month	1.9	1.8	1.8	1.7	1.8	2.0
Talk about studies at home	3.4	3.5	3.5	3.4	3.6	3.5
Traditional math beliefs	1.9	1.8	1.8	1.9	1.7	1.9
Does not like math	16	16	19	19	20	19
Likes math	47	43	39	41	41	45
School factors:						
School lunch (1–6 scale)	4.1	2.0	1.8	1.5	1.4	4.2

Mean number of home resources	3.7	4.4	4.2	4.3	4.2	3.7
Percent minority	31	20	18	16	21	45
Percent LEP (1–6 scale)	1.8	1.1	1.0	1.0	1.2	1.7
Percent large city	14	28	18	14	23	36
Percent rural/small town	38	12	19	30	14	14
Percent schools in Northeast	17	33	3	17	15	5
Percent schools in South	33	18	19	45	46	29
Percent schools in West	23	14	12	20	22	40
Percent schools in Midwest	27	35	66	18	17	27
School enrollment (1–4 scale)	2.3	1.5	1.1	1.4	1.4	1.9
Class size (1–4 scale)	3.6	3.3	2.0	1.8	2.0	3.4
Teacher morale	-0.2	0.5	0.4	0.5	0.5	0.1
School conflict	0.1	-0.4	-0.5	-0.4	-0.5	-0.0
Parents involved	-0.1	0.6	0.0	0.2	0.5	-0.1
Parents volunteer	-0.1	0.5	-0.1	0.1	-0.0	0.6
Percent certified teachers	91	77	75	49	73	70
Percent new teachers	21	22	13	29	19	42
Professional development	3.2	2.5	1.8	2.2	2.3	3.4
Time on math	3.2	3.7	3.6	3.5	3.4	3.2
Emphasis on geometry, measurement, data, algebra	8.6	7.7	7.5	7.7	8.1	8.6
Emphasis on number/ops	2.9	2.9	2.8	2.9	3.0	2.9
Multiple choice	0.9	0.7	0.7	0.8	0.4	0.8
Calculators	1.6	1.2	1.1	0.7	1.1	1.2

Note: Sample sizes reflect the unweighted National Assessment of Educational Progress reporting samples; however, the means and percentages reported are for the samples weighted to represent U.S. students and schools.

Table A8: NAEP sample sizes, achievement, student demographics, and school location by school type: Grade 8 HLM sample (119,364 students from 4,870 schools)

	Public (noncharter), n = 114,561 students, 4,403 schools	Catholic, n = 1,862 students, 179 schools	Lutheran, n = 418 students, 71 schools	Conservative Christian, n = 440 students, 59 schools	Other private, n = 981 students, 97 schools	Charter, n = 1,072 students, 61 schools
Student factors:						
Mean student achievement	277	291	299	287	302	274
Percent black	16	10	6	13	8	30
Percent Hispanic	15	10	5	3	4	17
Percent American Indian	1	0	1	0	0	3
Percent Asian	4	3	4	4	8	3
Percent female	50	53	50	49	49	54
Percent LEP	5	1	0	0	0	5
Percent with IEPs	11	3	2	2	2	11
Percent free/ reduced-price lunch	36	14	9	0	14	48
Mean number of home resources (of six items)	4.3	5.1	5.1	4.9	5.1	4.4
Days absent from school	1.9	1.8	1.8	1.8	1.8	2.0
Talk about studies at home	3.0	2.2	2.3	2.5	2.2	2.5
Traditional math beliefs	2.4	2.2	2.3	2.5	2.2	2.5
Likes math	3.2	3.3	3.1	3.0	3.3	3.3
School factors:						
School lunch (1–6 scale)	4.0	2.3	1.5	1.3	1.8	3.9
Mean number of home resources	4.2	4.9	5.1	4.7	4.9	4.3
Percent minority	28	21	9	20	24	38
Percent LEP (1–6 scale)	1.4	1.1	1.0	1.0	1.1	1.2
Percent large city	11	29	24	14	21	20
Percent rural/small town	50	11	20	23	25	25
Percent schools in Northeast	17	29	4	7	21	10
Percent schools in South	35	21	16	38	39	35
Percent schools in West	17	14	16	23	14	40
Percent schools in Midwest	31	36	64	32	25	14
School enrollment (1–5 scale)	2.4	1.5	1.1	1.3	1.4	1.6
Teacher morale	−0.4	0.5	0.6	0.4	0.5	0.4
School conflict	0.3	−0.5	−0.6	−0.3	−0.4	−0.1
Drugs/alcohol	0.3	−0.6	−0.7	−0.5	−0.2	−0.3
Parents involved	−0.4	0.9	0.3	0.2	0.4	0.2
Parents volunteer	−0.4	0.8	0.3	0.4	0.2	0.6
Percent certified teachers	84	70	67	58	58	54
Math majors	1.1	0.7	0.6	0.8	0.8	0.9
Percent new teachers	26	26	26	46	28	47
Professional development	5.5	4.8	3.2	3.3	3.8	5.3
Time on math	3.7	3.8	3.5	3.7	3.7	3.5
Calculators	2.6	2.5	2.9	2.4	2.4	2.5

Note: Sample sizes reflect the unweighted National Assessment of Educational Progress reporting samples; however, the means and percentages reported are for the samples weighted to represent U.S. students and schools.

(2) measurement error associated with the matrix sampling scheme. These challenges and the ways they were addressed are described briefly here.[3]

1. MULTISTAGE CLUSTER SAMPLING

The 2003 NAEP national sample is a combination of data from pooled state samples along with a selection of additional schools to ensure that the sample represents the nation as a whole. In creating the samples, schools were stratified based on urbanicity, minority population, size, and area income, and then schools within each stratum were selected at random. Finally, students were selected randomly within schools. Deliberate oversampling of certain strata, such as private schools and those with high enrollments of minority students, resulted in more reliable estimates for the oversampled subgroups, but the resulting samples must be weighted to provide accurate estimates of the U.S. school population. Weights are adjusted for both unequal probabilities of selection and nonresponse.

2. MATRIX SAMPLING SCHEME

In order to reduce the test-taking burden on individual students, no student takes the entire NAEP battery of items, and individual students are not assigned a single score. Instead, a distribution of plausible values for each student's proficiency is estimated, based on the student's responses to administered items and other student characteristics. Five plausible values are drawn at random from the conditional distribution of proficiency scores for each student. Hence, when analyzing NAEP achievement data, the results of separate analyses must be obtained for each of the five plausible values and then synthesized, following Rubin on the analysis of multiply imputed data.[4] This procedure accounts for the additional uncertainty arising from the use of five plausible values rather than a single observed outcome.

Throughout this project, the appropriate weights and statistical techniques were used to address these special features of NAEP data.[5] Although most data management tasks were conducted within SPSS, most statistical analyses were conducted with the use of two software programs, AM and HLM 6.0,[6] which were designed to address the needs of complex data sets such as NAEP. We also tested some of the mixed regression models using the Stata 9.1 program xtmixed to confirm the results obtained within HLM; only minor differences were observed.

Specifically, student achievement means by school type were generated with the cross tabulation feature of AM Statistical Software, designed by the American Institutes for Research.[7] AM is designed to handle the weighting and jackknifing needs of NAEP and was used to calculate basic achievement means and standard errors.

However, the bulk of the analyses focused on the main research question about the relationship between school type and achievement. Because of the nested nature of the data (students within schools), we used HLM to create two-level hierarchical linear models to examine achievement by school type while controlling for potential student- and school-level confounding variables. A school-level weight was used at level 2; no level 1 weight was used because students were randomly selected within schools. The plausible values feature of HLM was used (prompting the program to run models for each of the five plausible values internally and producing their average value and correct standard errors). A detailed explanation of the data analysis methods used by the HLM software is available from Raudenbush and Bryk.[8]

One final issue to consider is the low-stakes nature of NAEP. Students are not rewarded for their performance on the assessment, raising concerns about NAEP's ability to accurately measure student achievement. However, this issue has been of greatest concern when NAEP also collects data on grade 12, where student and school participation rates have tended to be lower, than at grades 4 and 8.[9] Hence, this is not a major concern for this study.

NAEP Variables

The achievement analyses reported in Chapter 4 utilized a variety of NAEP variables, including school type, student and school demographic variables, and school location. The analyses of potential achievement-related factors discussed in Chapter 6 also utilized school size, class size, school climate, teacher education/experience, time spent on math, teaching methods, and student attitudes regarding mathematics. Both sets of analyses used NAEP scale scores for mathematics as the outcome variable.

SCHOOL TYPE

Binary variables were used to distinguish among Catholic, Lutheran, conservative Christian, other private schools, and charter schools (which by default allowed comparisons with noncharter public schools).

STUDENT DEMOGRAPHICS

Binary variables were used for black, Hispanic, American Indian, Asian/Pacific Islander,[10] and female students, as well as for students with limited English proficiency (LEP) and those with an Individualized Education Program (IEP).[11]

Two variables were used to approximate students' socioeconomic status (SES): their resources at home and free/reduced lunch eligibility. The home-resources composite was created by summing the six relevant items available in the NAEP data set. Specifically, students reported whether they had each of the following at home:[12]

- Magazines (received regularly)
- Newspaper (received at least four times weekly)
- Computer
- Encyclopedia (in book form or on computer)
- Atlas (a book of maps or on computer)
- Books (0–10 coded as 0, 11–25 books coded as .33, 26–100 books coded as .67, and more than 100 coded as 1)[13]

Survey information about individual students' eligibility for free or reduced lunch posed a challenge, given that a disproportionate number of private school administrators reported that the school did not participate in the program (the percentage was over half for some types of private schools). Although these schools generally appeared to be of high SES on other measures,[14] we did not assume that every student in such schools was ineligible for lunch. To preserve data while also being cautious in imputing eligibility status, such students were recoded as ineligible only if their school administrator also reported (on a separate question) that less than 5% of the school was eligible for lunch or if the student reported having at least five of the six resources that made up the home resources composite (five was higher than the mean of

4.1 at grade 4 and of 4.7 for grade 8, for *ineligible* students). Overall, the recoded students' mean achievement was higher than that of the other lunch-ineligible students within their school type, providing further evidence that the recoding was warranted and did not negatively bias the performance of private schools. The final lunch variable was binary, with 0 = ineligible and 1 = eligible for free or reduced lunch.[15]

SCHOOL DEMOGRAPHICS

School administrators reported the percentage of students eligible for free or reduced lunch in their schools, as well as the percentage of LEP students, using the categories: 0%, 1%–5%, 6%–10%, 11%–25%, 26%–50%, 51%–75%, 76%–90%, and above 90%. The two top and bottom categories were collapsed to create a more evenly spaced 6-point scale. In order to preserve data, the variable "percent eligible for school lunch" was imputed based on student home environment variables for those schools that did not report this information (similar to the method described above for the student-level imputation). The percentage of students with IEPs was also included in initial models but was ultimately deleted owing to lack of significance.

The home resources composite was aggregated to the school level to provide a school-level mean home resources measure. Additionally, school administrators reported the percentage of students who were black, Hispanic, and American Indian (on a 0%–100% scale), and these percentages were summed and then divided by 100 to create a percent minority variable for each school.[16]

SCHOOL LOCATION

A binary variable denoted schools located within large cities, while another indicated whether schools were in a rural or small-town locale. Similarly, binary variables were used to distinguish among schools in the Northeastern, Southern, and Western (and by default Midwestern) portions of the United States.

SCHOOL SIZE

School administrators reported student enrollment by selecting one of several categories, which differed at grades 4 and 8. At grade 4, the four options (coded from 1 to 4) were as follows: 1–299, 300–499, 500–699, and 700 or more. At grade 8, there were five options (coded from 1 to 5): 1–399, 400–599, 600–799, 800–999, and 1,000 or more.

CLASS SIZE

Grade 4 teachers were asked to report the number of students in their math class, using the following categories (coded from 1 to 5): 0–15, 16–18, 19–20, 21–25, and 26 or more. Grade 8 teachers were not asked about class size. Although this variable was reported by fourth-grade teachers for each participating student, it was aggregated to the school level to create a school-level estimate of average class size for inclusion in the HLM models.

SCHOOL CLIMATE

There were roughly two dozen NAEP variables that pertained directly or indirectly to the climate of the school, including parents' involvement in their children's schooling. In order to reduce the number of variables in the models and to avoid collinearity among the variables, factor analyses were used to identify clusters of correlated variables—those that ultimately loaded onto a single factor (with an eigenvalue greater than 1) when the cluster of variables was put into a factor analysis. Each of the five identified clusters was then averaged and standardized to create a z-score composite for inclusion in the HLM models. Some variables included in initial factor analyses did not cluster with others. Some of these isolated variables were then entered into the HLM models individually (as in the case of school size and class size), and others were deemed less important for the purposes of this study and were simply deleted (e.g., student health). Two student-reported variables—talking about schoolwork at home and school attendance—did not cluster with others but were sufficiently related to some of the school climate composites (e.g., parent involvement) to merit including as individual measures of school climate.

Teacher Morale

Four administrator-reported measures of teacher morale were (1) percentage of teachers absent on an average day; (2) extent to which teacher absenteeism is a problem in the school (response options being "not a problem," "minor," "moderate," and "serious"; (3) general teacher morale; and (4) teachers' expectations for student achievement, with the latter two variables measured on a 4-point scale ranging from "very negative" to "very positive."

Conflicts/Student Behavior

Administrators were asked to report the extent to which gang activities, physical conflicts among students, student/teacher physical conflicts, race/culture conflicts, vandalism, disregard for school property, and student misbehavior were problematic within their schools. Response options were "not a problem," "minor," "moderate," and "serious."

Drugs/Alcohol (Grade 8 Only)

At grade 8, three administrator-reported variables indicated the extent to which student use of drugs, alcohol, and tobacco was a problem within the school (again using the 4-point scale ranging from "not a problem" to "serious").

Parents Involved

There were five administrator-reported variables pertaining to parent involvement that clustered together: (1) parents attending open house/back to school night, (2) parents attending parent-teacher conferences, (3) parents in parent-teacher organizations, (4) parental support for student achievement, and (5) whether lack of parent involvement is a problem. All of these variables were on a 4-point scale; the first three of these variables used a quartile scale (0%–25%, 26%–50%, 51%–75%, and 76%–100%); the response options for the fourth variable ranged from "very negative" to "very positive"; and the options for the final variable ranged from "not a problem" to "severe."

Parent Volunteers

At both grades 4 and 8, factor analyses revealed that variables pertaining to parent volunteerism within the school were *not* highly correlated with the five variables pertaining to the other forms of parent involvement outlined above. However, four variables pertaining to volunteerism did cluster together and were combined into a single composite. Specifically, the three variables indicating how often ("routinely," "occasionally," or "no") parents served as guest teachers, were used as aides in classrooms, or worked in volunteer programs were combined with the percentage of parents who participated in volunteer programs (4-point quartile scale).

Parents Talk about Schoolwork with Students at Home

Students were asked how often they talked about their studies at home with a parent or other adult. Response options (coded from 1 to 5) were 1 = never or hardly ever, 2 = 1–2 times a month, 3 = once a week, 4 = 2–3 times a week, 5 = every day. Again, this variable and student attendance (below) seem less of a direct measure of school climate than the others, but they fit conceptually with the other measures of parent involvement in students' schooling and could be viewed as outgrowths of, and contributors to, school climate. Hence, these two variables were included under the school climate umbrella.

Student Attendance

Students were asked the number of days they were absent from school in the previous month. Response options (coded from 1 to 5) were none, 1–2 days, 3–4 days, 5–10 days, or more than 10 days. Although this information was student reported and entered at the student level of the HLM models, it was included as one of the seven measures of school climate.

TEACHER EDUCATION AND EXPERIENCE

Certified Teachers

This binary variable was created from teacher-reported data that were originally tied to the student data (as is always the case for teacher-reported data because NAEP randomly samples students within a school—not teachers). Teachers were considered "certified" if they held regular state certification or probationary state certification (with only a probationary period to complete before gaining a regular certificate). Teachers who held emergency, temporary, or other provisional forms of certification were not considered certified. This variable was aggregated to the school level, indicating the percentage of students in the school who had a certified teacher (which, assuming equal class sizes across teachers, provides an estimate of the percentage of certified teachers).

New Teachers

This binary variable, based on teacher-reported data, indicated whether teachers had 0–4 years of experience. This variable was aggregated to the school level, indicating the percentage of students within a school who had such teachers.

Professional Development

Teachers were asked whether they had each of twelve different forms of professional development within the prior two years, including workshops, mentoring, coteaching, research projects, and consultation with a mathematics specialist. The twelve binary variables were simply summed. Hence, the final variable is a measure of the number of the twelve activities encountered within the prior two years (0–12 scale). This is obviously a very rough measure of professional development, providing no indication of the amount of time spent in such activities nor their focus and quality. Again, this variable was aggregated to the school level.

TIME ON MATH

Fourth grade teachers were asked how much time they spend on mathematics instruction weekly. Response options (coded from 1 to 4) were "less than 1 hour," "at least 1 hour," "at least 2 hours," and "3 hours or more." This variable was aggregated to the school level. Eighth grade teachers did not report the amount of time spent on mathematics instruction (and consequently there were only eleven HLM models created for grade 8, compared with twelve models for grade 4).

TEACHING METHODS

NAEP asked fourth grade teachers about their curricular emphases, as well as their use of multiple choice assessments and calculators. These instruction-related variables were aggregated to the school level to provide estimates of instructional emphases within each school.

Emphasis on Geometry, Measurement, Algebra, and Data Analysis (Grade 4 Only)

Teachers responded to four questions (1–3 scale) asking whether they place "little/no emphasis," "moderate emphasis," or "heavy emphasis" on each of the four nonnumber mathematics strands. The resulting four variables were summed to form a composite measure of teachers' emphasis on nonnumber mathematics content areas.

Emphasis on Number and Operations (Grade 4 Only)

For this single variable, teachers indicated whether they placed "little/ no emphasis," "moderate emphasis," or "heavy emphasis" (1–3 scale) on number and operations when teaching mathematics. This variable did not closely correlate with the other four content emphasis variables.

Multiple Choice Assessments (Grade 4 Only)

Fourth grade teachers were asked how often they used multiple choice assessments. Responses were coded on a 3-point scale, with 0 = less than twice per year, 1 = 1–2 times per month, and 2 = 1–2 times per week.

Calculators

The variables pertaining to calculator use varied by grade level. At grade 4, teachers were asked whether they provide instruction in the use of calculators and whether their students have access to school calculators. These two binary variables were summed to produce a variable (on a 0–2 scale) that indicated whether teachers provided (0 points) no calculator instruction and no student access to calculators,

(1 point) either calculator instruction or student access to calculators, or (2 points) both instruction and access to calculators. At grade 8, teachers were not asked about calculator use, but students were asked how often they use calculators on tests, for class work, and for mathematics more generally. These variables were coded as follows: 1 = never or hardly ever, 2 = 1–2 times a month, 3 = 1–2 times a week, and 4 = almost every day.

STUDENT BELIEFS/ATTITUDES REGARDING MATHEMATICS

Students were surveyed regarding their beliefs about and attitudes toward mathematics. These variables were included because they likely relate to the mathematics instruction occurring in the schools. Although the questions were similar at both the fourth and eighth grades, the scales differed, with fourth graders asked to indicate whether a statement was "not like me" (coded as 1), "a little like me" (coded as 2), or "a lot like me" (coded as 3). However, at eighth grade, students were given a 1–5 scale, with 1 = strongly disagree and 5 = strongly agree.

Using these response options, fourth and eighth graders rated two statements regarding the nature of mathematics: "Learning mathematics is mostly memorizing facts" and "There is only one correct way to solve a mathematics problem." Both of these statements represent relatively rigid, rule-bound views of mathematics learning and are contrary to the spirit of recent reforms in mathematics education.[17] For the sake of brevity, agreement with these statements is termed "traditional mathematics beliefs."

Students also indicated their agreement with the statement "I like mathematics" at both fourth and eighth grades. Given the 3-point scale at grade 4 for this single variable, we converted it to two binary variables (this was not done for other 3-point-scaled variables that were aggregated to the school level because the aggregation created a more continuous variable). The grade 8 variable on the 5-point scale remained as originally coded.

NAEP MATHEMATICS ACHIEVEMENT SCORES

To understand the results discussed here, some information about NAEP scores is necessary. NAEP mathematics results are reported with scale scores, with the 2003 mean scores being 235 at grade 4 and 278 at grade 8. The NAEP mathematics scale was originally designed to allow cross-grade comparisons, indicating that a 43-point difference between grade 4 and grade 8 would mean that a gap of 10 or 11 points represents a difference of roughly "one grade level." NCES no longer maintains that the scale is consistent across grades, however, the idea that "10–11 points translates to approximately one grade level" is still often used as a helpful, albeit rough, guide for interpreting score differences. Another way to interpret the magnitude of these disparities is in terms of effect sizes. Standard deviations for school achievement means were 14.7 at grade 4 and 19.3 at grade 8.[18] In these terms, a 10–11 point difference represents a moderate to large effect (roughly .5–.7 standard deviations).

Data Analysis

EXAMINING ACHIEVEMENT BY SCHOOL TYPE (CHAPTER 4)

A sequence of two-level HLM models was created at both the fourth and eighth grades to examine the relationship between school type and mathematics achievement while controlling for demographic variables and school location. We began by running a traditional null model, followed by a model with school sector variables only, to allow for comparisons of achievement means by school type before and after demographic/location differences were controlled. We then added student and school demographics to examine how much the demographics "explained" the school achievement disparities evident in the prior model. Finally, we added school location variables to examine the additional impact of rural/urban and U.S. region on the school type coefficients.[19] Binary variables were entered uncentered, and the remaining variables (italicized below) were entered grand mean centered.

The HLM equations for the full model are as follows:

Level 1 Model

Y = B0 + B1*(BLACK) + B2*(HISP) + B3*(INDIAN) + B4*(ASIAN) + B5*(FEMALE) + B6*(LEP) + B7*(IEP) + B8*(LUNCH) + B9*(*HOME RESOURCES*) + R.

Level 2 Model

B0 = G00 + G01*(CATHOLIC) + G02*(LUTHERAN) + G03*(CONSERVATIVE
CHRISTIAN) + G04*(OTHER PRIVATE) + G05*(CHARTER) +
G06*(*PCTLUNCH*) + G07*(*MEAN HOME RESOURCES*) + G08*(*PCT
MINORITY*) + G09*(*PCTLEP*) + G010*(LARGE CITY) + G011*(RURAL) +
G012*(NORTHEAST) + G013*(SOUTH) + G014*(WEST) + U0.

Given that previous studies indicated that some achievement inequities were smaller in Catholic schools than in public schools,[20] interactions between school type and race- and SES-related achievement gaps were included in additional HLM models to determine whether the gaps were larger or smaller in public, charter, Catholic, or other private schools. No significant interactions were found, and therefore the detailed results of that examination are not reported here. Still, it is possible small differences could be detected if sample sizes of racial minority groups were larger in private schools.

EXAMINING ACHIEVEMENT-RELATED VARIABLES AND
SCHOOL TYPE (CHAPTER 6)

After finding disparities in achievement by school type, we extended our NAEP analysis to examine correlates of achievement that could help explain the school sector differences in achievement. Hence, we created a series of additional models that began with the models outlined above but then added school size, class size, school climate, teacher education, mathematics instruction, and student beliefs/attitudes. As these factors were added to the models, we were able to determine both whether these factors correlate with achievement and the effect of the addition of these factors on the school coefficients, thereby shedding light on possible explanations for school achievement differences.

Results of HLM Analyses

The results of the first set of achievement-focused analyses were explained in some detail in Chapter 4. Here we provide details of the results from the analyses underlying the discussion in Chapter 6. Descriptive statistics for variables used in the HLM analyses are presented in Table A7. Tables A9 and A10 report the HLM results for fourth and eighth grades, respectively. Standard errors are reported for the intercept and school type coefficients only, but significance levels are included for all coefficients.

The first three models are similar to those discussed in Chapter 4 and are summarized only briefly here. According to Model 1 in Table A9, the traditional HLM null model, school mathematics achievement across all schools averaged 235.9 points in fourth grade, with 29% of the variance in achievement between schools and 71% within schools. Model 2 indicates that, in comparison to public schools, fourth grade mathematics achievement averaged 8.6 points higher in Catholic schools, roughly 11 points higher in Lutheran and "other private" schools, 5 points higher in conservative Christian schools, and 6.5 points lower in charter schools. However, Model 3 reveals that after adjusting for demographic differences among schools, public school means were significantly higher than the means for all other school types, with coefficients ranging from −3.7 (Lutheran) to −11.3 (conservative Christian). The addition of the demographic variables to the model explained over 74% of the variance in achievement between schools and 18% of the variance within schools. This very large reduction in the variance between schools drastically diminishes the additional variance for which the remaining models (Models 4–12) can account.

As explained previously, each intercept in table A9 is the estimated mean achievement of a fourth grade student who is 0 on all of the binary predictors and at the mean of all of the continuous predictors. As a specific example, Model 3's intercept of 247.6 is the estimated mean achievement for white, non-IEP, non-LEP, lunch-ineligible males with average home resources, in a Midwestern, suburban (or small city) public school of average minority, LEP, and SES populations. In a Catholic school of similar demographics, the estimated achievement of such a student would be 7.5 points lower, or 240.1.

Overall, Model 3 indicates that the apparent private school advantage evident in Model 2 reverses after accounting for the higher proportions of advantaged students attending private schools. One can see in Table A10 that the grade 8 results are similar, with public schools scoring roughly equal to or higher than the various private school types after controlling for demographics. This certainly raises the question of why public schools are scoring so well in comparison with their demographically similar counterparts of other school types.

Table A9: NAEP school-, teacher-, and student-reported variables predicting fourth-grade mathematics achievement (157,161 students, 6,288 schools)

	Model 1: null model	Model 2: school sector	**Model 3: + demographics + location**	Model 4: + school enrollment	Model 5: + class size	Model 6: + school climate
Fixed effects:						
Intercept	235.9*** (0.3)	234.5*** (0.3)	**247.6*** (0.4)**	247.6*** (0.4)	247.8*** (0.4)	247.4*** (0.4)
School level:						
Catholic School		8.6*** (1.2)	**−7.5*** (0.9)**	−7.5*** (0.9)	−7.4*** (0.9)	−7.5*** (0.9)
Lutheran		11.0*** (2.0)	**−3.7** (1.4)**	−3.7** (1.4)	−4.4** (1.4)	−3.4* (1.5)
Conservative Christian[a]		5.0* (2.3)	**−11.3*** (1.8)**	−11.3*** (1.8)	−12.1*** (1.9)	−11.6*** (1.9)
Other private[a]		10.6*** (2.2)	**−6.1*** (1.5)**	−6.1*** (1.5)	−7.0*** (1.6)	−6.2*** (1.5)
Charter		−6.5** (2.5)	**−4.1* (1.7)**	−4.1* (1.7)	−4.2* (1.7)	−4.7** (1.6)
Percent lunch			**−2.0*****	−2.0***	−2.1***	−1.4***
Home resources			**5.1*****	5.1***	5.2***	4.5***
Percent minority			**−3.1****	−3.1**	−3.2**	−2.2*
LEP			**1.7*****	1.7***	1.7***	1.5***
In large city			**0.2**	0.2	0.2	0.1
Rural			**−2.1*****	−2.1***	−2.3***	−1.7***
Northeast			**−0.6**	−0.6	−0.8	−0.5
South			**2.7*****	2.7***	2.6***	2.3***
West			**−2.4*****	−2.4***	−2.2***	−2.3***
School enrollment				0.0	0.3	0.3
Class size					−0.7**	−0.7***
Teacher morale						0.5*
Conflicts						−0.4*
Parents involved						1.3***
Parents volunteer						0.6*
Certified teachers						
New teachers						

Professional development						
Time on math						
Geometry measurement, algebra, data						
Number/operations						
Multiple choice						
Calculators						
Student level (slopes):						
Black			**-15.8*** **	-15.8***	-15.8***	-15.9***
Hispanic			**-6.6*** **	-6.6***	-6.6***	-6.7***
American Indian			**-4.1*** **	-4.1***	-4.2***	-3.7***
Asian			**6.3*** **	6.3***	6.3***	5.7***
Female			**-4.4*** **	-4.4***	-4.4***	-4.3***
LEP			**-11.3*** **	-11.3***	-11.3***	-11.4***
IEP			**-20.9*** **	-20.9***	-20.9***	-20.5***
Lunch			**-7.3*** **	-7.3***	-7.3***	-6.9***
Home resources			**2.4*** **	2.4***	2.4***	2.3***
Absences						-2.4***
Talk at home						0.1*
Traditional math beliefs						
Not like math						
Like math						
Random effects:						
Intercept (variance between schools)	212.5***	200.1***	**51.1*** **	51.1***	50.6***	47.1***
Level 1 (variance within schools)	517.7	517.7	**423.3**	423.3	423.3	417.8
Intraclass Correlation	0.29	0.28	**0.11**	0.11	0.11	0.10

Table A9: *continued*

	Model 7: + teacher education	Model 8: + time on math	Model 9: + teaching methods	Model 10: + student beliefs	Model 11: + students like math	Model 12: keeping $p<.05$
Fixed effects:						
Intercept	247.4*** (0.4)	247.4*** (0.4)	247.4*** (0.4)	246.3*** (0.4)	243.6*** (0.4)	243.6*** (0.4)
School level:						
Catholic School	−6.9*** (0.9)	−6.9*** (0.9)	−5.6*** (0.9)	−4.9*** (0.9)	−4.5*** (0.9)	−4.5*** (0.9)
Lutheran	−2.6 (1.5)	−2.7 (1.5)	−1.3 (1.5)	−0.8 (1.5)	−0.2 (1.5)	−0.2 (1.5)
Conservative Christian[a]	−10.3*** (2.0)	−10.4*** (1.9)	−8.6*** (2.0)	−7.1** (1.9)	−6.7** (1.8)	−6.7** (1.8)
Other private[a]	−5.6** (1.6)	−5.6* (1.6)	−4.6** (1.5)	−4.2** (1.5)	−3.4* (1.5)	−3.5* (1.5)
Charter	−4.2* (1.6)	−4.2* (1.6)	−3.9* (1.6)	−3.6* (1.5)	−3.2* (1.5)	−3.0* (1.5)
Percent lunch	−1.5***	−1.5***	−1.4***	−1.3***	−1.3***	−1.3***
Home resources	4.4***	4.4***	4.3***	3.8***	3.9***	3.9***
Percent minority	−2.2*	−2.1*	−2.8**	−2.5**	−3.1**	−3.4***
LEP	1.5***	1.5***	1.5***	1.4***	1.4***	1.4***
In large city	0.2	0.2	0.0	−0.2	−0.1	−0.1
Rural	−1.6*	−1.6*	−1.6***	−1.3**	−1.2**	−1.2**
Northeast	−0.6	−0.6	−0.8	−1.0*	−1.0*	−1.0*
South	2.2***	2.2***	1.9***	1.9***	1.9***	2.0***
West	−2.4***	−2.4***	−2.1***	−1.9**	−1.6**	−1.6**
School enrollment	0.3	0.3	0.4*	0.4	0.4	0.4
Class size	−0.7***	−0.7***	−0.8***	−0.7***	−0.7***	−0.7***
Teacher morale	0.5*	0.5*	0.5*	0.5**	0.5**	0.6**
Conflicts	−0.4*	−0.4*	−0.4	−0.3	−0.3	
Parents involved	1.3***	1.3***	1.3***	1.2***	1.2***	1.4***
Parents volunteer	0.5*	0.5*	0.4	0.3	0.3	
Certified teachers	2.3*	2.3*	2.4*	2.4**	2.4**	2.4**
New teachers	−0.3	−0.3	−0.1	−0.3	−0.1	
Professional development	0.3**	0.3**	0.2*	0.1	0.1	
Time on math		0.2	0.2	0.2	0.2*	
Geometry measurement, algebra, data			1.1***	1.0***	1.0***	1.0***

Number/operations	−1.2*	−1.2*	−1.1	−1.6*	
Multiple choice	−0.3	−0.3	−0.2	−0.4	
Calculators	0.6*	0.5	0.6	0.8**	
Student level (slopes):					
Black	−15.0***	−15.0***	−15.0***	−16.0***	−15.9***
Hispanic	−5.7***	−5.7***	−5.5***	−6.6***	−5.7***
American Indian	−3.3***	−3.2***	−3.2*	−3.7***	−3.7***
Asian	5.0***	5.0***	6.2***	5.7***	5.7***
Female	−3.6***	−3.6***	−4.3***	−4.3***	−4.3***
LEP	−10.6***	−10.6***	−10.2***	−11.4***	−11.4***
IEP	−18.4***	−18.4***	−19.1***	−20.5***	−20.5***
Lunch	−6.2***	−6.2***	−6.2***	−6.9***	−6.9***
Home resources	1.9***	1.9***	2.1***	2.3***	2.3***
Absences	−2.1***	−2.1***	−2.4***	−2.5***	−2.5***
Talk at home	−0.3***	−0.3***	0.1*	0.1*	0.1*
Traditional math beliefs	−9.1***	−9.1***	−8.7***		
Not like math	−5.7***	−5.7***			
Like math	6.8***	6.8***			
Random effects:					
Intercept (variance between schools)	39.1***	38.9***	39.8***	44.2***	46.5***
Level 1 (variance within schools)	397.1	397.1	397.2	417.8	417.8
Intraclass Correlation	0.09	0.09	0.09	0.10	0.10

Note: Data are coefficient (standard error) unless otherwise specified. Model 3 results are bold faced because they provide a baseline for comparison with later models that include specific school and teacher characteristics.

[a] Participation rates did not meet NCES reporting requirements. Results for these subsamples should be interpreted with caution.

*p < .05.

**p < .01.

***p < .001.

Table A10: NAEP school-, teacher-, and student-reported variables predicting eighth-grade mathematics achievement (119,364 students, 4,870 schools)

	Model 1: null model	Model 2: school sector	Model 3: + demographics + location	Model 4: + school enrollment	Model 5: + class size	Model 6: + school climate
			Fixed effects			
Intercept	280.3*** (0.6)	276.1*** (0.4)	**292.9*** (0.8)**	292.8*** (0.8)	292.8*** (0.8)	292.5*** (0.7)
School level:						
Catholic School		13.9*** (1.7)	**−3.3* (1.5)**	−2.5 (1.6)		−5.2* (1.5)
Lutheran		22.1*** (2.5)	**0.3 (2.2)**	1.2 (2.3)		1.1 (2.1)
Conservative Christian		5.1 (4.2)	**−11.7*** (3.1)**	−10.8** (3.1)		−10.1** (3.0)
Other private[a]		15.7*** (3.8)	**−0.2 (2.8)**	−0.5 (2.8)		−1.0 (2.6)
Charter[a]		2.5 (4.4)	**3.5 (2.0)**	4.1 (2.1)		2.2 (2.0)
Percent lunch			**−1.6*****	−1.6***		−0.9*
Home resources			**4.2*****	4.1***		3.0**
Percent minority			**−7.7*****	−7.8***		−6.4**
Percent LEP			**1.2***	1.1*		0.8
In large city			**0.6**	0.6		0.2
Rural			**−2.0***	−1.5		−1.4
Northeast			**−1.4**	−1.5		−1.0
South			**−0.7**	−1.0		−0.5
West			**−2.0**	−2.1		−1.7
School enrollment				0.5		0.5
Teacher morale						0.4
Conflicts						−0.9
Drugs/alcohol						0.2
Parents involved						3.0***
Parents volunteer						−0.0

Certified teachers				
Math major				
New teachers				
Professional development				
Time on math				
Calculators				
Student level (slopes):				
Black		−19.8***	**−19.8*** **	−20.3***
Hispanic		−9.4***	**−9.4*** **	−9.8***
American Indian		−6.4***	**−6.5*** **	−5.9***
Asian		7.1**	**7.1*** **	5.9***
Female		−4.4***	**−4.4*** **	−4.5***
LEP		−14.6***	**−14.5*** **	−15.1***
IEP		−34.7***	**−34.7*** **	−33.8***
Lunch		−6.7***	**−6.7*** **	−6.3***
Home resources		4.5***	**4.5*** **	4.0***
Absences				−3.4***
Talk at home				0.8***
Traditional math beliefs				
Like math				
			Random effects	
Intercept	363.4***	316.0***	**103.1*** **	91.9***
(variance between schools)				
Level 1	633.5	633.8	**481.9**	473.8
(variance within schools)				
Intraclass correlation	0.36	0.33	**0.18**	0.16

Table A10: *continued*

	Model 7: + teacher education	Model 8: + time on math	Model 9: + teaching methods	Model 10: + student beliefs	Model 11: + students like math	Model 12: Keeping p<.05
			Fixed effects			
Intercept	292.2*** (0.7)	292.2*** (0.7)	291.6*** (0.7)	291.1*** (0.7)	290.8*** (0.7)	290.9*** (0.7)
School level:						
Catholic School	-4.5** (1.5)	-4.6** (1.5)	-3.8* (1.5)	-3.8* (1.5)	-3.8** (1.4)	-3.9** (1.3)
Lutheran	1.8 (2.2)	2.1 (2.2)	1.7 (2.1)	2.0 (2.1)	3.2 (2.1)	3.4 (2.1)
Conservative Christian	-8.8** (3.1)	-8.8** (3.0)	-8.3** (2.9)	-7.0* (2.8)	-5.8* (2.8)	-6.0* (2.8)
Other private[a]	0.1 (2.6)	0.1 (2.6)	0.9 (2.6)	0.9 (2.5)	1.4 (2.4)	1.6 (2.4)
Charter[a]	3.4 (2.0)	3.6 (2.1)	3.6 (2.0)	3.7 (1.9)	2.9 (1.8)	2.7 (1.8)
Percent lunch	-1.0*	-1.0*	-1.0*	-0.9*	-0.9*	-0.9*
Home resources	2.9**	2.9**	2.5*	2.4**	2.3*	2.2*
Percent minority	-5.9**	-5.8**	-4.7*	-4.3*	-5.3**	-5.5**
Percent LEP	0.9	0.9*	0.9*	0.8	0.9*	0.9*
In large city	0.5	0.5	0.8	0.7	0.6	0.5
Rural	-1.4	-1.3	-1.1	-1.1	-0.9	-0.7
Northeast	-0.9	-0.9	-0.6	-1.2	-1.0	-1.0
South	-0.5	-0.5	0.1	0.1	0.3	0.1
West	-1.4	-1.4	-0.5	-0.4	0.1	-0.2
School enrollment	0.5	0.5	0.5	0.5*	0.6*	0.6*
Teacher morale	0.4	0.4	0.4	0.3	0.3	
Conflicts	-0.9	-0.8	-0.9	-0.9	-0.9*	-1.1**
Drugs/alcohol	0.1	0.1	0.1	0.1	0.1	
Parents involved	3.0***	3.0***	3.0***	2.9***	2.8***	2.7***
Parents volunteer	-0.1	-0.1	-0.3	-0.3	-0.3	
Certified teachers	2.9*	2.9*	2.6*	2.6*	2.4*	2.8*
Math major	0.5	0.4	0.2	0.2	0.1	
New teachers	-1.6	-1.6	-1.8	-1.6	-1.6	

Professional development	0.0	0.0	−0.0	−0.0	−0.1
Time on math	1.0*	0.9*	0.9***	0.8*	0.8*
Calculators		3.0***	2.9***	2.5***	2.5***
Student level (slopes):					
Black	−20.2***	−20.3***	**−19.4***	−20.1***	−20.1***
Hispanic	−9.7***	−9.7***	**−8.8***	−9.1***	−9.1***
American Indian	−6.0***	−5.9***	**−5.1**	−5.0**	−5.0**
Asian	5.9***	6.0***	**6.3***	4.6***	4.7***
Female	−4.5***	−4.5***	**−4.6***	−3.9***	−4.0***
LEP	−15.1***	−15.0***	**−13.8***	−14.3***	−14.4***
IEP	−33.7***	−33.7***	**−32.2***	−31.7***	−31.7***
Lunch	−6.3***	−6.3***	**−6.0***	−6.4***	−6.4***
Home resources	4.0***	4.0***	**3.9***	3.5***	3.5***
Absences	−3.4***	−3.4***	**−3.3***	−2.8***	−2.8***
Talk at home	0.8***	0.8***	**0.8***	−0.1	
Traditional math beliefs			**−5.6***	−5.8***	−5.8***
Like math				5.3***	5.2***
Random effects					
Intercept (variance between schools)	90.1***	86.4***	79.5***	77.0***	77.4***
Level 1 (variance within schools)	473.8	473.8	460.9	432.9	432.9
Intraclass correlation	0.16	0.15	0.15	0.15	0.15

Note: Data are coefficient (standard error) unless otherwise specified. Model 3 results are bold faced because they provide a baseline for comparison with later models that include specific school and teacher characteristics.

[a] Participation rates did not meet NCES reporting requirements. Results for these subsamples should be interpreted with caution.

*$p < .05$.

**$p < .01$.

***$p < .001$.

As we add variables to Models 4–12 (in Tables A9 and A10), we can examine the impact of various factors on the private school coefficients. If a variable correlates positively with achievement and is more prevalent in private schools than in demographically similar public schools, then the private school coefficients would decrease after adding that variable because an advantage of private schools has been controlled for. For example, if smaller class size is both a predictor of achievement and more prevalent in private schools than in their public school counterparts, we would expect private school scores to decrease after we control for class size, indicating that once we hold class size constant, the disparities between public and private school achievement are even larger. On the other hand, if another variable, such as teacher certification, correlates positively with achievement, and the private school coefficients increase when the variable is added, then the variable is explaining some of the achievement disparities favoring public schools, revealing that it is important that more certified teachers are employed in public schools than in comparable private schools.[21]

Model 4 indicates that school size is not a significant predictor of achievement at either the fourth or eighth grade (although it was marginally significant and crossed into statistical significance in some later models), and the addition of the variable did not account for any additional variance in achievement at either grade. Still, because it is a nearly significant, positive predictor of achievement at grade 8, and because private schools are, on average, smaller than public schools, we see a small (less than 1 point) rise in most private school coefficients when comparing Model 3 with Model 4 in Table A10.

Model 5 (grade 4 only) indicates that class size is a significant negative predictor of achievement. As a specific example of the meaning of the −.7 coefficient, schools reporting average class sizes of greater than 25 students (5 on the 1–5 scale) scored an estimated .7 points lower than demographically equivalent schools reporting class sizes of 21–24 students (4 on the scale). It is important to note that the NAEP class size variable provides only a rough proxy for the class sizes encountered by the students actually assessed; if more sensitive measures were used, it is likely that the relationship between class size and achievement would be even stronger. In comparing school type coefficients in Models 4 and 5, we see a decrease ranging from .7 to .9 points for the three school types with the smallest class sizes: conservative Christian, Lutheran, and other private schools. The addition of class size explained an additional 1% of the remaining variance in achievement between schools.

Model 6 includes a set of school climate variables (again, very broadly defined), revealing several patterns. First, although parent involvement (i.e., participation in parent-teacher conferences, open houses, PTA) was a highly significant predictor of achievement at grades 4 and 8, parents volunteering in the schools was not correlated at all with achievement at grade 8 and was barely significant (and insignificant in later models) at grade 4. Teacher morale was positively associated with achievement, while conflicts were negatively associated, however, these relationships were significant at grade 4 only. At grade 8, drugs/alcohol was not related to achievement. Student absences were consistently strongly negatively related to achievement in both grades, while talking about studies at home was positively correlated (although at both grades, the addition of the "I like math" variable reversed the latter correlation, indicating some collinearity issues between talking about studies at home and liking mathematics). The climate variables correlating positively with achievement tended to be those that were more prevalent in private schools. Hence, we might expect to see substantial decreases in the coefficients of the private schools when these variables are added to Model 6. However, the pattern is not consistent, indicating that although school climate factors, such as parent involvement, teacher morale, and student attendance, might seem more favorable in private schools, it appears that in many cases this might simply be due to the advantaged demographics of those schools, particularly at grade 4. However, at grade 8, Catholic schools show a 2.7-point decrease when school climate variables are included, indicating that those schools might have relatively positive climates when compared with other demographically similar schools. Overall, the addition of the school climate variables explained an additional 7% of the remaining variance between schools and 1% within schools.

Model 7 adds teacher background variables, including certification, whether teachers majored or minored in mathematics (grade 8 only), whether teachers were new, and the number of different professional development activities in which teachers participated. Of these four variables, only the employment of certified teachers was a significant, positive predictor of achievement at both grades 4 and 8. As a specific example of the meaning of the 2.3-point coefficient (2.9 at grade 8) reported in Model 7, schools in which 80% of assessed fourth graders had certified teachers scored an average of .23 points higher than schools with only 70% of students with certified teachers. This appears to be a small effect, but as will be discussed later, the relationships identified here between student achievement and the teacher-reported data, in particular, are likely conservative estimates of the relationships that exist and would be identified by using more sensitive measures over time. Still, it is important to note the significant, positive relationship between fourth-grade student achievement and teachers' exposure to a variety of professional development forms (a variable that is correlated with reform-oriented student beliefs about mathematics, given the change in the professional development coefficient seen in Model 10). Overall, the teacher education variables accounted for an additional 1.3% of the remaining variance between schools. Despite the small amount of variance explained, there is a strikingly consistent pattern in that all of the private school coefficients increased between .6 and 1.3 points from Model 6 to Model 7, with the largest increases occurring for the conservative Christian schools at both the fourth and eighth grades.

Model 8 includes the time on math variable, which was significant at grade 8 but not at grade 4. This variable explained virtually no additional variance in achievement at either grade. The addition of the variable had little effect on the school type coefficients. The weakness of this variable could be due to the insensitivity of the response scale, which topped out at "3 or more hours per week."

Instruction-related variables were added to create Model 9. At grade 4 these included curricular emphases, use of multiple choice assessments, and calculator use. Of these, the strongest, most persistent predictor of achievement was teachers' emphasis on nonnumber mathematics strands. Specifically, the 1.1 coefficient indicates that if teachers in a school said they had a "strong" emphasis on geometry, measurement, algebra, and data analysis/probability (therefore averaging 12 on the 1–12 scale), the school mean was an estimated 4.4 points higher than that of schools in which teachers, on average, reported a "moderate" emphasis on the four strands (thereby averaging 8 on the scale). Moreover, an emphasis on number/operations correlated negatively with achievement, while calculator instruction correlated positively. The effect of the addition of these variables on the fourth grade private school coefficients was consistent, with the various private school coefficients increasing between 1.0 and 1.8 points, with the largest gain made by conservative Christian schools, whose coefficient changed from −10.4 points in Model 8 to −8.6 points in Model 9.

At grade 8, the only instruction-related variable included was a calculator composite, which was positively correlated with mathematics achievement. However, the change in private school coefficients from Model 8 to Model 9 was mixed. The inclusion of the teaching-related variables explained 5% of the remaining variance between schools at grade 4 and 4% at grade 8.

Model 10 reveals that students' traditional beliefs about mathematics correlate very strongly and negatively with achievement at grades 4 and 8.[22] Private school coefficients generally increased, with conservative Christian schools again showing the greatest increases of 1.3–1.5 points. The increases in the private school coefficients from Model 9 to Model 10 (with the exception of Catholic schools at grade 8) suggest that students in private schools tend to hold more traditional beliefs about mathematics than students in demographically similar public schools. Overall, the addition of student beliefs to the fourth grade models explained an additional 10% of the remaining variance between schools (8% at grade 8) and 5% of the remaining variance within schools (3% at grade 8).

Finally, the "I like mathematics" variable was added to Model 11. Liking mathematics was a significant, positive correlate of mathematics achievement at both grades. Most private school coefficients increased slightly with the addition of this variable, with Lutheran and conservative Christian schools showing the greatest gains of 1.2 points at grade 8. This suggests that public school students tend to like mathematics more than students in demographically similar private schools. This variable explained 2%–3% of the remaining variance between schools at grades 4 and 8 and 6% within schools at grade 8 but no additional within-school variance at grade 4.

The final Model 12 retained all school type and demographic/location variables, as well as those school size, climate, and instruction-related variables (from Models 4–11) that were significant ($P<.05$).[23] This final model is slightly weaker than Model 11 in terms of explaining variance but is more parsimonious in its inclusion of only those school climate/instruction-related variables that are statistically significant. Overall, the final grade 4 model explains 82% of the between-school variance and 23% of the within-school variance, or 40% of the total variance in achievement (79%, 32%, and 49%, respectively at grade 8).

It is important to note that across all of the models, large race- and SES-related inequities persisted across all schools types. For example, within schools, black fourth graders scored an average of 15–16 points (20 points at grade 8) lower than their white peers of similar SES, LEP, and disability status across all twelve models. Overall, demographic issues accounted for the vast majority of the variance in achievement between schools, while school type accounted for very little (and would likely account for even less if added at the end of the series of models instead of the beginning). School climate and instruction-related factors explained roughly 5%–7% of the total variance between schools, or 20%–25% of the between-school variance that remained after adding demographics and school type.

Given that the vast majority of schools are public and had relatively little variation in key aspects such as teacher certification, it is not surprising that the percentage of variance explained by such variables is small. The purpose of this study was not to provide definitive measures of the exact strength of the relationships between the variables and the differences between models, but instead to identify factors that might explain the rather surprising disparities found between public and private school achievement scores in the first phase of our NAEP analysis. Given the cross-sectional nature of NAEP data, the coefficients in the various models were viewed as suggestive of relationships that might be important and merit further examination with longitudinal data. Hence, these NAEP analyses laid the foundation for our additional analyses conducted with the Early Childhood Longitudinal Study, Kindergarten Class of 1998–99.

Appendix B: Details about Early Childhood Longitudinal Study, Kindergarten Class of 1998–99 Data and Analyses

WITH CORINNA CRANE, PH.D.

The Early Childhood Longitudinal Study, Kindergarten Class of 1998–99 (ECLS-K) data set was used to examine student achievement gains by sector (discussed in Chapter 5) and to determine potential explanations for differential patterns in achievement by sector (discussed in Chapter 6). The ECLS-K data set and achievement-focused analysis were discussed in some detail in Chapter 5. However, fewer details of the more complicated analyses of school- and teacher-related factors were discussed in Chapter 6. Given that the Chapter 6 analyses both confirm the findings from Chapter 5 and extend them to discuss possible explanations for those findings, it is particularly important to provide details of the Chapter 6 analyses. Hence, this appendix provides an overview of ECLS-K data and briefly recaps the data and methods used for the analyses reported in Chapter 5 but then focuses primarily on the details of the more comprehensive analyses reported in Chapter 6.

ECLS-K Samples and Missing Data

The ECLS-K data were collected using a multistage probability sample design in order to obtain a nationally representative sample of children attending kindergarten in the fall of 1998, with data collection completed in their kindergarten, first, third, fifth, and eighth grade years. In total, 22,782 children were followed, and certain students were oversampled in order to obtain sufficient information on smaller population subgroups. For example, Asian-Pacific Islander students were oversampled by 2.5 times.[1] Sampling weights were assigned to students, teachers and schools to adjust for unequal probabilities of selection, nonresponse, and attrition.

Any longitudinal study faces student attrition and mobility issues. The number of children who participated in all stages of the ECLS-K data collection (base year, first grade, third grade, fifth grade, and eighth grade) is 9,725. This represents roughly 50 percent of the base year respondents. However, the majority of attrition was the result of students moving to other schools, as opposed to refusing to continue in the study. The National Center of Education Statistics (NCES) did not follow all students who moved to other schools, but to reduce bias and to preserve sample sizes, a stratified random subsample of movers was followed each year, with particular groups (such as language minority students) followed at higher rates to maintain a viable sample. The sampling weights assigned for each year take these factors into account, weighting the subsample of movers appropriately to represent the contingent of students who moved. In this way, the effects of attrition are greatly reduced.

ECLS-K ACHIEVEMENT ANALYSIS (CHAPTER 5)

The full fifth-grade ECLS-K sample consisted of 11,820 students. The sample used for the achievement analysis reported in Chapter 5 contained the 9,791 students who had the necessary K–5 achievement and who remained in the same school sector (although some did switch schools within sector). The students in the analytic sample were spread across 1,531 public and private schools—1,273 public, 140 Catholic, and 118 other private schools.

ECLS-K ANALYSIS OF ACHIEVEMENT-RELATED FACTORS (CHAPTER 6)

The full first- through third-grade ECLS-K sample contained 13,964 children from 6,093 classrooms and 3,019 schools. The ECLS-K sample was refreshed in the first grade to make it a representative sample but not again in later waves. Therefore the results of the first- through third-grade analysis can be considered representative of students who began first grade in the fall of 1999. We removed students, classrooms, and schools that were not public or Catholic. This reduced the number of schools by 204. At the classroom level, data from 113 teachers were removed because the teacher reported that she or he does not teach mathematics. Student-level cases missing either the mathematics first- or third-grade *t*-score, school sector information, or teacher ID were removed from the analysis. Finally, only students who were in the same school sector in first and third grade were used in the analysis, further reducing the student-level file by 261 cases.[2] The final hierarchical linear modeling (HLM) sample included 11,860 students, 4,911 classrooms, and 1,972 schools.[3]

Given the large number of variables involved in the first- through third-grade analysis of achievement-related factors, missing data were a particular concern. In order to preserve cases, missing data were imputed in a number of ways. First, whenever possible, missing data were imputed using other similar variables from the same grade. For example, when total class size was missing, it was imputed using the sum of the number of boys plus the number of girls. Next, for student-level variables such as student race/ethnicity, socioeconomic status (SES), and learning problem diagnosed, missing data were first imputed using the same students' first-grade information if available, and, if not, then the fifth-grade information. Similarly, school-level missing data such as school size and security variables were first imputed using first-grade information if available, and then fifth-grade information. Missing school-level free and reduced-price lunch eligibility information was imputed using aggregated class-level data when no first-, third-, or fifth-grade school-level data were available. Finally, any remaining missing cases were assigned the value of the mean for the school type. When this was done, a new binary variable was created indicating whether the variable was imputed or not, and this variable was entered into the HLM models as its corresponding variable was added. In each case, the "missing" indicator variable was insignificant when included in the HLM model, and therefore a final model was rerun without the missing indicator included.

Addressing ECLS-K Data Complexities

The ECLS-K data set includes various sample weights to adjust for differential selection probabilities and reduce the bias associated with nonresponse. Denton and West explain that "weighting the data adjusts for unequal selection probabilities at the school and child levels and then adjusts for school, child, teacher, and parent non-response."[3]

For example, Asian and private school students were oversampled in order to ensure large enough samples, so they must be weighted accordingly. In addition, not all students who transferred out of their original school were retained in the sample, and the ECLS-K weights at each wave are adjusted to take this into account in the remaining sample.

The correct ECLS-K sample weights were used in all analyses. For the first through third grade analysis of potential explanations for achievement patterns by sector, we used the direct child assessment longitudinal weight C45CW0, which is appropriate for analyses of assessment data from both spring–first grade and spring–third grade in conjunction with child characteristics, third grade teacher questionnaire data, and data from the administrator questionnaire. Weights were adjusted by being multiplied by the number of positive weights divided by the sum of the weights and were additionally divided by the design effect for any analysis conducted using SPSS. This was done to correct for the fact that SPSS calculates standard errors assuming a simple random sample, as opposed to the clustered sampling design of ECLS-K.[4]

ECLS-K Assessments

In order to gauge children's mathematical skills, the ECLS-K Direct Child Assessment was used. Various sources were utilized in the creation of the ECLS-K Direct Child Assessment for mathematics, including state/national standards, elementary content specialists, and multicultural experts. The items assess five strands of mathematical content, as advocated by the National Council of Teachers of Mathematics *Standards*.[5] The mathematics assessment was administered through an hour-long one-on-one testing session using computer-assisted interviews. Test items measured conceptual knowledge, procedural knowledge, and problem-solving skills. Test scores were provided in *t*-score format (with a mean of 50 and a standard deviation of 10) and item response theory (IRT) scale scores, which can be used to estimate achievement gains between different assessment periods. In addition to the *t*-scores and IRT scores, the ECLS-K also provides data on student proficiency levels in different areas: (1) number and shape, (2) relative size, (3) ordinality and sequence, (4) addition/subtraction, (5) multiplication/division, (6) place value, (7) rate and measurement, (8) fractions, and (9) area and volume.

ECLS-K Variables

This ECLS-K data set is valuable not only because of its longitudinal and large-scale nature, but also because of the wide scope of information collected from multiple sources including children, families, teachers, principals, and outside observers.

ECLS-K ACHIEVEMENT ANALYSIS (CHAPTER 5)

A variety of demographic controls were used in the analysis of K–5 achievement:

- Student SES composite—a z-score, created by NCES based on parents' level of education, occupational status, and total household income.[6]
- Race (binary coded variables for Black, Latino/a, Asian).
- Whether a language other than English is spoken at home (to account for the fact that some students are fluent in English but speak another language at home, we excluded students from this category if they scored in the top 10% of the English language test given to students to assess their readiness to take the test in English).
- Gender.
- Parent-reported disability status of the student (a student was defined as having a disability if a parent reported that his/her child "obtained a diagnosis of a problem from a professional"—with possibilities being a learning problem, activity problem, behavior problem, speech problem, hearing problem, or vision problem—or that the child received therapy services or participated in a program for children with disabilities. Although this definition might be broader than some might like, this parent-reported variable alleviates concerns that critics previously raised about the Individualized Education Program (IEP) variable in the National Assessment of Educational Progress unfairly biasing results in favor of public schools, given that only public schools are required to have IEPs for their students with disabilities).
- Age of student when starting kindergarten.

We also used the following school-level variables as predictors:

- The SES of a school (the average SES of the students sampled from a school, using the student SES variable).
- The percentage of white and Asian students at a school, as reported by the principal.
- Whether a school is located in an urban or rural area.
- School geographic region (West, South, Northeast, or Midwest).

Table 5.1 in Chapter 5 presented the means of student demographic variables by school type.

ECLS-K ANALYSIS OF ACHIEVEMENT-RELATED FACTORS (CHAPTER 6)

The variables used in the first through third grade analyses were grouped into three sets: student-level, classroom-level, and school-level. The average number of sampled students per classroom was 2.41 (maximum of 21), and the average number of sampled classrooms per school was 2.49 (maximum of 12). The ECLS-K questionnaire asked teachers, administrators, and outside observers to each answer hundreds of questions, and from those we drew the items that past research suggested might differ by school sector and be related to student achievement. In order to further reduce the number of variables in the final analysis as well as avoid issues of multicollinearity, we created composite variables when there were several related variables. Reliability analyses were conducted to confirm scale reliability for all composite variables. Finally, each variable's relationship to mathematics achievement growth was examined, and variables were recoded when necessary so that they would have a linear relationship with achievement. This was necessary because the HLM models created in this analysis assume a linear relationship between predictor variables and achievement.

Third Grade Student-Level Variables

Student-level variables in the Chapter 6 analysis included those measuring student mathematics performance (as discussed above) and student demographic characteristics, including the ECLS-K SES composite, gender, race/ethnicity, age, and whether a learning problem has been diagnosed.[7] Given that demographics by school type are discussed

Table B1: Composite variables and their Cronbach's alpha reliability scores

Composite	Alpha coefficient
School security composite (items) (1 = yes, 0 = no)	
Presence of security guards	
Presence of door bars in the school	.51
School climate composite (outside observer ratings) (1 = strongly disagree, 4 = strongly agree):	
Decorated hallways	
Attentive teachers	
Personable principal	
Helpful staff	
Order in hallways	
Order in classrooms	.81
Neighborhood climate composite (1 = strongly disagree, 4 = strongly agree):	
Absence of litter or trash near the school (outside observer rating)	
Absence of graffiti near the school (outside observer rating)	
Absence of boarded-up buildings near the school (outside observer rating)	
Absence of people congregating near the school (outside observer rating)	
Absence of substance abuse near the school (principal rating)	
Absence of gangs near the school (principal rating)	
Absence of unkempt areas near the school (principal rating)	
Absence of heavy traffic near the school (principal rating)	
Absence of violent crime near the school (principal rating)	
Absence of general crime near the school (principal rating)	.86
Administrative support composite (teacher ratings)(1 = strongly disagree, 5 = strongly agree):	
School administration prioritizes well	
School administration handles outside pressure	
School administration communicates vision	
School administration encourages staff	.90
Student misbehavior composite (teacher ratings) (1 = strongly disagree, 5 = strongly agree):	
Physical conflicts are a serious problem	
Bullying is a serious problem	
Child misbehavior affects teaching	.79
Teacher satisfaction composite (teacher ratings) (1 = strongly disagree, 5 = strongly agree):	
Teacher would choose teaching again	
Teacher enjoys present teaching job	
Teacher makes a difference in children's lives	.71

Table B1: *continued*

Composite	Alpha coefficient
Staff support composite (teacher ratings) (1 = strongly disagree, 5 = strongly agree):	
Staff continually learning and seeking new ideas	
Staff accept me as a colleague	
Staff have school spirit	.73
Traditional practices composite (math teacher ratings) (1 = strongly disagree, 5 = strongly agree):	
Frequency children take math tests	
Frequency solve math problems on worksheets	
Frequency solve math problems from textbooks	.28
Reform practices composite (math teacher ratings) (1 = strongly disagree, 5 = strongly agree):	
Frequency discuss solutions to math problems with others	
Frequency talk to class about math work	
Frequency work on problems that reflect real-life situations	
Frequency write about how to solve a math problem	
Frequency use measuring instruments	
Frequency work with manipulatives	
Frequency math in groups	
Frequency work on math projects or write reports	.78
Nonnumber teaching focus (teacher ratings) (1 = none, 4 = a lot):	
Frequency focus on measurement	
Frequency focus on geometry and spatial relations	
Frequency focus on data analysis, statistics and probability	
Frequency focus on algebra and functions	.74

in both Chapters 4 and 5 and are not focal in this analysis, additional descriptive data of demographics are not provided here.[8]

In this analysis, race was treated in a slightly different manner than in the mainstream literature in that the default comparison group of students is African American as opposed to white. This means that binary variables were created for white, Asian, Hispanic, and "other races", so when these variables are included in the HLM equations, the default omitted category that these groups are all being compared with is black students. This affects the interpretation of intercepts, but the coefficients for the variables of interest in the models are the same as they would be otherwise.

Third Grade Classroom-Level Variables

Classroom-level variables included those related to classroom demo-graphics, curriculum and instruction, parental involvement, profes-sional development, class climate, and teacher characteristics. Only third grade classroom-level variables were examined because the first grade mathematics test score that was included as a control variable was from the spring of first grade and therefore would already reflect first grade classroom effects. A full list of classroom-level variables and their descriptive statistics by school type is provided in Table 6.4. Composites of classroom- and school-level variables are detailed in Table B1.

Classroom Demographics

The classroom variables included in the analysis that were related to student composition were the percentage of students with disabilities in the classroom and the total number of students in the classroom.

Curriculum and Instruction

Mayer and Stipek and Byler found that teachers' responses to survey questions regarding their teaching practices in mathematics were strongly correlated with data from classroom observations, indicating that teachers' responses reflect their practice relatively well.[9] The cur-riculum and instruction variables included in the analysis were teacher reports of their classroom layout, computer access, calculator use, and use of traditional or reform-oriented teaching methods.[10]

The ECLS-K classroom layout variable had four response options for teachers, including rows facing front, circle/semicircle, small groups, and no set arrangement. Means of first through third test score gains by response indicated that rows facing front had a negative *t*-score change (−.30), while the other three response options had a positive *t*-score change (between .30 and .36); therefore this variable was con-verted into a binary indicating whether desks were arranged in rows facing the front of the classroom or not.

The number of computers per child was calculated by taking the teacher-reported number of computers in the classroom that children could use and dividing it by the total class enrollment. Finally, the

ECLS-K teacher survey included eleven questions about the frequency with which teachers used various teaching practices in mathematics instruction. These items seemed to logically break down into two categories: traditional teaching practices and reform-oriented practices (see Table B1 for item groupings and Cronbach's alpha reliability scores). The reform-oriented practices variables included the frequency with which students in the class use measuring instruments and manipulatives, solve problems in small groups, write about how they solved a math problem, talk to the class about mathematics work, work on math projects, discuss solutions to math problems with other students, and work on math problems that reflect real life situations. When combined, these had a Cronbach's alpha coefficient of .78. The items that were combined into the traditional practices composite include the frequency with which children in the class use a math textbook, work on math worksheets, and take math tests.[11] When combined, these had a Cronbach's alpha coefficient of .28.[12]

Teacher Autonomy

Teachers were asked several questions that could help gauge how much autonomy they had in the classroom. These were a rating of how much the teacher controls the curriculum, how much paperwork interferes with teaching, and whether job security is based on state and local tests. The Cronbach's alpha reliability score for these three was low so they were kept separate.

Parental Involvement

Several questions in the ECLS-K teacher survey can be used to measure parental involvement, including the percentage of parents who attend conferences, volunteer regularly, and attend other school activities, and whether the teacher reports that parents support school staff. The percentage of parents who attend conferences and other school activities appeared to have a linear relationship with achievement when examining t-score gain means by category, so these were left in ordinal categories (1 = none, 2 = 1%–25%, 3 = 26%–50%, 4 = 51%–75%, 5 = 76%+). The relationship between achievement and both the percentage of parents volunteering regularly and whether parents support school staff appeared less linear so they were converted into binaries, with the volunteering variable coded as either at least one parent in the class-room volunteers regularly versus none do and the supporting school staff variable coded as 1 for agree or strongly agree and 0 for neither agree nor disagree, disagree, and strongly disagree.

Professional Development

The only math-related variable that measured the amount of professional development given to math teachers was one asking teachers how many hours during the past year they had spent in staff development workshops, seminars, or university courses relating to mathematics or math teaching. Owing to the skewed nature of this variable, with most responses concentrated in the lower numbers and few responses reaching out into the tens or hundreds, this variable was recoded into four ordinal categories, each with approximately 25% of the responses: 0 hours, 1–3 hours, 4–8 hours, and 9 or more hours. For those teachers in the highest category, the mean number of hours attended was 25, while the median was 16.

Climate

There were several questions answered by teachers that were related to the class and school climate. Factor analysis was run to examine which variables were most closely related, and results indicated that there were four different clusters of variables: administrative support, student misbehavior, teacher satisfaction, and staff support. The administrative support composite included four items asking teachers whether the administration encourages staff, prioritizes well, handles outside pressure, and communicates the school vision. The student misbehavior composite included items about whether physical conflicts, bullying, and child misbehavior are a problem. The teacher satisfaction composite included teachers' opinions as to whether they enjoy their present teaching job, would choose teaching again, and feel they make a difference in children's lives. Finally, the staff support composite variable includes teacher's ratings on whether staff members accept them as a colleague, have school spirit, and continually learn and seek new ideas. These groupings made sense theoretically and were therefore used to create composite variables.

Teacher Characteristics

The variables related to the teacher characteristics that were used include the highest education level the teacher achieved and the type of certification the teacher has. Many studies have found that there is not necessarily a linear trend between teacher education and student achievement particularly in elementary school.[13] Therefore, the variable indicating a teacher's highest education level achieved was not treated as ordinal but instead was recoded into two binary variables: whether a teacher has a bachelor's degree or less and whether a teacher has had education beyond a master's degree. Teacher certification type was given as five categories in the ECLS-K: none, temporary/probational certification, alternative program certification, regular or standard state certification, and advanced professional certification. Only 1% of students in the sample had a teacher with alternative program certification (thirty-three teachers), and their students' mean *t*-score increase was not statistically significantly different from that of the students with teachers with temporary certification so these were grouped together into a binary variable called Temporary/Alternative Certification. Although there were also few teachers with no certification, their students' mean *t*-score increase was not comparable to the other categories and combining them with other types of certified teachers did not make theoretical sense, so they were left as a separate category. Finally, studies have generally found that the newest and also the most veteran teachers tend to have students who perform more poorly than teachers in the middle range,[14] so the variable indicating a teacher's number of years as a school teacher was recoded into two binaries: three years of teaching experience or less and twenty-five or more years of experience. Thus results indicate how teachers in these two categories compare with the default omitted category of teachers with four to twenty-four years of experience.

Third Grade School-Level Variables

School-level variables used in the analyses included descriptive and demographic variables, building characteristics, and school climate variables.

SCHOOL DESCRIPTORS AND DEMOGRAPHICS

Several variables were included in this group:

- School sector was recoded as a binary variable with Catholic = 1 and public = 0.
- School location was recoded into binary variables with large city as the default omitted category.
- School size was converted from an ordinal 1–5 scale as given in the ECLS-K into two binary variables indicating whether a school is small (<150 students) or large (750+ students) because past research has been mixed regarding whether small or large schools are more beneficial, and some researchers have argued that there may be a nonlinear trend.[15] In addition, preliminary analysis of the ECLS-K data examining mean mathematics t-scores by student enrollment category indicated a nonlinear trend, with students in the lowest (<150) and highest (>750) categories having the lowest t-scores (mean of 49.72 and 49.34, respectively).
- Free and reduced-price lunch-eligible student percentage was calculated using principal survey responses, and for cases where the response was missing, it was imputed using the teacher-reported classroom free and reduced-price lunch eligibility data aggregated to the school level.
- Average daily attendance as reported by the principal.

BUILDING CHARACTERISTICS

The building characteristics included in the analysis are the school's percent capacity and the principal's response to whether classroom facilities meet student needs. The school percent capacity was calculated by subtracting the principal-reported number of students the school can accommodate from the number enrolled and dividing this by the number the school can accommodate. A comparison of means by eight rank categories as well as a partial correlation controlling for the school's free and reduced-price lunch eligibility percentage indicated that there was a significantly positive correlation between percent capacity and students' mean math test score gain from first to third grade (r = .052, p = .02) so this variable was left as a continuous variable.

The principal also responded to a question indicating whether the classroom facilities meet the needs of the children in the school with response options including "never adequate," "often not adequate," "sometimes not adequate," and "always adequate." There were very few responses in the first two categories (about 5% of responses overall), and about half of responses were in the last "always adequate" category, so this variable was recoded into a binary variable with always adequate versus not always adequate.

SCHOOL CLIMATE VARIABLES

Several variables were included to help gauge the school climate, including a principal report of the presence of safety measures (security guards, metal detectors, and window and door bars). Almost no schools had metal detectors (0.8%) so this item was left out of the analysis. The variables indicating the presence of security guards and window and door bars were combined into a security composite. These two had a Cronbach's alpha reliability score of 0.51. In addition, six questions measuring school climate were combined into a School Climate composite variable, which had a Cronbach's alpha score of .81. These included an outside observers' response to whether they observed decorated hallways, attentive teachers, personable principal, helpful staff, order in hallways, and order in classrooms. Eleven questions relating to the neighborhood around the school also had a high Cronbach's alpha score (.86) and so were combined into a Neighborhood Climate composite variable. These included an outside observers' rating of the absence of litter or trash near the school, graffiti near the school, boarded-up buildings near the school, and people congregating near the school, as well as principal-reported variables indicating the extent to which the neighborhood has difficulties with substance abuse, gangs, unkempt areas, heavy traffic, violent crime, and general crime in the area.

Data Analysis

The results discussed in Chapter 6 are based on a series of relatively complex analyses that merit detailed discussion here. The analyses were organized around three questions.[16]

QUESTION 1—HOW DO PUBLIC AND CATHOLIC SCHOOLS DIFFER IN THE THIRD GRADE?

To determine whether public and Catholic schools differ in teacher and administrator responses to the class- and school-level variables outlined above, *t*-tests were first run to compare the raw means by school sector. The results of these analyses give a snapshot of what an average public or Catholic school might report on these variables. Binary logistic regressions were also run to determine whether a relationship between each variable and school type existed after controlling for the demographic composition of schools and classrooms. The control variables used in the logistic regressions were student lunch eligibility percentages as reported at the school and classroom level and special education percentage at the classroom level.[17] Each variable of interest was run in a separate logistic regression to avoid collinearity issues: Tables 6.1 and 6.2 contain the results of these analyses.

QUESTION 2—HOW DO ANY DIFFERENCES FOUND IMPACT STUDENTS' MATHEMATICS TEST SCORE GAINS BETWEEN FIRST AND THIRD GRADES?

Based on the results of the binary logistic regressions, the school-level variables that were not significantly different by school sector after controlling for demographic information were removed from the analysis of this second question. Once the variables were narrowed down, the remaining variables were entered into a series of fifteen three-level HLM models (students nested within classrooms, nested within schools) to examine the relationship between school type and mathematics test score gains while controlling for the student, classroom, and school demographic variables outlined above.[18] HLM was used because it allows for nesting, which is important to take into account when examining students who are clustered within classrooms and/or schools. The program used was HLM 6.0.[19]

In the models, binary demographic variables were entered uncentered, and continuous variables were grand mean centered at all levels.[20] The variables were entered in groups of related variables, beginning with demographic variables in the first six models, which would serve as a baseline for comparison of the Catholic school estimate. As variables pertaining to school and classroom climate, building characteristics, curriculum and teaching practices, parental involvement, professional development, and teacher characteristics were added, we could determine the effect the addition of these factors had on the Catholic school estimate, thereby shedding light on possible explanations for the difference in math test score gains. The dependent variable for this portion of the study was the third grade mathematics t-score, with a control included for first grade spring mathematics test scores. Interaction terms of race/ethnicity and SES by sector were also included to examine whether there were significant differential effects. The HLM equation for the full model was as follows. Variables that were grandmean centered are italicized.

LEVEL 1 MODEL

Y = P0 + P1*(1st Grade Math t-score) + P2*(SES) + P3*(Male) + P4*(White) + P5*(Hispanic) + P6*(Asian) + P7*(Other Race) + P8*(Age) + P9*(Learning Problem Diagnosed) + E.

LEVEL 2 (CLASS) MODEL

P0 = B00 + B01*(Percentage Special Education) + B02*(Total Enrollment) + B03*(Desks Facing Front) + B04*(Number of Computers per Child) + B05*(Never or Hardly Ever Use Calculators) + B06*(Traditional Practices Composite) + B07*(Reform Practices Composite) + B08*(% Parents Attend Other School Activities) + B09*(Time in Math Workshop) + B010*(Administrator Support Composite) + B011*(Student Misbehavior Composite) + B012*(Teacher Satisfaction Composite) + B013*(Staff Support Composite) + B014*(Paperwork Interferes with Teaching) + B015*(How Much Curriculum Control) + B016*(Job Security Based on Tests) + B017*(Bachelor's Degree or Less) + B018*(Beyond Master's Degree) + B019*(Temporary/Alternative Certification) + B020*(No Certification) + R0.

LEVEL 3 (SCHOOL) MODEL

B00 = G000 + G001(Catholic School) + G002(Mid-sized City) + G003(Large Suburb) + G004(Mid-sized Suburb) + G005(Small Town)

+ G006(Rural) + G007(Small School) + G008(Large School) + G009
(*% Free/Reduced Price Lunch*) + G0010(*Percent Capacity*) + G0011(Classrooms
Meet Needs) + G0012(*Neighborhood Climate Composite*) + U00.

Once the full model was run, a reduced model was examined that
included all student demographic variables as well as school location
and demographic composition variables as controls, along with all explanatory variables with a *p*-value of .10 or below. The cutoff of .10 was
chosen to increase the chances that no variables were dropped that
might have turned out to be significant once all of the other nonsig-
nificant variables were removed. The full model was also run with a
reduced sample that included only students who remained in the same
school between first and third grades, to ensure that the results were
consistent across samples.

QUESTION 3—HOW DO PUBLIC AND CATHOLIC SCHOOL STUDENTS DIFFER IN THEIR PERFORMANCE ON ECLS-K MATHEMATICS ASSESSMENT SUBSCALES, AND TO WHAT EXTENT ARE THE SMALLER GAINS IN CATHOLIC STUDENTS' OVERALL MATHEMATICS TEST SCORES FROM FIRST THROUGH THIRD GRADE DUE TO A DIFFERENCE IN THE FREQUENCY OF ITEMS FROM THE VARIOUS SUBSCALES?

In order to examine whether there was a difference in the type of curriculum taught to Catholic and public school students, we examined
both teacher-reported curriculum foci as well as student performance
on various mathematics subscales. The purpose of this was to examine
whether disparities in overall mathematics gains were concentrated
within particular strands of mathematics and whether teacher reports
indicated differential emphasis on those strands by sector.

Curricular Emphasis

Teachers were asked about the emphasis they placed on the National
Council of Teachers of Mathematics (NCTM's) five curriculum areas:
(1) numbers and operations, (2) measurement, (3) geometry and spatial relations, (4) data analysis, statistics, and probability, and (5) algebra and functions.[21] Teachers were asked to report how often they
addressed each (from "none" to "a lot").

Teacher responses were analyzed using *t*-tests to examine whether there were differential responses by school sector. However, given that teaching emphases can vary based on school characteristics, HLM models were run examining teacher focus as the outcome in order to examine whether teachers' curricular emphases varied by school sector after controlling for student, class, and school demographics. Lastly, a final HLM model was run to examine whether teacher education, experience, professional development, or certification status were significantly related to teacher focus in order to shed light on potential reasons for differences in teaching emphases by sector.

STUDENT SUBSCALE PERFORMANCE, TEACHER EMPHASIS, AND ECLS-K EMPHASIS

The ECLS-K assigns each child a proficiency probability rating on several mathematics subscales indicating the likelihood that the child is proficient in each area based on their responses to specific mathematics assessment questions.[22] The subscales include (1) count/number/shape, (2) relative size, (3) ordinality/sequence, (4) add/subtract, (5) multiply/divide, (6) place value, and (7) rate/measurement, fractions, and area/volume. For the first three subscales (count/number shape, relative size, and ordinality/sequence), the mean score for third graders was 99.9 or above, indicating that almost all third graders in the sample were proficient in these areas. Therefore these three subscales were left out of any further analysis.

As listed in the *User's Manual for the ECLS-K Third Grade Public-Use Data File and Electronic Code Book*,[23] the remaining four categories relate specifically to

4. Solving simple addition and subtraction problems;
5. Solving simple multiplication and division problems and recognizing more complex number patterns;
6. Demonstrating understanding of place value in integers to hundreds place;
7. Using knowledge of measurement and rate to solve word problems.

We compared the student proficiency rating for each subscale by school type to see whether there was a pattern of differences that might indicate a different focus in the classroom. This was done using *t*-tests at the student level as well as through three-level HLM models with subscale scores as the outcome variable. The *t*-tests were done to examine raw differences between sectors, but it is possible that these differences in teaching emphases reflect differences in demographics, as opposed to school sector. If the differences persist by sector after controlling for demographics, this then raises the questions of why and whether these patterns in teaching emphases are due to teacher characteristics, particularly in light of prior studies that found that public schools employ more certified teachers, offer more professional development, and have more teachers with higher levels of education.[24] In order to answer these questions, a series of three HLM models were run for each of the four subscale scores examined: a base model with only a first grade subscale score and the Catholic binary variable, a model with demographic information, and a model with the teacher focus variables examined above. Finally, we ran a series of HLM models with third grade math *t*-score as the outcome, first grade math *t*-score and demographic variables as controls, and teacher focus variables as the explanatory variables.

The results of question 1's comparisons of various school and teacher variables by school type, including both *t*-tests and logistic regressions, are explained in sufficient detail in Chapter 6. Hence, the results below focus on the remaining two questions involving the results of the HLM analyses of achievement by school type and public and Catholic school teachers' curricular emphases and the effects those might have on student achievement.

QUESTION 2 RESULTS—HLM ANALYSES OF ACHIEVEMENT
IN PUBLIC AND CATHOLIC SCHOOLS INITIAL BASELINE
MODELS

Initial baseline models with and without student and school demographics are shown in Table B2. The significant proportion of variance among classrooms and between classrooms in the null model as well as in subsequent models reveals that the use of multilevel models was sensible because the clustered data are related.

In order to interpret these HLM results, one can think of the intercept as the estimated mean achievement of a student who is 0 on all of the binary predictors (e.g., a black, female, public school student, etc.) and at the mean for all continuous predictors. According to Model 1,

Table B2: HLM results part 1—models 1–6: 1,972 schools, 4,911 classrooms, 11,860 students

Variable	Model 1: base model	Model 2: +school type	Model 3: +first grade math t-score	Model 4: + student demographics	Model 5: + school size/ location	Model 6: + school and class demographics
Intercept	49.38***	49.30***	50.37***	48.00***	48.29***	48.49***
School level:						
Catholic school (standard error)		1.88*	−1.07*	−2.08***	−2.18***	−2.81***
		(0.84)	(0.49)	(0.41)	(0.41)	(0.45)
Midsized city (all compared with large city)					0.10	0.11
Large suburb					0.03	−0.15
Midsized suburb					−0.34	−0.44
Small town					−1.06	−0.98
Rural					−0.73	−0.83
Small school					−1.46	−1.46
Large school					−0.77*	−0.79*
Percent free/reduced-price lunch eligible						−1.51**
Class level: Percent special education						−2.25*
Student level:						
First grade math t-score			0.79***	0.73***	0.73***	0.73***
SES				1.52***	1.49***	1.42***
Gender male				1.59***	1.59***	1.59***
White[a]				2.37***	2.46***	2.32***
Hispanic				1.73***	1.77***	1.75***
Asian				3.01***	3.05***	2.97***
Other race				1.88***	1.98***	1.90***

Age at assessment in months (1–5)				−0.17**	−0.16**	−0.16**
Learning problem diagnosed				−1.38***	−1.40***	−1.37***
Variance components:						
Level 1	51.33	51.35	24.19	23.13	23.20	23.23
Level 2	18.73	18.74	3.90	4.47	4.53	4.58
Level 3	35.52	35.30	10.32	6.35	5.82	5.44
Proportion of variance within classroom (child effect)	0.49	0.49	0.63	0.68	0.69	0.70
Proportion of variance between classrooms within schools (class effect)	0.18	0.18	0.10	0.13	0.14	0.14
Proportion of variance between schools (school effect)	0.34	0.33	0.27	0.19	0.17	0.16
Percent of within-classroom variation explained		0.0	52.9	54.9	54.8	54.7
Percent of between-classroom variation explained		−0.1	79.2	76.1	75.8	75.5
Percent of between-school variation explained		0.6	70.9	82.1	83.6	84.7
Deviance	86,040.42	86,036	75,413	74,617	74,581	74,548
Number of parameters	4	5	6	14	21	23
Chi-squared	0.0304	0.0304	0.0000	0.0000	0.0000	0.0000

[a] In a move away from having white students automatically serve as the default group, the default comparison group of students is African American in these analyses. This means that binary variables were created for white, Asian, Hispanic, and other race students, so when these variables are included in the HLM equations, the default omitted category that they are being compared with is African American students.

*$p < .05$.
**$p < .01$.
***$p < .001$.

the traditional null model, mathematics achievement across all the students in the sample averaged 49.38 points in third grade. This is sensible because the test scores being used are in the form of t-scores with a mean of 50 and standard deviation of 10.[25]

When school type was added in Model 2, the Catholic school estimate was significantly positive (1.88, $p < .05$) indicating that, on average, Catholic school students scored 1.88 points higher on the ECLS-K math test than public school students in third grade. However, adding school sector to the model did little to explain the variation in achievement between schools or classrooms.

When students' first grade math t-scores are added in Model 3, the Catholic school estimate "flips" and becomes significantly negative (-1.07, $p < .05$). This indicates that, while Catholic school students' raw mathematics t-scores are higher in third grade than public school students', public school students with similar first grade math t-scores actually make significantly greater gains than Catholic school students. After the addition of the first grade math t-score, the model explained a considerable portion (71%) of the variation in achievement between schools as well as between classrooms (79%) and within classrooms (53%). These large reductions in variance drastically diminish the amount of additional variance that can be explained using the remaining models.

STUDENT, CLASS, AND SCHOOL DEMOGRAPHICS

Student demographics were added in Model 4, and their inclusion further reduced the Catholic mathematics achievement estimate, showing that public school students, on average, had a 2.08 ($p<.001$) point advantage over Catholic school students with similar demographics (including SES, gender, race/ethnicity, age, and diagnosed learning problems). As a specific example of how to interpret the results of this model, Model 4's intercept of 48 is the estimated mean mathematics t-score for a black female public school student who is of average age and SES, had an average first grade math t-score, and does not have a learning problem diagnosed. In order to determine the estimated achievement for an Asian male with the other defaults, you would simply add 1.59 (the estimate for male) and 3.01 (the estimate for Asian). Examination of the gender, SES, and race coefficients is consistent with past research, namely, that boys made greater mathematics gains than girls, higher SES students made greater gains than lower SES students, and students in the other racial categories made greater gains than African American students.

Model 5 includes school size and location, revealing a negative estimate for the Large School binary variable (-0.77, $p < .05$), indicating that students in large schools with over 750 students have slightly smaller math test score gains than students in medium-sized schools (150–750 students), which is the default. It is also interesting to note that the estimate for small schools (<150 students) was about twice that for the large school variable, but it was not significant owing to the small number of schools in that group. Adding these variables caused the Catholic school estimate to decrease from -2.08 to -2.18, which is not a large change compared with both the Catholic school-level standard deviation of 6.1 or the Catholic school-level standard deviation of mathematics test score gains, which is 3.8. Throughout this analysis, the Catholic school estimates do not change drastically compared with these measures of standard deviation.

Finally, adding the school's percentage of free and reduced-price lunch eligible students and class percentage of students with special needs (in Model 6) reduced the Catholic estimate to -2.81. Prior research has found that a school's socioeconomic composition is related to student achievement within the school (or a "peer effect"),[26] and this is indeed seen in Model 6 when the school's percentage of free and reduced-price lunch eligible students and class percentage of students with special needs were added to the model. Students in schools with lower income populations had lower math test scores than students in schools with higher income populations, even after controlling for individual students' demographics. In addition, the percentage of students receiving special education services in the classroom was negatively associated with student mathematics gains even after controlling for a student's diagnosis of a learning problem.[27]

VARIABLES THAT APPEAR ADVANTAGEOUS FOR PUBLIC SCHOOLS

All of the variable groups that reduced the gap between public and Catholic schools when added to the models are shown in Table B3. If the negative Catholic coefficient is reduced in magnitude when a variable is added, then this variable helps to explain the difference in

Table B3: ECLS-K third grade HLM results part 2—models 7–11: 1,972 schools, 4,911 classrooms, 11,860 students

Variable	Model 7: + instructional practices	Model 8: + time in math workshop	Model 9: + class climate	Model 10: + teacher education	Model 11: + building meets needs
Intercept	48.52***	48.50***	48.51***	48.64***	48.90***
School level:					
Catholic School (standard error)	-2.62***	-2.58***	-2.54***	-2.27***	-2.25***
	(0.46)	(0.46)	(0.46)	(0.46)	(0.46)
Midsized city (all compared with large city)	0.14	0.15	0.15	0.11	0.08
Large suburb	-0.14	-0.13	-0.13	-0.14	-0.15
Midsized suburb	-0.38	-0.37	-0.37	-0.39	-0.43
Small town	-0.85	-0.79	-0.80	-0.88	-0.88
Rural	-0.72	-0.68	-0.66	-0.69	-0.71
Small school	-1.32	-1.30	-1.22	-1.24	-1.11
Large school	-0.79*	-0.79*	-0.79*	-0.77*	-0.88**
Percent free/reduced-price lunch eligible	-1.46**	-1.48**	-1.62**	-1.57**	-1.63***
School percent capacity					0.77
Classrooms meet needs (yes/no)					-0.22
Class level:					
Percent special education	-2.03*	-2.07*	-2.06*	-2.12*	-2.11**
Total class enrollment	0.03	0.03	0.03	0.03	0.02
Desks facing front	-0.45	-0.45	-0.45	-0.43	-0.42

Number of computers per child	0.69	0.70	0.75	0.72	0.74
Calculators never/hardly ever	-0.04	-0.02	-0.04	-0.03	-0.03
Traditional composite	0.18	0.19	0.19	0.18	0.17
Reform composite	0.52*	0.48*	0.48*	0.49*	0.49*
Time in math workshop, recoded		0.14	0.14	0.13	0.13
Administrator support composite			-0.02	-0.01	-0.00
Student misbehavior composite			0.18	0.18	0.19
Teacher satisfaction composite			0.14	0.14	0.14
Staff support composite			-0.18	-0.20	-0.20
Bachelor's degree or less				-0.18	-0.17
Beyond master's degree				-0.23	-0.23
Temporary/alternative certification				-0.56	-0.57
No certification				-2.59*	-2.66*
Student level:					
First grade math t-score	0.73***	0.73***	0.73***	0.73***	0.73***
SES	1.42***	1.42***	1.42***	1.41***	1.41***
Gender male	1.59***	1.59***	1.58***	1.58***	1.58***
White	2.33***	2.32***	2.34***	2.30***	2.30***
Hispanic	1.75***	1.74***	1.76***	1.74***	1.74***
Asian	2.98***	2.98***	2.99***	2.95***	2.94***
Other race	1.90***	1.91***	1.91***	1.88***	1.87***
Age at assessment in months (1–5)	-0.16**	-0.16**	-0.16**	-0.17**	-0.17**
Learning problem diagnosed	-1.36***	-1.36***	-1.35***	-1.35***	-1.35***

Table B3: *continued*

Variable	Model 7: + instructional practices	Model 8: + time in math workshop	Model 9: + class climate	Model 10: + teacher education	Model 11: + building meets needs
Variance components:					
Percent of variance within classroom (child effect)	70.3	70.4	70.5	70.3	70.3
Percent of variance between classrooms (class effect)	13.6	13.6	13.6	13.5	13.4
Percent of variance between schools (school effect)	16.1	16.0	15.9	16.2	16.3
Percent of within-classroom variation explained	54.7	54.6	54.6	54.7	54.8
Percent of between-classroom variation explained	75.9	76.0	76.0	76.2	76.3
Percent of between-school variation explained	85.0	85.1	85.2	85.0	84.8
Deviance	74,522	74,519	74,512	74,498	74,493
Number of parameters	29	30	34	38	40
Chi-squared	0.0003	0.0566	0.1464	0.0083	0.0821

*p < .05.
**p < .01.
***p < .001

performance between sectors. This means that either the variable is an advantage for public schools (i.e., positively correlated with student achievement and also more common in public schools) or a disadvantage for Catholic schools (i.e., negatively correlated with student achievement and more common in Catholic schools). When these variables are added to the model, they are in a sense controlled for, and the Catholic coefficient then indicates the average test score difference between public and Catholic schools when all the other variables in the model are equal. These categories of variables are discussed below.

Teaching Practices

One group of variables that increase the Catholic school estimate (and thus help explain the Catholic school lag) were the teaching practices variables, which were added in Model 7. These narrowed the gap, increasing the Catholic estimate from −2.81 (in Model 6) points to −2.62 points (in Model 7). Adding these variables to the model did reduce the deviance statistic significantly ($p < .001$) so Model 7 is a better fitted model than Model 6. Of the variables added, the only one that was significant was the estimate for the reform-oriented practices composite. This variable had an estimate of 0.52 ($p < .05$), which indicates that those teachers who reported using reform-oriented practices more often had students with higher mathematics test score gains after controlling for demographics and prior test scores.

Professional Development

When the variable measuring how much time teachers spent in mathematics workshops was added in Model 8, the Catholic school estimate was further increased from −2.62 to −2.58. The professional development estimate itself, although positive, was not statistically significantly related to student achievement gains.

Class Climate

The class climate variables measuring administrator and staff support, student misbehavior, and teacher satisfaction were added in Model 9. These variables slightly increased the Catholic school estimate from

−2.58 to −2.54, but none of the variables were significantly related to student test score gains.

Teacher Education

Adding the three teacher education variables to the equation in Model 10 increased the Catholic school estimate from −2.54 to −2.27. The only variable that was significant, however, was the one indicating that a teacher was not certified ($p < .05$), which had an estimate of −2.59, indicating that, all other factors being equal, students who had a third grade teacher who was not certified would be expected to have a test score that was 2.59 points lower than those with fully certified teachers who were both demographically similar and had identical test scores two years earlier. Because Catholic school teachers are less likely to be certified than public school teachers, it makes sense that adding this variable to the model would increase the Catholic school estimate and might explain some of the difference in mathematics test score gains between public and Catholic school students. The change in the deviance statistic is significant ($p = .008$), indicating that the model with the teacher education variables is a better fitted model.

Building Characteristics

Model 11 adds the school's percent capacity and the principal report of whether classrooms meet student needs. We see that the Catholic school estimate increases very slightly (from −2.27 to −2.25). However, neither of these variables is significantly related to achievement.

VARIABLES THAT HELP CATHOLIC SCHOOLS

Table B4 shows the categories of variables that, when added to the model, reveal a decrease in the Catholic school estimate for student mathematics test scores. This indicates that these variables were either positive correlates with achievement and also more prevalent in Catholic schools or negative correlates that were less prevalent in Catholic schools. When ratings of the neighborhood climate were added in Model 12, the Catholic school estimate decreased from −2.25 to −2.28. This is not a large change in the Catholic school estimate, and the

Table B4: ECLS-K third grade HLM results part 3—models 12–15: 1,972 schools, 4,911 classrooms, 11,860 students

Variable	Model 12: neighborhood climate	Model 13: +parent involvement	Model 14: teacher autonomy	Model 15: reduced only <.10
Intercept	48.90***	48.90***	48.90***	48.62***
School level:				
Catholic School (standard error)	−2.28***	−2.30***	−2.32***	−2.43***
	(0.47)	(0.47)	(0.47)	(0.45)
Midsized city (all compared with large city)	0.09	0.09	0.09	0.09
Large suburb	−0.14	−0.14	−0.16	−0.15
Midsized suburb	−0.42	−0.42	−0.44	−0.39
Small town	−0.88	−0.89	−0.90	−0.95
Rural	−0.70	−0.72	−0.71	−0.79
Small school	−1.11	−1.12	−1.12	−1.44
Large school	−0.88**	−0.88*	−0.88**	−0.77*
Percent free/reduced-price lunch eligible	−1.69**	−1.62**	−1.60**	−1.44**
School percent capacity	0.76	0.76	0.74	
Classrooms meet needs (yes/no)	−0.22	−0.22	−0.23	
Neighborhood climate composite	−0.12	−0.12	−0.13	
Class level:				
Percent special education	−2.11**	−2.11**	−2.15**	2.18**
Total class enrollment	0.02	0.02	0.02	
Desks facing front	−0.43	−0.42	−0.40	
Number of computers per child	0.74	0.73	0.69	
Calculators never/hardly ever	−0.03	−0.02	−0.02	

Table B4: *continued*

Variable	Model 12: neighborhood climate	Model 13: +parent involvement	Model 14: teacher autonomy	Model 15: reduced only <.10
Traditional composite	0.17	0.18	0.19	
Reform composite	0.49*	0.48*	0.48*	0.57**
Percent of parents attend other school activities		0.08	0.07	
Time in math workshop, recoded	0.13	0.13	0.13	
Administrator support composite	−0.01	−0.01	−0.01	
Student misbehavior composite	0.18	0.20	0.21	
Teacher satisfaction composite	0.14	0.13	0.11	
Staff support composite	−0.20	−0.20	−0.22	
Paperwork interferes with teaching			0.06	
How much teacher controls curriculum			0.08	
Job security based on state/local tests			−0.09	
Bachelor's degree or less	−0.18	−0.17	−0.15	
Beyond master's degree	−0.23	−0.22	−0.22	
Temporary or alternative certification	−0.57	−0.57	−0.55	−0.55
No certification	−2.61*	−2.61*	−2.59*	−2.75*
Student level:				
First grade Math *t*-score	0.73***	0.73***	0.73***	−0.73***
SES	1.41***	1.41***	1.41***	1.42***

Gender male	1.58***	1.58***	1.58***	1.58***
White	2.30***	2.29***	2.28***	2.29***
Hispanic	1.74***	1.73***	1.73***	1.74***
Asian	2.94***	2.93***	2.93***	2.95***
Other race	1.87***	1.87***	1.87***	1.87***
Age at assessment in months (1–5)	−0.17**	−0.17**	−0.17**	−0.16**
Learning problem diagnosed	−1.35***	−1.35***	−1.34***	−1.38***
Variance components:				
Percent of variance within classroom (child effect)	70.3	70.3	70.4	69.9
Percent of variance between classrooms (class effect)	13.4	13.4	13.4	13.5
Percent of variance between schools (school effect)	16.3	16.3	16.3	16.7
Percent of within-classroom variation explained	54.8	54.8	54.7	54.8
Percent of between-classroom variation explained	76.3	76.3	76.4	76.1
Percent of between-school variation explained	84.8	84.8	84.9	84.4
Deviance	74,493	74,492	74,489	74,517
Number of parameters	41	42	45	26
Chi-squared	1.0000	0.3173	0.3916	0.0000

*$p < .05$.
**$p < .01$.
***$p < .001$.

estimate for the neighborhood climate composite is also not a statistically significant predictor of achievement in the model.

Likewise, adding the parental involvement variable in Model 13, which indicates the percentage of parents that attend other school activities, did not change the Catholic estimate significantly (reducing it another .02 points to 2.30), and the estimate for parental involvement in other school activities was not a statistically significant predictor of mathematics achievement.

Finally, adding the variables indicating how much autonomy the teacher has in the classroom (Model 14) only decreased the Catholic estimate by .02 (to 2.32), and autonomy was not related to achievement. For each of these categories of variables, the Chi-squared tests examining the deviance statistics are not significant, indicating that adding these groups of variables to the model does not reduce the lack of fit.

FINAL MODEL

A final model was run that includes all of the demographic and school descriptor variables but only includes those explanatory variables that had a *p*-value of .10 or below in the full model. The explanatory variables included in the model are the reform-oriented practices composite, the temporary or alternative certification variable, and the no certification variable. The reduced model (Model 15) is shown in Table B4. The Catholic school estimate in this model is −2.43, which is up from −2.81 in Model 6. While the deviance statistic is significantly different between Model 6 and Model 15 as seen by the significant Chi-squared value, the percentages of variation explained in Model 6 and Model 15 are similar. The percent of between-class variation explained did increase from 75.5% to 76.1%, or about 2.5% of the remaining unexplained variation.[28]

SCHOOL SECTOR AND RACE/ETHNICITY INTERACTIONS

As shown in Table B5, interaction terms were included in Model 5 to examine whether there are racial or socioeconomic interactions by sector as suggested by some past studies.[29] However, none of the interaction terms were significant. Still, the sample sizes for Catholic school students in several of the racial categories were small. Specifically, out of 1,492 Catholic school students in the sample, 78 were black, 197 were

Table B5: ECLS-K two-level HLM interaction term results—1,972 schools, 11,860 students

Variable	Model 1: base model	Model 2: school type only	Model 3: first grade score	Model 4: demographics	Model 5: race interactions
Intercept	49.54***	49.45***	50.38***	48.34***	48.35***
School level:					
Catholic School		1.87*	−1.12*	−2.58***	−3.00**
(standard error)		(0.84)	(0.49)	(0.43)	(1.05)
Small school				−1.76*	−1.76*
Large school				−0.68*	−0.68*
Percent free/reduced price lunch eligible				−1.37**	−1.37**
Student level:					
First grade math t-score			0.79***	0.74***	0.74***
SES				1.45***	1.45***
SES × Catholic					0.02
Gender male				1.54***	1.54***
White				2.23***	2.22***
White × Catholic					0.43
Hispanic				1.74***	1.72***
Hispanic × Catholic					0.74
Asian				2.95***	3.02***
Asian × Catholic					−0.94
Other race				1.82**	1.78***
Other race × Catholic					1.18
Age at assessment in months (1–5)				−0.17**	−0.17**
Learning problem diagnosed				−1.37***	−1.37***
Variance components					
Level 1	65.44	65.46	27.38	26.72	26.72
Intercept	40.83	40.65	11.48	7.35	7.37
Intraclass correlation	0.38	0.38	0.30	0.22	0.22
Percent of between-school variation explained		0	72	82	82
Percent of within-school variation explained		0	58	59	59

*$p < .05$.
**$p < .01$.
***$p < .001$.

Hispanic, and 82 were Asian. Hence, it is difficult to draw firm conclusions about the lack of interaction effects, but our analysis does suggest that such effects are not significant.[30]

Results of Analyses of Teachers' Curricular Focus

CONTENT OF THE ECLS-K MATHEMATICS ASSESSMENT

ECLS-K test items are not available for scrutiny, so we rely on manuals and psychometric reports for information about the content of the mathematics assessment. The K-1st Grade Psychometric Report states the following:

> The mathematics test specifications . . . are primarily based on the Mathematics Framework for the 1996 National Assessment of Educational Progress (National Assessment Governing Board [NAGB] 1996a). The NAEP mathematics framework is itself largely based on the curriculum standards from the Commission on Standards for School Mathematics of the National Council of Teachers of Mathematics (NCTM 1989).[31]

Hence, the assessment was heavily influenced by the NCTM curricular reforms, and, as mentioned previously, the questions covered NCTM's five strands: number/operations, algebra/patterns, statistics/probability, geometry, and measurement. Even in the category of number/operations, which could be viewed as relatively traditional content, at least half of the items involved "some aspect of estimation or mental mathematics."[32]

TEACHER-REPORTED CURRICULUM FOCUS BY SECTOR

The ECLS-K asked teachers to report how often they focus on several different mathematics curricular areas, and t-tests indicate that public school teachers reported focusing more on all areas ($p < .001$) except for numbers and operations (see Table B6). More specifically, almost all public (96.2%) and Catholic (97.9%) school teachers reported that they focus on numbers and operations "a lot" (or 4 on a 1–4 scale), and there was no significant difference in rating by school sector. However, public school teachers reported focusing significantly more on mea-

Table B6: ECLS-K curricular emphasis: Descriptive statistics and *t*-test results: Catholic (*n* = 234) and public (*n* = 3,427) school third grade teachers

Variable		Descriptive Statistics		*T*-test Results	
	Sector	Mean	Standard deviation	*t*-value	
Frequency numbers and operations	Public	3.96	0.20	−1.81	
	Catholic	3.98	0.14		
Frequency measurement	Public	3.18	0.62	5.40***	
	Catholic	2.96	0.70		
Frequency geometry and spatial relations	Public	3.05	0.63	6.78***	
	Catholic	2.74	0.69		
Frequency data analysis, statistics and probability	Public	2.93	0.76	5.57***	
	Catholic	2.65	0.76		
Frequency algebra and functions	Public	2.79	0.90	3.84***	
	Catholic	2.54	0.94		

*$p < .05$.
**$p < .01$.
***$p < .001$.

surement, geometry and spatial relations, data analysis, statistics and probability, and algebra and functions. Again, these four nonnumber strand variables were combined into a composite (see Table B1).

PREDICTORS OF TEACHERS' CURRICULAR FOCUS

A series of four HLM models were run with the nonnumber mathematics composite as the outcome in order to examine differences in teachers' curricular focus by sector before and after controlling for demographic information, as well as after controlling for teacher characteristics. This was done in order to determine whether curricular differences by school sector can be explained by differences in school populations or teacher characteristics. In addition, a similar set of HLM models were run with the numbers and operations classroom focus rating as the outcome.

Predictors of a Nonnumber Focus

As reported in Table B7, Catholic school teachers reported significantly less focus on nonnumber strands ($p < .001$) in all of the models. Also,

Table B7: ECLS-K HLM results: predictors of teachers' curricular emphases (1,509 schools, 3,649 classrooms)

Variable	Frequency nonnumber mathematics focus				Frequency numbers and operations focus			
	Base model	Add Catholic	Add demographic etc.	Add explanatory teacher-level variables	Base model	Add Catholic	Add Demographic etc.	Add explanatory teacher-level variables
Intercept	2.97***	2.99***	3.08***	3.06***	3.06***	3.96***	3.94***	3.94***
School level:								
Catholic school (standard error)		−0.24*** (0.04)	−0.21*** (0.05)	−0.18*** (0.05)		0.02* (0.01)	0.02(0.01)	0.02* (0.01)
Mid-sized city			−0.09*	−0.07*			0.01	0.01
Large suburb			−0.08*	−0.06			0.01	0.01
Mid-sized suburb			−0.14**	−0.12**			0.01	0.02
Small town			−0.22***	−0.17***			0.03	0.04**
Rural			−0.17***	−0.14**			0.04**	0.04**
Small school			−0.11	−0.12			0.00	0.00
Large school			0.04	0.05			0.02	0.02
Percent free/reduced-price lunch eligible			0.11**	0.11**			−0.01	−0.01
Class level:								
Percent special education			−0.19*	−0.19*			0.00	
Time in math workshop, recoded				0.07***				0.00

Bachelor's degree or less				−0.02				−0.01
Beyond master's degree				0.01				−0.01
Temporary or alternative certification				0.02				−0.01
No certification				0.02				0.00
New teacher (3 years or less)				−0.10**				0.01
Veteran teacher (25+ years)				0.04				−0.00
Variance components:								
Level 1	0.24	0.24	0.24	0.23	0.03	0.03	0.03	0.03
Intercept	0.08	0.07	0.06	0.06	0.005	0.005	0.005	0.005
Intraclass correlation	0.25	0.23	0.20	0.21	0.14	0.14	0.14	0.14
Percent of between-school variation explained	0	13	25	25	0	0	0	%
Percent of within-school variation explained	0	0	0	4	0	0	0	0

Table B8: ECLS-K HLM results: curricular emphases as predictors of third grade achievement (1,509 schools, 3,649 classrooms, 9,720 students)

Variable	Model A: only first t-score	Model B: + demographics	Model C: + frequency non-number focus	Model D: frequency numbers and operations	Model E: frequency measurement	Model F: frequency geometry	Model G: frequency statistics	Model H: frequency algebra
Intercept	50.95***	49.22***	49.11***	49.21***	49.16***	49.16***	49.17***	49.17***
School level:								
Catholic School (standard error)	-1.10*	-2.97***	-2.80***	-2.96***	-2.91***	-2.84***	-2.89***	-2.91***
	0.50	0.48	0.47	0.48	0.48	0.48	0.48	0.47
Midsized city (all compared with large city)		-0.17	-0.12	-0.16	-0.14	-0.16	-0.17	-0.13
Large suburb		-0.42	-0.36	-0.41	0.37	-0.39	-0.40	-0.40
Midsized suburb		-0.55	-0.44	-0.54	-0.49	-0.48	-0.47	-0.53
Small town		-1.66**	-1.51*	-1.64**	-1.62**	-1.58**	-1.61**	-1.56**
Rural		-1.29*	-1.14*	-1.28*	-1.23*	-1.21*	-1.21	-1.22*
Small school		-1.26	-1.24	-1.25	-1.26	-1.27	-1.26	-1.23
Large school		-0.70	-0.70	-0.70	-0.68	-0.69	-0.72*	-0.69
Percent free/reduced-price lunch eligible		-1.91**	-1.99**	-1.91**	-1.95**	-1.93**	-1.96**	-1.95**
Class level:								
Percent special education		-2.11*	-1.91*	-2.11*	-2.00*	-1.98*	-2.04*	-2.01*
Frequency numbers and operations			-0.61	-0.42				
Frequency measurement					0.37*			
Frequency geometry and spatial relations						0.40*		

	(1)	(2)	(3)	(4)	(5)	(6)	(7)
Frequency data analysis, statistics and probability						0.40**	
Frequency algebra and functions							0.31*
Frequency nonnumber combined		0.68**					
Student level:							
First grade math subscale score	0.80***	0.73***	0.73***	0.73***	0.73***	0.73***	0.73***
SES	1.40***	1.40***	1.40***	1.40***	1.40***	1.40***	1.40***
Gender male	1.73***	1.74***	1.73***	1.74***	1.74***	1.73***	1.73***
White	2.28***	2.30***	2.28***	2.28***	2.29***	2.30***	2.29***
Hispanic	1.75***	1.71***	1.75***	1.74***	1.74***	1.75***	1.73***
Asian	2.53***	2.54***	2.53***	2.53***	2.53***	2.55***	2.53***
Other race	1.76**	1.76**	1.76**	1.75**	1.76**	1.76**	1.75**
Age at assessment in months (1–5)	−0.14*	−0.14*	−0.14*	−0.14*	−0.14*	−0.14*	−0.14*
Learning problem diagnosed	−1.41***	−1.40***	−1.42***	−1.41***	−1.41***	−1.41***	−1.39***

*p < .05.
**p < .01.
***p < .001

when the teacher characteristics were added to the last model, results indicate that the amount of time a teacher had spent in mathematics workshops was significantly positively related to a focus on nonnumber mathematics strands ($p < .001$) and that being a new teacher with three years of experience or less was significantly negatively associated with a focus on nonnumber mathematics ($p < .01$). Finally, schools with a higher percentage of free and reduced-price lunch eligible students focused more on nonnumber strands ($p < .01$), while classrooms with a greater percentage of special education students focused less on these strands ($p < .01$).

Predictors of a Numbers and Operations Focus

First, it is important to reiterate that almost all teachers reported focusing on this strand "a lot," so there is little variability in the results. Still, Catholic school teachers reported slightly more focus on numbers and operations, with the difference being significant ($p < .05$) in both the model with only school sector and the final model with all the demographic and explanatory teacher-level variables. Other interesting findings are that teachers in small and rural town schools focused more on numbers and operations and less on the other nonnumber strands than teachers in large city schools.[33]

The percentage of test items related to number and operations decreased between grades 1 and 3. It is important to note that public school teachers report focusing more on the nonnumber strands, which became more prominent in the third-grade assessment (e.g., measurement and geometry) and could help explain why public school gains are higher.

INFLUENCE OF TEACHER FOCUS ON MATHEMATICS ACHIEVEMENT

We created a series of HLM models to examine whether differences in Catholic and public school mathematics gains can be explained by teachers' curricular emphases (see Table B8). Students' third-grade math t-score served as the outcome, with first-grade math t-score and demographic variables serving as controls and teacher curricular focus variables serving as explanatory variables.

When entered separately into the models (Models E–H), each of the nonnumber teacher focus items were significant, positive predictors of students' mathematics gains ($p < .05$), with estimates between .31 and .40. However, the numbers and operations focus was insignificant. This indicates that, when demographics and prior test score are equal, teachers who report focusing on nonnumber strands tend to have students with greater third grade mathematics t-test scores than those who report focusing less on these. A model was also run with both the numbers and operations focus variable and the nonnumber focus composite (see Model C). The frequency of numbers and operations focus was negative but not significant, but the nonnumber composite was .68 and significant ($p < .01$). Also, the Catholic estimate increased from −2.97 to −2.80 after adding the curricular focus variables, indicating that teachers' curricular focus partially explains the Catholic school students' smaller ECLS-K test score gains.

Notes

PREFACE

1   Michael J. Sandel, *What Money Can't Buy: The Moral Limits of Markets* (New York: Farrar, Straus and Giroux, 2012).

2   Gary S. Becker and G. Nashat (1997). *The Economics of Life: From Baseball to Affirmative Action to Immigration, How Real-World Issues Affect Our Everyday Life* (New York, McGraw-Hill, 1997); S.E. Landsburg, *More Sex Is Safer Sex: The Unconventional Wisdom of Economics* (New York, Free Press, 2007); S. D. Levitt and S. J. Dubner (2005). *Freakonomics: A Rogue Economist Explores the Hidden Side of Everything* (New York, William Morrow, 2005).

3   Jeffrey M. Jones, "Confidence in U.S. Public Schools at New Low," *Gallup*, June 20 2012.

4   Diana Jean Schemo, "Charter Schools Trail in Results, U.S. Data Reveals," *New York Times*, August 17, 2004, A1.

5   Diane Ravitch, "Every State Left Behind," *New York Times*, November 7, 2005; U.S. Department of Education, *The Nation's Report Card: America's Charter Schools* (Washington, DC: National Assessment of Educational Progress, 2004).

6   Although there was the distinct possibility that charter schools were serving more disadvantaged children, the authors of the study instituted some rudimentary measures to compare similar students in charter and public schools but still found charters to be underperforming. See F. Howard Nelson, Bella Rosenberg, and Nancy Van Meter, *Charter School Achievement on the 2003 National Assessment of Educational Progress* (Washington, DC: American Federation of Teachers, 2004).

7   Various Scholars and Center for Education Reform, "Charter School Evaluation Reported by the *New York Times*, Fails to Meet Professional Standards," *New York Times*, August 25, 2004, http://www.edreform.com/_upload/NewYorkTimesAd.pdf.

8   For two excellent reviews of this controversy, see Martin Carnoy, Rebecca Jacobsen, Lawrence Mishel, and Richard Rothstein, *The Charter School Dust-Up: Examining the Evidence on Enrollment and Achievement* (Washington,

DC: Economic Policy Institute, 2005); Jeffrey R. Henig, *Spin Cycle: How Research Is Used in Policy Debates—The Case of Charter Schools* (New York: Russell Sage Foundation, 2007).

9   On incentivist reforms, see Jay P. Greene, Thomas W. Carroll, Andrew J. Coulson, Robert Enlow, E. D. Hirsch, Matthew Ladner, Neal McCluskey, Diane Ravitch, and Sol Stern, "Is School Choice Enough?" *City Journal*, January 24, 2008, http://www.city-journal.org/2008/forum0124 .html.

10   In this book we distinguish not only between public and private schools but also between public and charter schools. We are aware that charter schools are a form of public schools in that they are publicly funded, chartered by public authorities, and (usually) open to the public. However, for the sake of brevity and analytic clarity, we use the terms "public" and "charter" to distinguish between these two models.

11   See, e.g., Christopher Lubienski and Sarah Lubienski, *Re-Examining a Primary Premise of Market Theory: An Analysis of NAEP Data on Achievement in Public and Private Schools* (New York: National Center for the Study of Privatization in Education, 2005); Sarah Theule Lubienski and Christopher Lubienski, "A New Look at Public and Private Schools: Student Background and Mathematics Achievement," *Phi Delta Kappan*, May 2005, 696–99; Joshua Benton, "Can Cash Buy Good Schools?" *Dallas Morning News*, June 26, 2005; Teresa Méndez, "Public Schools: Do They Outperform Private Ones?" *Christian Science Monitor*, May 10, 2005.

CHAPTER ONE

1   "One out of every seven teachers . . . " and competing nations, see Benjamin Fine, *Our Children Are Cheated: The Crisis in American Education* (New York: H. Holt, 1947), 22; "educational wastelands" . . . see Arthur Bestor, *Educational Wastelands: The Retreat from Learning in Our Public Schools* (Chicago & Urbana, IL: University of Illinois Press, 1953); in New York City, see Albert Lynd, *Quackery in the Public Schools* (Boston, MA: Little, Brown, 1953), 21–22; on college freshman, see Benjamin Fine, "Ignorance in U.S. History Shown by College Freshmen," *New York Times*, April 4, 1943, 1; "Our democracy . . . " see Fine, *Our Children Are Cheated*, xi; see also Bernard Iddings Bell, *Crisis in Education: A Challenge to American Complacency* (New York: Whittlesey House, 1949), and Bestor, *Educational Wastelands*.

2   Quoted in Naomi Klein, *The Shock Doctrine: The Rise of Disaster Capitalism* (New York: Metropolitan Books/Henry Holt, 2007), 174.

3   Matt Miller, "First, Kill All the School Boards," *Atlantic Monthly*, January/ February, 2008.

4   Jay P. Greene, *Education Myths: What Special Interest Groups Want You to Believe about Our Schools—And Why It Isn't So* (Lanham, MD: Rowman & Little-

field Publishers, 2005); M. Lemke, A. Sen, E. Pahlke, L. Partelow, D. Miller, T. Williams, D. Kastberg, and L. Jocelyn, *International Outcomes of Learning in Mathematics Literacy and Problem Solving: PISA 2003 Results from the U.S. Perspective* (Washington, DC: National Center for Education Statistics, 2004); Herbert J.Walberg and Joseph L. Bast, *Education and Capitalism: How Overcoming Our Fear of Markets and Economics Can Improve America's Schools* (Stanford, CA: Hoover Institution Press, 2003).

5   See, e.g., http://www.all4ed.org/whats_at_stake/crisis.html and Greene, *Education Myths.*

6   Walberg and Bast, *Education and Capitalism*, 9.

7   Christopher Jencks and Meredith Phillips, *The Black-White Test Score Gap* (Washington, DC: Brookings Institution Press, 1998); Tommy G. Thompson, Roy E. Barnes, and The Commission on No Child Left Behind, *Beyond NCLB: Fulfilling the Promise to Our Nation's Children* (Washington, DC: Aspen Institute, 2007).

8   David B. Tyack and Larry Cuban, *Tinkering Toward Utopia: A Century of Public School Reform* (Cambridge, MA: Harvard University Press, 1995).

9   Walberg and Bast, *Education and Capitalism*, 4.

10   Steven Brill, *Class Warfare: Inside the Fight to Fix America's Schools* (New York: Simon & Schuster, 2011); Karin Chenoweth, *How It's Being Done* (Cambridge, MA: Harvard Education Press, 2009).

11   John E. Chubb and Terry M. Moe, *Politics, Markets, and America's Schools* (Washington, DC: Brookings Institution, 1990), 3; see also New Commission on the Skills of the American Workforce, *Tough Choices or Tough Times* (Washington, DC: National Center on Education and the Economy, 2006); Paul E. Peterson, "A Report Card on School Choice," *Commentary* 104, no. 4 (1997): 29–34; Paul E. Peterson, "School Choice: A Report Card," in *Learning from School Choice*, ed. P. E. Peterson and B. C. Hassel (Washington, DC: Brookings Institution Press, 1998).

12   See, e.g., Samuel Bowles and Herbert Gintis, *Schooling in Capitalist America: Educational Reform and the Contradictions of Economic Life* (New York: Basic Books, 1976); Michael B. Katz, *Class, Bureaucracy, and Schools: The Illusion of Educational Change in America* (New York: Praeger, 1971).

13   See Herbert J. Walberg, "Market Theory of School Choice," *Education Week*, July 12, 2000, 46–49; Walberg and Bast, *Education and Capitalism.*

14   Paul E. Peterson, "Monopoly and Competition in American Education," *Choice and Control in American Education, Volume 1: The Theory of Choice and Control in Education*, ed. W. H. Clune and J. F. Witte (London, UK: Falmer Press, 1990).

15   David F. Labaree, *Education, Markets, and the Public Good: The Selected Works of David F. Labaree* (New York: Routledge, 2007).

16   Chubb and Moe, *Politics, Markets, and America's Schools*; Labaree, *Education, Markets, and the Public Good.*

17　Milton Friedman, *Public Schools: Make Them Private* (Washington, DC: Cato Institute, 1995); Walberg and Bast, *Education and Capitalism.*

18　Philip E. Tetlock, *Expert Political Judgment: How Good Is It? How Can We Know?* (Princeton, NJ: Princeton University Press, 2005).

19　There are, of course, other aspects of purer markets that are not represented in markets for education, such as price competition and consumers directly shouldering the costs of the goods or services they use. Consequently, some have described education markets as "quasi-markets" to reflect these shortcomings. See Nick Adnett and Peter Davies, "Schooling Reforms in England: From Quasi-Markets to Co-opetition?" *Journal of Education Policy* 18, no. 4 (2003): 393–406; W. Bartlett, "Quasi-Markets and Educational Reforms," in *Quasi-Markets and Social Policy,* ed. J. LeGrand and W. Bartlett (London, UK: Macmillan, 1993); Christopher Lubienski, "Public Schools in Marketized Environments: Shifting Incentives and Unintended Consequences of Competition-Based Educational Reforms," *American Journal of Education* 111, no. 4 (2005): 464–86; Geoffrey Walford, *School Choice and the Quasi-Market, Oxford Studies in Comparative Education* (Oxford, UK: Triangle, 1996); Geoff Whitty, "Creating Quasi-Markets in Education: A Review of Recent Research on Parental Choice and School Autonomy in Three Countries," in *Review of Research in Education,* ed. W. L. Boyd and J. G. Cibulka (Washington, DC: American Educational Research Association, 1997).

20　Christopher Lubienski, "Public Schools in Marketized Environments."

21　David L. Kirp, *Shakespeare, Einstein, and the Bottom Line: The Marketing of Higher Education* (Cambridge, MA: Harvard University Press, 2003).

22　The degree to which markets cause or alleviate poverty—particularly through patterns of development—is, of course, a topic of serious debate. See, for instance, Niall Ferguson, *Civilization: The West and the Rest* (New York: Allen Lane, 2011); Christopher Snowdon, *The Spirit Level Delusion: Fact-Checking the Left's New Theory of Everything* (Ripon and London: Little Dice and Democracy Institute, 2010); Hernando de Soto, *The Mystery of Capital: Why Capitalism Triumphs in the West and Fails Everywhere Else* (New York: Basic Books, 2000); Richard G. Wilkinson and Kate Pickett, *The Spirit Level:Why Greater Equality Makes Societies Stronger* (New York: Bloomsbury Press, 2010).

23　Jeffrey R. Henig, *Spin Cycle: How Research Is Used in Policy Debates—The Case of Charter Schools* (New York: Russell Sage Foundation, 2007); Christopher Lubienski, Peter Weitzel, and Sarah T. Lubienski, "Is There a 'Consensus' on School Choice and Achievement? Advocacy Research and the Emerging Political Economy of Knowledge Production," *Educational Policy* 23, no. 1 (2009): 161–93.

24　Geoffrey Goodman et al., *School Choice Yearbook 2008–09* (Washington, DC: Alliance for School Choice, Advocates for School Choice, 2009).

25   In making this argument, we are borrowing from the logic used by Laba-
      ree, *Education, Markets, and the Public Good.*

26   Charles M. Tiebout, "A Pure Theory of Local Expenditures," *Journal of Politi-
      cal Economy* 64, no. 4 (1956): 416–24.

27   Albert O. Hirschman, *Exit, Voice, and Loyalty: Responses to Decline in Firms,
      Organizations, and States* (Cambridge, MA: Harvard University Press, 1970).

28   Hirschman, *Exit, Voice, and Loyalty,* 122.

29   Since he did not focus specifically on education, Hirschman did not ad-
      dress the role of scientific expertise.

30   Famous examples, such as Summerhill School, tend to focus on internal
      democratic processes, or—like much of the current charter school move-
      ment—giving enhanced voice to the local community of users rather than
      to the wider community of citizens. See Alexander Sutherland Neill, *Sum-
      merhill: A Radical Approach to Child Rearing* (New York: Hart Publishing Co.,
      1960).

31   Caroline M. Hoxby, *School Choice and School Productivity (or Could School
      Choice Be a Tide That Lifts All Boats?)* (Cambridge, MA: National Bureau of
      Economic Research, 2002).

32   E.g., W. Clark Durant, "The Gift of a Child: The Promise of Freedom:
      Creative Approaches to Learning, Teaching, and Schooling," *Freeman* 47,
      no. 6 (1997): 360–64; John Stossel, *Give Me a Break: How I Exposed Hucksters,
      Cheats, and Scam Artists and Became the Scourge of the Liberal Media* (New
      York: HarperCollins, 2004).

33   William J. Bennett, *The De-Valuing of America: The Fight for Our Culture and
      Our Children* (New York: Summit Books, 1992); John Stossel, "Stupid in
      America," *Fox Business News,* November 6, 2011.

CHAPTER TWO

1   John E. Chubb and Terry M. Moe, *Politics, Markets, and America's Schools*
      (Washington, DC: Brookings Institution, 1990); see also Paul E. Peterson,
      "A Report Card on School Choice," *Commentary* 104, no. 4 (1997), 29–34.

2   Diane Ravitch, "US Schools: The Bad News Is Right," *Washington Post,*
      November 17, 1991, C7.

3   Joel I. Klein, Condoleeza Rice, and Council on Foreign Relations, *U.S.
      Education Reform and National Security* (New York: Council on Foreign Rela-
      tions, 2012); New Commission on the Skills of the American Workforce,
      Tough Choices or Tough Times (Washington, DC: National Center on Educa-
      tion and the Economy, 2006).

4   Robert Compton, *2 Million Minutes,* True South Studios, http:\\www
      .2mminutes.com\about.html.

5   Michael E. Porter, "Why America Needs an Economic Strategy," *Business
      Week,* October 30, 2008.

6   Jonah Goldberg, "Do Away with Public Schools," *Los Angeles Times*, June 12, 2007.

7   Milton Friedman, "The Promise of Vouchers," *Wall Street Journal*, December 5, 2005, A20.

8   While some see government as inherently ineffective, other observers see these examples as the results of an intentional strategy to eviscerate the capacity of government to work effectively; see Greg Anrig, *The Conservatives Have No Clothes: Why Right-Wing Ideas Keep Failing* (Hoboken, NJ: John Wiley & Sons, 2007); Thomas Frank, *The Wrecking Crew: How Conservatives Rule* (New York: Metropolitan Books, 2008).

9   See, e.g., Terry M. Moe, "Private Vouchers," in *Private Vouchers*, ed. T. M. Moe (Stanford, CA: Hoover Institution Press, 1995).

10   Daniel Yergin and Joseph Stanislaw, *The Commanding Heights: The Battle between Government and the Marketplace That Is Remaking the Modern World* (New York: Simon & Schuster, 1998).

11   Milton Friedman, "The Role of Government in Education," in *Economics and the Public Interest*, ed. R. A. Solo (New Brunswick, NJ: Rutgers University Press, 1955); Milton Friedman, *Capitalism and Freedom* (Chicago, IL: University of Chicago Press, 1962); Milton Friedman, *Public Schools: Make Them Private* (Washington, DC: Cato Institute, 1995); for a more recent version of this thinking, see Herbert J. Walberg and Joseph L. Bast, *Education and Capitalism: How Overcoming Our Fear of Markets and Economics Can Improve America's Schools* (Stanford, CA: Hoover Institution Press, 2003).

12   E.g., Chester E. Finn Jr., "Lessons Learned," *Education Week*, February, 2008, 27, 28, 36; William G. Howell and Paul E. Peterson, *The Education Gap: Vouchers and Urban Schools* (Washington, DC: Brookings Institution Press, 2002), 15; Matthew Ladner and Matthew J. Brouillette, *The Impact of Limited School Choice on Public School Districts* (Midland, MI: Mackinac Center for Public Policy, 2000).

13   On public choice theory, see James M. Buchanan, "What Is Public Choice Theory?" *Imprimis* 32, no. 3 (2003), 1–7; James M. Buchanan, Robert D. Tollison, and Gordon Tullock, *Toward a Theory of the Rent-Seeking Society* (College Station: Texas A&M University, 1980); George J. Stigler, "The Theory of Economic Regulation," in *The Foundations of Regulatory Economics*, ed. R. B. Ekelund (Cheltenham, UK: E. Elgar, 1998); Gordon E. Tullock, "Public Choice in Practice," in *Collective Decision Making: Applications from Public Choice Theory*, ed. C.S. Russell (Baltimore, MD: Published for Resources for the Future by the Johns Hopkins University Press, 1979).

14   Dennis C. Mueller, *Public Choice* (Cambridge, UK: Cambridge University Press, 1979).

15   On the classic case of overuse use of common resources, or the "tragedy of the commons," see G. Hardin, "The Tragedy of the Commons," *Science*

162 (1968): 1243–48; D. Pearce and J. Warford, *World without End: Economics, Environment, and Sustainable Development* (New York: Oxford University Press, 1993).

16   Ronald Reagan, *First Inaugural Address* (Washington, DC), January 20, 1981.

17   James M. Buchanan, *The Limits of Liberty: Between Anarchy and Leviathan* (Indianapolis, IN: Liberty Fund, 2000); James M. Buchanan and Gordon Tullock, *The Calculus of Consent: Logical Foundations of Constitutional Democracy* (Indianapolis, IN: Liberty Fund, 1999); Thomas Romer and Howard Rosenthal, "Bureaucrats versus Voters: On the Political Economy of Resource Allocation by Direct Democracy," *Quarterly Journal of Economics* 93, no. 4 (1979): 63–587; Joseph P. Kalt and Mark A. Zupan, "Capture and Ideology in Economic Theory of Politics," *American Economic Review* 74, no. 3 (1984): 279–300.

18   E.g., Scott Davies, Linda Quirke, and Janice Aurini, "The New Institutionalism Goes to the Market: The Challenge of Rapid Growth in Private K-12 Education," in *The New Institutionalism in Education*, ed. H. D. Meyer and B. Rowan (Albany, NY: State University of New York Press, 2006); Howell and Peterson, *The Education Gap*; Kevin B. Smith, *The Ideology of Education: The Commonwealth, the Market, and America's Schools* (Albany, NY: State University of New York Press, 2003); Herbert J. Walberg, "Market Theory of School Choice," *Education Week*, July 12, 2000, 46, 49.

19   Gary Becker, "Competition" (Paper, the Heritage Foundation 25th Anniversary Leadership for America Lectures, Chicago, IL, September 12, 1999); Edwin G. West, *Education and the State: A Study in Political Economy* (London, UK: The Institute of Economic Affairs, 1970); Edwin G. West, "The Public Monopoly and the Seeds of Self-Destruction," in *Family Choice in Schooling: Issues and Dilemmas*, ed. M. E. Manley-Casimir (Lexington, MA: Lexington Books, 1982).

20   Paul E. Peterson, "Monopoly and Competition in American Education," in *Choice and Control in American Education, Volume 1: The Theory of Choice and Control in Education*, ed. W. H. Clune and J. F. Witte (London, UK: Falmer Press, 1990); James Tooley, *Disestablishing the School: Debunking Justifications for State Intervention in Education* (Aldershot Hants, UK: Avebury, 1995).

21   Varun Gauri, *School Choice in Chile: Two Decades of Educational Reform* (Pittsburgh, PA: University of Pittsburgh Press, 1998); Naomi Klein, *The Shock Doctrine: The Rise of Disaster Capitalism* (New York: Metropolitan Books/Henry Holt, 2007).

22   William Niskanen, *Bureaucracy and Representative Government* (Chicago, IL: Aldine, 1971); Romer and Rosenthal, "Bureaucrats versus Voters."

23   E.g., Foundation for Excellence in Education, *State Education Chiefs Form "Chiefs for Change": A Unified Voice for Bold Education Reform* (Tallahasee, FL: Foundation for Excellence in Education, 2010).

24   Jeffrey D. Greene, "Cities and Privatization: Examining the Effect of Fiscal Stress, Location, and Wealth in Medium-Sized Cities," *Policy Studies Journal* 24, no. 1 (1996): 135–45; Stigler, "The Theory of Economic Regulation."

25   Thomas E. Lehman, "Government Schooling: The Bureaucratization of the Mind," *Freeman* 48, no. 7 (1997): 266–69; Niskanen, *Bureaucracy and Representative Government.*

26   Friedman, *Public Schools.*

27   E.g., David Harmer, *School Choice: Why You Need It—How You Get It* (Washington, DC: Cato Institute, 1994); West, *Education and the State: A Study in Political Economy*; Edwin G. West, "The Spread of Education before Compulsion: Britain and America in the Nineteenth Century," *Freeman* 46, no. 7 (1996), http://www.fee.org/freeman/96/9607/WEST.html.

28   Chubb and Moe, *Politics, Markets, and America's Schools.*

29   Chubb and Moe, *Politics, Markets, and America's Schools*; Walberg and Bast, *Education and Capitalism.*

30   Milton Friedman, "The Case for Choice," in *Voices on Choice: The Education Reform Debate*, ed K. L. Billingsley (San Francisco, CA: Pacific Research Institute for Public Policy, 1994), 101.

31   Buchanan, Tollison, and Tullock, *Toward a Theory of the Rent-Seeking Society*; Buchanan and Tullock, *The Calculus of Consent: Logical Foundations of Constitutional Democracy.*

32   Mancur Olson, *The Logic of Collective Action: Public Goods and the Theory of Groups*, Harvard Economic Studies, vol. 124 (Cambridge, MA: Harvard University Press, 1965); "free-riders" are people who take advantage of opportunities where the costs of their use of a service are shifted to others—for instance, people who listen to public radio but do not donate funds. In free-rider situations, the misalignment of users and funding can lead to overuse and undersupply, often necessitating state intervention to provide the service or to require funding, either from users or taxpayers.

33   E.g., Terry M. Moe, "Beyond the Free Market: The Structure of School Choice," *Brigham Young University Law Review* 2008, no. 1 (2008): 557–92.

34   See, e.g., David Osborne and Ted Gaebler, *Reinventing Government: How the Entrepreneurial Spirit Is Transforming the Public Sector* (New York: Plume, 1992); Richard H. Thaler and Cass R. Sunstein, *Nudge: Improving Decisions about Health, Wealth, and Happiness* (New Haven, CT: Yale University Press, 2008).

35   Gauri, *School Choice in Chile.*

36   Friedman, *Public Schools*; David Harmer, "Teach Our Children Well/Parents Are United about the Goal: We Want Our Youngsters to Have the Best Education Possible. The Sticking Point Is How./Abolish the Public Schools," *San Francisco Chronicle*, August 27, 2000.

37   Walberg and Bast, *Education and Capitalism.*

38 A. O. Hirschman, *Exit, Voice, and Loyalty: Responses to Decline in Firms, Organizations, and States* (Cambridge, MA: Harvard University Press, 1970); Charles M. Tiebout, "A Pure Theory of Local Expenditures," *Journal of Political Economy* 64, no. 4 (1956): 416–24.

39 Christopher Lubienski, Janelle Scott, and Elizabeth DeBray, "The Rise of Intermediary Organizations in Knowledge Production, Advocacy, and Educational Policy," *Teachers College Record*, http://www.tcrecord.org (ID Number: 16487); see, e.g., Jay P. Greene, Thomas W. Carroll, Andrew J. Coulson, Robert Enlow, E. D. Hirsch, Matthew Ladner, Neal McCluskey, Diane Ravitch, and Sol Stern, "Is School Choice Enough?" *City Journal*, January 24, 2008, http://www.city-journal.org/2008/forum0124.html.

40 E.g., Sam Dillon, "Incentives for Advanced Work Let Pupils and Teachers Cash," *New York Times*, October 2, 2011; Marilyn Geewax, "Does Paying for Good Grades Cheapen Education?" NPR *Weekend Edition Sunday*, August 30, 2009; Donald B. Gratz, *The Peril and Promise of Performance Pay: Making Education Compensation Work* (Lanham, MD: Rowman & Littlefield, 2009); Michael J. Sandel, *What Money Can't Buy: The Moral Limits of Markets* (New York: Farrar, Straus and Giroux, 2012).

41 Chubb and Moe, *Politics, Markets, and America's Schools*; James S. Coleman, "The Design of Schools as Output-Driven Organizations," in *Autonomy and Choice in Context: An International Perspective*, ed. R. Shapira and P. W. Cookson (Oxford, UK: Pergamon, 1997); Walberg and Bast, *Education and Capitalism*.

42 Moe, "Beyond the Free Market."

43 Christopher Lubienski and Peter Weitzel, *The Charter School Experiment: Expectations, Evidence, and Implications* (Cambridge, MA: Harvard Education Press, 2010).

44 David Dodenhoff, *Fixing the Milwaukee Public Schools: The Limits of Parent-Driven Reform* (Thiensville, WI: Wisconsin Policy Research Institute, 2007); Christopher Lubienski and Gregg Garn, "Evidence and Ideology on Consumer Choices in Education Markets: An Alternative Analytical Framework," *Current Issues in Education* 13, no. 3 (2010): 1–31; Virginia R. Weidner, "Information and Information Use for School Choice under a Statewide Voucher Program," *Politics of Education Association Bulletin* 29, no. 2 (2005): 1–5.

45 Vicki Carpenter, "Bloodlines' Aim for Schools Unfair," *New Zealand Herald*, April 19, 2011, http://www.nzherald.co.nz/opinion/news/article.cfm?c_id=466&objectid=10720196; S. Waslander and M. Thrupp, "Choice, Competition and Segregation: An Empirical Analysis of a New Zealand Secondary School Market, 1990–93," *Journal of Education Policy* 10, no. 1 (1995): 1–26; Sue Watson, David Hughes, and Hugh Lauder, "'Success' and 'Failure' in the Education Marketplace: An Example from New Zealand," *Journal of Educational Change* 4, no. 1 (2003): 1–24.

46   Friedman, *Public Schools.*

47   Caroline Minter Hoxby, "School Choice and School Productivity: Could School Choice Be a Tide That Lifts All Boats?" in *The Economics of School Choice,* ed. C.M. Hoxby (Chicago, IL: University of Chicago Press, 2003).

48   Hoxby quoted in John Stossel, "Stupid in America: How Lack of Choice Cheats Our Kids out of a Good Education," *20/20,* January 13, 2006; Marcus A. Winters, "Data Proves Charter Schools Work," *Washington Examiner,* October 28, 2009, http://www.washingtonexaminer.com/opinion /columns/Manhattan-Moment/Data-proves-charter-schools-work -8444859-66412077.html.

49   See, e.g., Steven Brill, *Class Warfare: Inside the Fight to Fix America's Schools* (New York: Simon & Schuster, 2011).

50   E.g., Atila Abdulkadiroglu, John Angrist, Sarah Cohodes, Susan Dynarski, Jon Fullerton, Thomas Kane, and Parag Pathak, *Informing the Debate: Comparing Boston's Charter, Pilot and Traditional Schools* (Boston, MA: Boston Foundation, 2009); Jeanne Allen, *Charter Schools Could Help Revitalize Ohio's Public Schools* (Dayton, OH: Buckeye Institute for Public Policy Solutions, 1996); Buckeye Institute, *15% of Eligible Cleveland Public School Children Apply for Vouchers* (Dayton, OH: Buckeye Institute for Public Policy Solutions, 1996); Center for Education Reform, *Dramatic Parent Choice Growth in 2008* (Washington, DC: Center for Education Reform, 2008); Dan Lips, *The Impact of Tuition Scholarships on Low-Income Families: A Survey of Arizona School Choice Trust Parents* (Phoenix, AZ: Goldwater Institute, 2003); John F. Witte, *The Market Approach to Education: An Analysis of America's First Voucher Program* (Princeton, NJ: Princeton University Press, 2000).

51   Catherine Candisky, "Dann Sues 2 Charter Schools," *Columbus Dispatch,* September 13, 2007.

52   Robert Bifulco and Helen F. Ladd, "School Choice, Racial Segregation, and Test-Score Gaps: Evidence from North Carolina's Charter School Program," *Journal of Policy Analysis and Management* 26, no. 1 (2006): 31–56; Varun Gauri, *School Choice in Chile*; John J. Janssen, "Public School Finance, School Choice, and Equal Educational Opportunity in Texas: The Enduring Importance of Background Conditions," *Review of Litigation* 19, no. 1 (2000): 1–20; Bretten Kleitz, Gregory R. Weiher, Kent Tedin, and Richard Matland, "Choice, Charter Schools, and Household Preferences," *Social Science Quarterly* 81, no. 3 (2000): 846–54; Mark Schneider and Jack Buckley, "What Do Parents Want from Schools? Evidence from the Internet," in *Occasional Paper Series* (New York: National Center for the Study of Privatization in Education, 2001); Kevin B. Smith and Kenneth J. Meier, *The Case against School Choice: Politics, Markets, and Fools* (Armonk, NY: M. E. Sharpe, 1995).

53   William J. Burshaw and Shane Lopez, "The 42nd Annual Phi Delta Kappa/ Gallup Poll of the Public's Attitudes Toward the Public Schools," *Phi Delta Kappan,* September, 2010, 8–26; Willian J. Burshaw and Shane J. Lopez,

"The 29th Annual Phi Delta Kappa/Gallup Poll of the Public's Attitudes Toward the Public Schools," *Phi Delta Kappan*, September, 2011, 9–26; Lowell C. Rose and Alec M. Gallup, "The 37th Annual Phi Delta Kappa/Gallup Poll of the Public's Attitudes Toward the Public Schools," *Phi Delta Kappan*, September, 2005, 41–57; Stossel, "Stupid in America."

54   National Commission on Excellence in Education, *A Nation at Risk: The Imperative for Educational Reform* (Washington, DC: U.S. Government Printing Office, 1983).

55   Andrew J. Rotherham, "Building on Mass. Charter Schools' Success," *Providence Journal*, January 10, 2010.

56   C.F. Kaestle, *Pillars of the Republic: Common Schools and American Society, 1780–1860* (New York: Hill & Wang, 1983); e.g., H. Mann, *Fifth Annual Report of the Board of Education Together with the Fifth Annual Report of the Secretary of the Board* (Boston, MA: Dutton and Wentworth, 1842).

57   David F. Labaree, "Public Goods, Private Goods: The American Struggle over Educational Goals," *American Educational Research Journal* 34, no. 1 (1997): 39–81.

58   David F. Labaree, *How to Succeed in School without Really Learning: The Credentials Race in American Education* (New Haven, CT: Yale University Press, 1997).

59   See National Public Radio, *Candidates Try to Woo Latinos*, July 6, 2008.

60   E.g., Margaret Spellings, "Save D.C.'s Vouchers," *Washington Post*, July 8, 2008, A15.

61   E.g., Roland S. Martin, "Commentary: McCain Right, Obama Wrong on School Vouchers," *CNN.com*, July 16, 2008.

62   For instance, Indiana Governor Daniels declared that "teacher quality has been found to be twenty times more important than any other factor, including poverty, in determining which kids succeed"; Michael Puente, "Indiana Governor Calls for Education Reforms," WBEZ, January 12, 2011.

63   This all assumes a static relationship between the public and various goods, treating education like consumable goods and services such as water or phone service. However, we would point out that the relationship between consumers and the service of education is much more dynamic and complex, with the type of consumers, and the nature of their preferences for education, influencing not only "demand" in a generic sense (as with water or telecommunication), but the quality of the good itself.

64   Indeed, popular culture also elevates the organizational effects of schools as the primary consideration in student success. A steady stream of Hollywood films over the last fifty years—from *Blackboard Jungle* and *To Sir, with Love* to *Lean on Me*, *Stand and Deliver*, and *Dangerous Minds*—promote the notion that students fail because of dysfunctional organizations, while more effort (and discipline) on the part of teachers and administrators

can "make a difference" for students regardless of larger social and systemic forces.

65   Economist Eric Hanushek argues that "All sides of the educational policy debate now accept that the key determinant of school effectiveness is teachers—that effective teachers get good achievement results for all children, while ineffective teachers hurt all students, regardless of background"; Eric A. Hanushek, "There Is No 'War on Teachers,'" *Wall Street Journal*, October 19, 2010, A17.

66   Seyward Darby, "Education Wars," *New Republic*, December 5, 2008.

67   Detroit News, "Editorial: House Cheats Detroit Kids by Protecting Schools," *Detroit News*, December 4, 2008; see Nolan Finley, "Radical Changes Needed for Detroit Public Schools," *Detroit News*, August 10, 2008, 5C.

68   Jay Mathews, "Bad Rap on the Schools," *Wilson Quarterly*, Spring (2008).

69   Chubb and Moe, *Politics, Markets, and America's Schools*, 19.

70   George Will, "Where Paternalism Makes the Grade," *Washington Post*, August 21, 2008, A15.

71   J. Carl, "Parental Choice as National Policy in England and the United States," *Comparative Education Review* 38, no. 3 (1994): 301.

72   Chubb and Moe, *Politics, Markets, and America's Schools*, 14.

73   Chubb and Moe, *Politics, Markets, and America's Schools*, 217 (italics in original).

74   E.g., David F. Labaree, "No Exit: Public Education as an Inescapably Public Good," in *Reconstructing the Common Good in Education: Coping with Intractable American Dilemmas*, ed. L. Cuban and D. Shipps (Stanford, CA: Stanford University Press, 2000).

CHAPTER THREE

1   E.g., William J. Bennett, Willard Fair, Chester E. Finn, Floyd H. Flake, E. D. Hirsch, Will Marshall, and Diane Ravitch, "A Nation Still at Risk," *Policy Review* 90 (1998): 23–29; Robert Compton, *2 Million Minutes*. True South Studios (2008); Davis Guggenheim, *Waiting for Superman*, film, directed by Davis Guggenhiem (2011); Paul E. Peterson, "School Choice: A Report Card," in *Learning from School Choice*, ed. P. E. Peterson and B. C. Hassel (Washington, DC: Brookings Institution Press, 1998); Diane Ravitch and Chester E. Finn, *What Do Our 17-Year-Olds Know? A Report on the First National Assessment of History and Literature* (New York: Harper & Row, 1987); John Stossel, "Stupid in America: How Lack of Choice Cheats Our Kids out of a Good Education," *20/20*, January 13, 2006.

2   D. C. Berliner and B. J. Biddle, *The Manufactured Crisis: Myths, Fraud, and the Attack on America's Public Schools* (New York: Addison-Wesley, 1995);

I. Rotberg, "I Never Promised You First Place," *Phi Delta Kappan*, December, 1990: 296–303.

3   Milton Friedman, "The Role of Government in Education," in *Economics and the Public Interest*, ed. R.A. Solo (New Brunswick, NJ: Rutgers University Press, 1955).

4   See also Milton Friedman, *Capitalism and Freedom* (Chicago, IL: University of Chicago Press, 1962).

5   Virgil C. Blum, *Freedom of Choice in Education* (Glen Rock, NJ: Paulist Press, 1958).

6   Benjamin Justice, "The Blaine Game: Are Public Schools Inherently Anti-Catholic?" *Teachers College Record* 109, no. 9 (2007): 2171–206; Henry M. Levin and Thomas James, *Public Dollars for Private Schools: The Case of Tuition Tax Credits* (Philadelphia, PA: Temple University Press, 1983).

7   Patrick J. McCloskey, and Joseph Claude Harris. "Catholic Education, in Need of Salvation." *New York Times*, January 6, 2013.

8   James S. Coleman, E. Q. Campbell, C. J. Hobson, J. McPartland, A. M. Mood, F. D. Weinfeld, and R. L. York, *Equality of Educational Opportunity* (Washington, DC: U.S. Office of Education, 1966).

9   E.g., Christopher Jencks, Marshall Smith, Henry Acland, Mary Jo Bane, David K. Cohen, Herbert Gintis, Barbara Heyns, and Stephan Michelson, *Inequality: A Reassessment of the Effect of Family and Schooling in America* (New York: Basic Books, 1972); Michael B. Katz, *Class, Bureaucracy, and Schools: The Illusion of Educational Change in America* (New York: Praeger, 1971).

10   Karl L. Alexander, and Aaron M. Pallas, "School Sector and Cognitive Performance: When Is a Little a Little?" *Sociology of Education* 58, no. 2 (1985): 115–28; Anthony S. Bryk, "Disciplined Inquiry or Policy Argument?" *Harvard Educational Review* 51, no. 4 (1981): 497–510; James S. Coleman, Thomas Hoffer, and Sally Kilgore, "Questions and Answers: Our Response," *Harvard Educational Review* 51, no. 4 (1981): 526–45; James S. Coleman, Thomas Hoffer, and Sally Kilgore, *High School Achievement: Public, Catholic, and Private Schools Compared* (New York: Basic Books, 1982), Thomas Hoffer, Andrew M. Greeley, and James S. Coleman, "Achievement Growth in Public and Catholic Schools," *Sociology of Education* 58, no. 2 (1985): 74–97; Richard J. Murnane, "Evidence, Analysis, and Unanswered Questions," *Harvard Educational Review* 51, no. 4 (1981): 483–90.

11   James S. Coleman and Thomas Hoffer, *Public and Private High Schools: The Impact of Communities* (New York: Basic Books, 1987); James S. Coleman, Thomas Hoffer, and Sally Kilgore, *Public and Private Schools: A Report to the National Center for Education Statistics* (Chicago, IL: National Opinion Research Center, 1981).

12   Even as these findings were being published, the results were challenged by a number of scholars who contested the methods, disputed the

implications the authors drew regarding school choice, or found little or no evidence of a private school effect in the data; see, e.g., Alexander and Pallas, "School Sector and Cognitive Performance"; Bryk, "Disciplined Inquiry or Policy Argument?"; James S. Catterall and Henry M. Levin, "Public and Private Schools: Evidence on Tuition Tax Credits," *Sociology of Education* 55, no. 2/3 (1982): 144–51; Arthur S. Goldberger and Glen G. Cain, "The Causal Analysis of Cognitive Outcomes in the Coleman, Hoffer and Kilgore Report," *Sociology of Education* 55, no. 2/3 (1982): 103–22; J. Douglas Willms, "Catholic-School Effects on Academic Achievement: New Evidence from the High School and Beyond Follow-Up Study," *Sociology of Education* 58, no. 2 (1985): 98–114.

13   Anthony S.Bryk, Peter B. Holland, Valerie E. Lee, and Ruben A. Carriedo, *Effective Catholic Schools: An Exploration* (Washington, DC: National Center for Research in Total Catholic Education, National Catholic Educational Association, 1984); Anthony S. Bryk, Valerie E. Lee, and Peter B. Holland, *Catholic Schools and the Common Good* (Cambridge, MA: Harvard University Press, 1993); Valerie E. Lee and Anthony S. Bryk, "A Multilevel Model of the Social Distribution of High School Achievement," *Sociology of Education* 62, no. 3 (1989): 172–92.

14   See also Andrew M. Greeley, *Catholic High Schools and Minority Students* (New Brunswick, NJ: Transaction Books, 1982).

15   John E. Chubb and Terry M. Moe, *Politics, Markets, and America's Schools* (Washington, DC: Brookings Institution, 1990).

16   Anthony S. Bryk and Valerie E. Lee, "Science or Policy Argument? A Rejoinder to Chubb and Moe," in *School Choice: Examining the Evidence*, ed. M. E. Rasell and R. Rothstein (Washington, DC: Economic Policy Institute, 1993); J. Henig, *Rethinking School Choice: Limits of the Market Metaphor* (Princeton, NJ: Princeton University Press, 1994); Kevin B. Smith and Kenneth J. Meier, *The Case against School Choice: Politics, Markets, and Fools* (Armonk, NY: M. E. Sharpe, 1995).

17   The National Education Longitudinal Study is a random sample of 25 eighth-graders in each of a thousand schools, supplemented by several subsequent rounds of data collection on these same students, providing multipoint data for comparison of students who attended public, Catholic, and other private schools. In the first follow-up two years later, researchers noted that Catholic and independent private schools outscored public schools, with a significant difference between types of private schools, with Catholic school gains outpacing those of independent private schools; Leslie A. Scott, Donald A. Rock, Judith M. Pollack, and Steven J. Ingels, *Two Years Later: Cognitive Gains and School Transitions of NELS: 88 Eighth Graders* (Washington, DC: National Center for Education Statistics, 1995).

18   Adam Gamoran, "Student Achievement in Public Magnet, Public Compre-

hensive, and Private City High Schools," *Educational Evaluation and Policy Analysis* 18, no. 1 (1996): 1–18.

19 Jeffrey Grogger and Derek Neal, "Further Evidence on the Effects of Catholic Secondary Schooling," in *Brookings-Wharton Papers on Urban Affairs 2000*, ed. W.G. Gale and J.R. Pack (Washington, DC: Brookings Institution Press, 2000).

20 The term "conservative Christian schools" is a category developed and used by the federal government for classifying schools.

21 Stephen P. Broughman and Nancy L. Swalm, *Characteristics of Private Schools in the United States: Results from the 2003–2004 Private School Universe Survey* (Washington, DC: National Center for Education Statistics, 2006); Grogger and Neal, "Further Evidence on the Effects of Catholic Secondary Schooling."

22 Similarly, tuition tax credit plans—or "neo-vouchers"—provide subsidies for private school attendance—albeit in a different form that foregoes direct public funding; Kevin Welner, *NeoVouchers: The Emergence of Tuition Tax Credits for Private Schooling* (Lanham, MD: Rowman & Littlefield, 2008). However, the research on academic impacts of such programs is virtually nonexistent compared with the more developed research on voucher impacts.

23 Greg Forster, *A Win-Win Solution: The Empirical Evidence on How Vouchers Affect Public Schools* (Indianapolis, IN: Friedman Foundation for Educational Choice, 2009); Friedman Foundation, *The ABCs of School Choice, 2007–2008 Edition* (Indianapolis, IN: Friedman Foundation, 2008); Jay P. Greene, "The Hidden Research Consensus for School Choice," in *Charters, Vouchers, and Public Education*, ed. P. E. Peterson and D. E. Campbell (Washington, DC: Brookings Institution, 2001); Shanea Watkins, "Are Public or Private Schools Doing Better? How the NCES Study Is Being Misinterpreted," *Heritage Foundation Backgrounder*, September 1, 2006, 1–4; Patrick J. Wolf, "School Voucher Programs: What the Research Says about Parental School Choice," *Brigham Young University Law Review* 2008, no. 1 (2006): 415–46.

24 Jay P. Greene, Paul E. Peterson, and J. Du, *The Effectiveness of School Choice in Milwaukee: A Secondary Analysis of Data from the Program's Evaluation* (Occasional Paper 96-3; Cambridge, MA: Program on Education Policy and Governance, Harvard University, 1996); Jay P. Greene, Paul E. Peterson, and Jianstao Du, "School Choice in Milwaukee: A Randomized Experiment," in *Learning from School Choice*, ed. P. E. Peterson and B. C. Hassel (Washington, DC: Brookings Institution Press, 1998).

25 William Howell, Patrick J. Wolf, Paul E. Peterson, and David E. Campbell, *Test-Score Effects of School Vouchers in Dayton, Ohio, New York City, and Washington, D.C.: Evidence from Randomized Field Trials* (Cambridge, MA: Harvard Program on Education Policy and Governance, 2000); Daniel P.

Mayer, Paul E. Peterson, David E. Myers, Christina Clark Tuttle, and William G. Howell, *School Choice in New York City after Three Years: An Evaluation of the School Choice Scholarships Program* (Princeton, NJ: Mathematica Policy Research Inc., 2002); David E. Myers, Paul Peterson, Daniel Mayer, Julia Chou, and William G. Howell, *School Choice in New York City after Two Years: An Evaluation of the School Choice Scholarships Program* (Princeton, NJ: Mathematica Policy Research Inc., 2000).

26   Alan B. Krueger and Pei Zhu, "Another Look at the New York City School Voucher Experiment," *American Behavioral Scientist* 47, no. 5 (2004): 658–98; Alan B. Krueger and Pei Zhu, "Inefficiency, Subsample Selection Bias, and Nonrobustness: A Response to Paul E. Peterson and William G. Howell," *American Behavioral Scientist* 47, no. 5 (2004): 718–28; Alex Molnar, *Educational Vouchers: A Review of the Research* (Milwaukee, WI: Center for Education Research, Analysis, and Innovation, University of Wisconsin-Milwaukee, 1999); John F. Witte, *Reply to Greene, Peterson and Du: "The Effectiveness of School Choice in Milwaukee: A Secondary Analysis of Data from the Program's Evaluation"* (Madison, WI: Department of Political Science and the Robert La Follette Institute of Public Affairs, University of Wisconsin-Madison, 1996).

27   Christopher Lubienski, "Innovation in Education Markets: Theory and Evidence on the Impact of Competition and Choice in Charter Schools," *American Educational Research Journal* 40, no. 2 (2003): 395–443; Christopher Lubienski and Peter Weitzel, "Two Decades of Charter Schools: Shifting Expectations, Partners, and Policies," in *The Charter School Experiment: Expectations, Evidence, and Implications.*, ed. C. Lubienski and P. Weitzel (Cambridge, MA: Harvard Education Press, 2010).

28   Jonah Goldberg, "Do Away with Public Schools," *Los Angeles Times*, June 12, 2007.

29   Eric P. Bettinger, "The Effect of Charter Schools on Charter Students and Public Schools," *Economics of Education Review* 24, no. 2 (2005): 133–47; Robert Bifulco and Helen F. Ladd, "The Impacts of Charter Schools on Student Achievement: Evidence from North Carolina," *Education Finance and Policy* 1, no. 1 (2006): 50–90; Robert Bifulco and Helen F. Ladd, "School Choice, Racial Segregation, and Test-Score Gaps: Evidence from North Carolina's Charter School Program," *Journal of Policy Analysis and Management* 26, no. 1 (2006): 31–56; Richard Buddin and Ronald Zimmer, "Student Achievement in Charter Schools: A Complex Picture," *Journal of Policy Analysis and Management* 24, no. 2 (2005): 351–71; Caroline M. Hoxby and Sonali Muraka, *New York City's Charter Schools Overall Report* (Cambridge, MA: New York City Charter Schools Evaluation Project, 2007); Margaret E. Raymond and Center for Research on Education Outcomes, *Multiple Choice: Charter School Performance in 16 States* (Stanford, CA: Stanford University, 2009).

30   Caroline M. Hoxby, *Achievement in Charter School and Regular Public Schools in the United States: Understanding the Differences* (Cambridge, MA: Harvard University and National Bureau of Economic Research, 2004); Caroline M. Hoxby, *A Straightforward Comparison of Charter Schools and Regular Public Schools in the United States* (Cambridge, MA: Department of Economics, Harvard University, 2004); Caroline M. Hoxby, Sonali Mararka, and Jenny Kang, *How New York City's Charter Schools Affect Achievement* (Stanford, CA: The New York City Charter Schools Evaluation Project, Stanford University, 2009); Caroline M.Hoxby and Jonah Rockoff, *The Impact of Charter Schools on Student Achievement: A Study of Students Who Attend Schools Chartered by the Chicago Charter School Foundation* (Cambridge, MA: Department of Economics, Harvard University, 2004).

31   Bruce D. Baker and Richard Ferris. *Adding up the Spending: Fiscal Disparities and Philanthropy among New York City Charter Schools.* Boulder: National Education Policy Center, 2011; Sean F. Reardon, *Review of "How New York City's Charter Schools Affect Achievement."* Boulder, CO: National Education Policy Center, 2009; Joydeep Roy and Lawrence Mishel. *Advantage None: Re-Examining Hoxby's Finding of Charter School Benefits* (Washington, DC: Economic Policy Institute, 2005).

32   E.g., Arne Duncan, "Keynote Address by U.S. Secretary of Education Arne Duncan" (presentation, National Charter Schools Conference: Leading Change in Public Education, Washington, DC, June 22, 2009).

33   Bryk, Lee, and Holland, *Catholic Schools and the Common Good*; Chubb and Moe, *Politics, Markets, and America's Schools.*

34   Greeley, *Catholic High Schools and Minority Students.*

35   Greg Forster, *Promising Start: An Empirical Analysis of How EdChoice Vouchers Affect Ohio Public Schools* (Indianapolis, IN: Friedman Foundation for Educational Choice, 2008); Jay P. Greene, "A Survey of Results from Voucher Experiments: Where We Are and What We Know," in *Can the Market Save Our Schools?*, ed. C. R. Hepburn (Vancouver, BC: The Fraser Institute, 2001); Jay P. Greene, "An Unfair Grade for Vouchers," *Wall Street Journal Online,* May 16, 2003, http://online.wsj.com/article_email/0%2C%2CSB10530 4733981768800%2C00.html; Patrick J. Wolf, "Research Findings on School Voucher Programs: Applications to Utah," in *Educational Choice: Emerging Legal and Policy Issues* (Provo, UT: Brigham Young University, 2007).

36   Jay P. Greene, Thomas W. Carroll, Andrew J. Coulson, Robert Enlow, E. D. Hirsch, Matthew Ladner, Neal McCluskey, Diane Ravitch, and Sol Stern, "Is School Choice Enough?" *City Journal,* January 24, 2008, http://www .city-journal.org/2008/forum0124.html; Bryan C. Hassel and Kathleen Kennedy Manzo, "Charter School Achievement: What We Know," *Education Week,* August 15, 2007; Herbert J. Walberg, *School Choice: The Findings* (Washington, DC: Cato Institute, 2007).

37   Hoxby, Mararka, and Kang, *How New York City's Charter Schools Affect Achievement*; Howell et al., *Test-Score Effects of School Vouchers in Dayton, Ohio, New York City, and Washington, D.C.*

38   E.g., Watkins, "Are Public or Private Schools Doing Better?"

39   In fact, "motivation may sometimes actually be a better predictor of academic achievement than IQ is"; Richard E. Nisbett, *Intelligence and How to Get It: Why Schools and Cultures Count* (New York: W.W. Norton & Co., 2009), 16.

40   E.g., William Carbonaro, "Public-Private Differences in Achievement among Kindergarten Students: Differences in Learning Opportunities and Student Outcomes," *American Journal of Education* 113, no. 1 (2006): 31–65; Sean F. Reardon, Jacob E. Cheadle, and Joseph P. Robinson, "The Effects of Catholic School Attendance on Reading and Math Achievement in Kindergarten through Fifth Grade," *Journal of Research on Educational Effectiveness* 2, no. 1 (2009): 45–87.

41   E.g., Deborah Kenny, "Opinion: Why Charter Schools Work," *Wall Street Journal*, June 24, 2012.

CHAPTER FOUR

1   John E. Chubb and Terry M. Moe, *Politics, Markets, and America's Schools* (Washington, DC: Brookings Institution, 1990).

2   Diane Ravitch, "Every State Left Behind," *New York Times*, November 7, 2005.

3   Anthony S. Bryk, Valerie E. Lee, and Peter B. Holland, *Catholic Schools and the Common Good* (Cambridge, MA: Harvard University Press, 1993); Stephen P. Heyneman, "Student Background and Student Achievement: What Is the Right Question?" *American Journal of Education* 112, no. 1 (2005): 1–9; Paul E. Peterson, "School Choice: A Report Card," in *Learning from School Choice*, ed. P. E. Peterson and B. C. Hassel (Washington, DC: Brookings Institution Press, 1998).

4   For instance, Grogger and Neal report that missing data on dropouts represented a substantial problem for researchers using the National Education Longitudinal Study of 1988 data; Jeffrey Grogger and Derek Neal, "Further Evidence on the Effects of Catholic Secondary Schooling," in *Brookings-Wharton Papers on Urban Affairs 2000*, ed. W. G. Gale and J. R. Pack (Washington, DC: Brookings Institution Press, 2000). Missing data issues also confounded efforts to evaluate the New York City voucher program; see Alan B. Krueger and Pei Zhu. "Another Look at the New York City School Voucher Experiment," *American Behavioral Scientist* 47, no. 5 (2004): 658–98; and, for examples, William G. Howell and Paul E. Peterson, *The Education Gap: Vouchers and Urban Schools* (Washington, DC: Brookings Institution Press, 2002); Daniel P. Mayer Paul E. Peterson,

David E. Myers, Christina Clark Tuttle, and William G. Howell, "School Choice in New York City after Three Years: An Evaluation of the School Choice Scholarships Program" (Princeton, NJ: Mathematica Policy Research Inc., 2002).

5   Sarah Theule Lubienski, "Examining Instruction, Achievement, and Equity with NAEP Mathematics Data," *Educational Policy Analysis Archives* 14, no. 14 (2006), http://epaa.asu.edu/epaa/v14n14/; Sarah Theule Lubienski, Eric Camburn, and Mack C. Shelley, *Reform-Oriented Mathematics Instruction, Achievement, and Equity: Examinations of Race and SES in 2000 Main NAEP Data* (Washington, DC: National Center for Education Statistics, 2004).

6   "Conservative Christian" is the label used in NAEP.

7   Stephen W. Raudenbush and Anthony S. Bryk, *Hierarchical Linear Models: Applications and Data Analysis Methods* (Thousand Oaks, CA: Sage Publications, 2002).

8   Descriptive comparisons of school differences are not the primary focus of this analysis, and therefore statistical differences among the many measures in Tables 4.1 and 4.2 are not discussed here. Those interested in a more detailed descriptive comparison of NAEP data by private school type should consult a report published by the National Center for Education Statistics, Stephen P. Broughman and Kathleen W. Pugh, *Characteristics of Private Schools in the United States: Results from the 2001–2002 Private School Universe Survey* (Washington, DC: National Center for Education Statistics, U.S. Department of Education, 2004).

9   We use NAEP's terminology for consistency with the data set.

10   Richard Arnot and J. Rowse, "Peer Group Effects and Educational Attainment," *Journal of Public Economics* 32, no. 3 (1987): 287–305; Eric A. Hanushek, Jacob M. Markman, John F. Kain, and Steven G. Rivkin, "Does Peer Ability Affect Student Achievement?" *Journal of Applied Econometrics* 18, no. 5 (2003): 527–44; Caroline M. Hoxby, *Peer Effects in the Classroom: Learning from Gender and Race Variation* (Cambridge, MA: National Bureau of Economic Research, 2000); Henry M. Levin, "Educational Vouchers: Effectiveness, Choice, and Costs," *Journal of Policy Analysis and Management* 17, no. 3 (1998): 373–92; Martin Thrupp, *Schools Making a Difference—Let's Be Realistic! School Mix, School Effectiveness, and the Social Limits of Reform* (Philadelphia, PA: Open University Press, 1999).

11   Despite the small changes in the coefficients and variance components, a multivariate hypothesis test revealed that the addition of location was significant ($p < .001$), indicating that Model 5 best fit the data when compared with our prior models.

12   One concern to consider is the effect of multicollinearity among the demographic predictors used in this study. Some demographic variables included were indeed highly correlated, such as home resources and lunch eligibility at both the student and school levels. If the main purpose of

this study was to disaggregate the effects of particular demographic factors on student achievement, then these correlations would be a concern. However, given that the focus was to simply control for demographic differences using a block of variables in order to better examine the relationship between school type and achievement, multicollinearity is not a substantial problem. However, readers are cautioned that the importance of some individual demographic variables would likely appear greater if closely related variables were omitted from this analysis.

13   As in grade 4, the addition of location was significant ($p < .001$), making Model 5 the best-fitting model.

14   Interestingly, market advocates re-analyzing the data came to the same conclusions regarding charter schools; see Paul E. Peterson and Elena Llaude, *On the Public-Private School Achievement Debate* (Cambridge, MA: Program on Education Policy and Governance, Harvard University, 2006).

15   See, for example, Joseph L. Bast and Herbert J. Walberg, "Can Parents Choose the Best Schools for Their Children?" *Economics of Education Review* 23, no. 4 (2004): 431–40.

16   Greg Forster, "'F' is for Failure," *National Review Online*, May 12, 2005.

17   John Stossel, "Smearing Education Choice," *Townhall.com*, July 26, 2006.

CHAPTER FIVE

1   Greg Forster, "'F' is for Failure," *National Review Online*, May 12, 2005.

2   Stephen P. Broughman and Nancy L. Swalm, *Characteristics of Private Schools in the United States: Results from the 2003–2004 Private School Universe Survey* (Washington, DC: National Center for Education Statistics, 2006).

3   Paul E. Peterson, "School Choice: A Report Card," in *Learning from School Choice*, ed. P. E. Peterson and B. C. Hassel (Washington, DC: Brookings Institution Press, 1998); see also Stephen P. Heyneman, "Student Background and Student Achievement: What Is the Right Question?" *American Journal of Education* 112, no. 1 (2005): 1–9.

4   ECLS-K assessments address what are known as "floor" and "ceiling" effects and are designed so that students, regardless of their initial achievement, have opportunities to make substantial gains on the assessment; Judith M. Pollack, Michelle J. Najarian, Donald A. Rock, and Sally Atkins-Burnett, *Early Childhood Longitudinal Study, Kindergarten Class of 1998–99 (ECLS-K), Psychometric Report for the Fifth Grade* (Washington, DC: National Center for Education Statistics, 2005); Karen Tourangeau, Christine Nord, Thanh Lê, Judith M. Pollack, and Sally Atkins-Burnett, *Early Childhood Longitudinal Study, Kindergarten Class of 1998–99 (ECLS-K), Combined User's Manual for the ECLS-K Fifth-Grade Data Files and Electronic Codebooks* (Washington, DC: National Center for Education Statistics, 2006).

5   To account for the fact that some students are fluent in English but speak another language at home, we excluded students from this category if they scored in the top 10% of the English language test.

6   A student was defined as having a disability if a parent reported on at least one survey/interview that his/her child "obtained a diagnosis of a problem from a professional" (with possibilities including a learning problem, activity problem, behavior problem, speech problem, hearing problem, or vision problem) or that the child received therapy services or participated in a program for children with disabilities. Although this definition might be broader than some might like, this parent-reported variable alleviates concerns that critics previously raised about the Individualized Education Program (IEP) variable in NAEP unfairly biasing results in favor of public schools (given that only public schools are required to have IEPs for their student with disabilities).

7   Forster, "'F' is for Failure."

8   We also ran this kindergarten analysis with the full ECLS-K sample and confirmed that the results are similar to what we obtained with the focal K–5 grade sample (containing students who remained in a single school sector). Specifically, all Catholic kindergarteners scored .8 points higher than comparable public school students, while all "other private" school students scored a statistically significant 1.2 points higher than their public school peers.

9   The ECLS-K models run for these Chapter 5 HLM analyses are similar to NAEP models 1–3 shown in Table A9, with the addition of the grade 1 baseline achievement measures in the ECLS-K models. This method is better than having students' K–5 gains serve as the outcome variable because it addresses the concern that students with higher initial achievement might be more or less likely to make gains on the ECLS-K assessment.

10   Another limitation of this ECLS-K study when compared with the NAEP study is that the smaller sample sizes force us to consider "other private" schools as one category, while with NAEP we were able to distinguish among Lutheran, conservative Christian, and the remaining private schools. Our NAEP results indicated that this is a very diverse group of schools, with Lutheran schools performing on par with public schools and conservative Christian schools performing lower than all other school types. Hence it is worth cautioning readers that there is much variation within the ECLS-K "other private schools" category and that the term refers to a modified set of schools compared with the meaning in the NAEP chapter.

11   Bruce Baker, "Private Schooling in the U.S.: Expenditures, Supply, and Policy Implications" (Boulder, CO: National Education Policy Center, 2009).

12   Henry Braun, "Are Private Schools Better Than Public Schools?" *Principal*, March/April, 2007, 22–25; Henry Braun, Frank Jenkins, and Wendy

Grigg, *A Closer Look at Charter Schools Using Hierarchical Linear Modeling* (Washington, DC: National Center for Education Statistics, 2006); Henry Braun, Frank Jenkins, and Wendy Grigg, *Comparing Private Schools and Public Schools Using Hierarchical Linear Modeling* (Washington, DC: National Center for Education Statistics, 2006).

13   Paul E. Peterson and Elena Llaudet, *On the Public-Private School Achievement Debate* (Cambridge, MA: Program on Education Policy and Governance, Harvard University, 2006); see also, Christopher Lubienski and Sarah Theule Lubienski, *Report on "On the Public-Private School Achievement Debate" from the Program on Education Policy and Governance at Harvard University* (Tempe, AZ: Educational Policy Research Unit, Education Policy Studies Laboratory, Arizona State University, 2006).

14   Christopher Lubienski, Sarah Theule Lubienski, and Corinna Crane, "What Do We Know about School Effectiveness? Academic Gains in Public and Private Schools," *Phi Delta Kappan*, May 2008: 689–95.

15   Sean F. Reardon, Jacob E. Cheadle, and Joseph P. Robinson, "The Effect of Catholic Schooling on Math and Reading Development in Kindergarten through Fifth Grade" (paper, annual meeting of the Society for Research on Educational Effectiveness, Arlington, VA, 2008).

16   William Carbonaro, "Public-Private Differences in Achievement among Kindergarten Students: Differences in Learning Opportunities and Student Outcomes," *American Journal of Education* 113, no. 1 (2006): 31–65.

CHAPTER SIX

1   John E. Chubb and Terry M. Moe, *Politics, Markets, and America's Schools* (Washington, DC: Brookings Institution, 1990).

2   Louis Chandler, *Traditional Schools, Progressive Schools: Do Parents Have a Choice?* (Washington, DC: Thomas B. Fordham Foundation, 1999).

3   Luis Benveniste, Martin Carnoy, and Richard Rothstein, *All Else Equal: Are Public and Private Schools Different?* (New York: RoutledgeFalmer, 2003).

4   Benveniste, Carnoy, and Rothstein, *All Else Equal*; James S. Coleman, "Equal Schools or Equal Students?" *Public Interest* 4 (1966): 70–75; Martin Thrupp, *Schools Making a Difference—Let's Be Realistic! School Mix, School Effectiveness, and the Social Limits of Reform* (Philadelphia, PA: Open University Press, 1999); see, e.g., Steven Brill, *Class Warfare: Inside the Fight to Fix America's Schools* (New York: Simon & Schuster, 2011); Arne Duncan, Keynote Address (National Charter Schools Conference: Leading Change in Public Education, Washington, DC, June 22, 2009).

5   E.g., Roland G. Fryer, *Injecting Successful Charter School Strategies into Traditional Public Schools: Early Results from an Experiment in Houston* (Cambridge, MA: EdLabs, Harvard University, 2012); Jay P. Greene, "Are Charter Schools Models of Reform for Traditional Public Schools?" in *Jay P. Greene's Blog*

(Fayetteville, Arkansas, 2012); Tom Vander Ark, "The Role of the Private Sector in Education," *Huffington Post*, September 4, 2009.

6   E.g., Anthony S. Bryk, Valerie E. Lee, and Peter B. Holland, *Catholic Schools and the Common Good* (Cambridge, MA: Harvard University Press, 1993); Andrew M. Greeley, *Catholic High Schools and Minority Students* (New Brunswick, NJ: Transaction Publishers, 2002).

7   Sean F. Reardon, Jacob E. Cheadle, and Joseph P. Robinson, "The Effects of Catholic School Attendance on Reading and Math Achievement in Kindergarten through Fifth Grade," *Journal of Research on Educational Effectiveness* 2, no. 1 (2009): 45–87.

8   In the initial analyses, we included a "charter/magnet/schools of choice" variable, but it was not significant so we omitted it in later analyses. With only fifty-nine charter schools in the full ECLS-K third grade sample, we did not examine charter schools separately.

9   E.g., James Bryant Conant, *The American High School Today*, (New York: McGraw-Hill, 1959).

10   E.g., Bill and Melinda Gates Foundation, *Annual Report: Responding to the Needs of Others* (Seattle, WA: Bill and Melinda Gates Foundation, 2003); Barbara Miner, "The Gates Foundation and Small Schools," *Rethinking Schools* 19, no. 4 (2005), http://www.rethinkingschools.org/ProdDetails .asp?ID=RTSVOL19N4&d=etoc; Thomas Toch, *High Schools on a Human Scale: How Small Schools Can Transform American Education* (Boston, MA: Beacon Press, 2003); Kathleen Vail, "Remaking High School," *American School Board Journal*, November, 2004, http://www.asbj.com/MainMenu Category/Archive/2004/November.

11   G.E. Conway, "Small Scale and School Culture: The Experience of Private Schools," in *ERIC Digest* (Charleston, WV: ERIC: Clearinghouse on Rural Education and Small Schools, 1994); Linda Darling-Hammond, "Teacher Quality and Student Achievement: A Review of State Policy Evidence," *Education Policy Analysis Archives* 8, no. 1 (2000); Jeremy D. Finn and K.E. Voelkl, "School Characteristics Related to Student Engagement," *Journal of Negro Education* 62, no. 3 (1993): 249–68; Douglas D. Ready and Valerie E. Lee, "Is Small Really Better? Testing Some Assumptions of School Size," in *Brookings Papers on Education Policy 2006/2007* (Washington, DC: Brookings Institution, 2006); Barbara Schneider, Adam E. Wyse, and Vanessa Keesler, "Optimal Context Size in Elementary Schools: Disentangling the Effects of Class Size and School Size," in *Brookings Papers on Education Policy*, ed. T. Loveless and F. M. Hess (Washington, DC: Brookings Institute, 2007).

12   Finn and Voelkl, "School Characteristics Related to Student Engagement."

13   For debates on such issues see, e.g., Craig B. Howley and Aimee A. Howley, "School Size and the Influence of Socioeconomic Status on Student Achievement: Confronting the Threat of Size Bias in National Data Sets," *Education Policy Analysis Archives* 12, no. 52 (2004), http://epaa.asu.edu

/ojs/article/view/207; Valerie E. Lee, "Effects of High-School Size on Student Outcomes: Response to Howley and Howley," *Education Policy Analysis Archives* 12, no. 53 (2004).

14   As discussed in more detail in Appendix B, adding school size and location variables to Model 5 in Table B2 caused the Catholic school estimate to decrease from −2.08 to −2.18. The fact that this coefficient decreased slightly reveals that the variables added pose (on average) a slight "advantage" for Catholic schools that has now been accounted for in the model. In interpreting the size of changes in the Catholic school coefficients, one method is to compare changes to the Catholic school-level standard deviation of mathematics test score gains, which is 3.8. In this case, a change of .1 represents an effect size of .1/3.8, or an effect of roughly .03 standard deviations. This is a particularly small change given the relatively small number of variables entered into the model thus far. It becomes increasingly difficult in later models to produce substantial changes in the Catholic school coefficient.

15   Jeremy D. Finn and Charles M. Achilles, "Tennessee's Class Size Study: Findings, Implications, Misconceptions," *Educational Evaluation and Policy Analysis* 21, no. 2 (1999): 97–110; Frederick Mosteller, "The Tennessee Study of Class Size in the Early School Grades," *Future of Children* 5, no. 2 (1996): 113–27; Frederick Mosteller, R. Light, and J. Sachs, "Sustained Inquiry in Education: Lessons from Skill Grouping and Class Size," *Harvard Educational Review* 66, no. 4 (1996): 797–842.

16   Eric A. Hanushek, "Some Findings from an Independent Investigation of the Tennessee STAR Experiment and from Other Investigations of Class Size Effects," *Educational Evaluation and Policy Analysis* 21, no. 2 (1999): 143–64; Caroline M. Hoxby, "The Effects of Class Size on Student Achievement: New Evidence from Population Variation," *Quarterly Journal of Economics* 115, no. 4 (2000): 1239–285; Alan B. Krueger and Diane M. Whitmore, "The Effect of Attending a Small Class in the Early Grades on College-Test Taking and Middle School Test Results: Evidence from Project STAR," *Economic Journal* 111, no. 468 (2001): 1–17; Alex Molnar, Philip Smith, John Zahorik, Amanda Palmer, Anke Halbach, and Karen Ehrle, "Evaluating the SAGE Program: A Pilot Program in Targeted Pupil-Teacher Reduction in Wisconsin," *Educational Evaluation and Policy Analysis* 21, no. 2 (1999): 165–78; Harold Wenglinsky, "How Money Matters: The Effect of School District Spending on Academic Achievement," *Sociology of Education* 70, no. 3 (1997): 221–37.

17   Bryk, Lee, and Holland, *Catholic Schools and the Common Good.*

18   Albert Bandura, "Perceived Self-Efficacy in Cognitive Development and Functioning," *Educational Psychologist* 28, no. 2 (1993): 117–48; Anthony S. Bryk and Barbara L. Schneider, *Trust in Schools: A Core Resource for Improvement, The Rose Series in Sociology* (New York: Russell Sage Foundation,

2002); R.G. Goddard, Wayne K. Hoy, and Anita Woolfolk-Hoy, "Collective Teacher Efficacy: Its Meaning, Measure, and Impact on Student Achievement," *American Educational Research Journal* 37, no. 2 (2000): 479–508.

19   Bryk and Schneider, *Trust in Schools.*

20   R.G. Goddard, M. Tschannen-Moran, and Wayne K. Hoy, "A Multilevel Examination of the Distribution and Effects of Teacher Trust in Urban Elementary Schools," *Elementary School Journal* 102 (2001): 3–17; Wayne K. Hoy, "Faculty Trust: A Key to Student Achievement," *Journal of School Public Relations* 23, no. 2 (2002): 88–103; Wayne K. Hoy, John C. Tarter, and Anita Woolfolk-Hoy, "Academic Optimism of Schools: A Force for Student Achievement," *American Educational Research Journal* 43, no. 3 (2006): 425–46.

21   A.T. Henderson and K.L. Mapp, *A New Wave of Evidence: The Impact of School, Family, and Community Connections on Student Achievement* (Austin, TX: National Center for Family and Community Connections with Schools, 2002).

22   James P. Comer, "The Reward of Parent Participation," *Educational Leadership* 62, no. 6 (2005): 38–42; James P. Comer, Norris M. Haynes, Edward T. Joyner, and Michael Ben-Avie, *Rallying the Whole Village: The Comer Process for Reforming Education* (New York: Teachers College Press, 1996).

23   C. Muller, "Parent Involvement in Education and School Sector" (paper, annual conference of the American Educational Research Association, Atlanta, GA, 1993).

24   J. Lee and N. K. Bowen, "Parent Involvement, Cultural Capital, and the Achievement Gap among Elementary School Children," *American Educational Research Journal* 43, no. 2 (2006): 193–218.

25   M.N. Alt and K. Peter, *Private Schools: A Brief Portrait* (Washington, DC: National Center for Education Statistics, 2002); Karen M. Anderson and Michael A. Resnick, *Careful Comparisons: Public and Private Schools in America* (Alexandria, VA: National School Boards Association, 1997); S. P. Choy, "Public and Private Schools: How Do They Differ?" in *Findings from "The Condition of Education, 1997"* (Berkeley, CA: MPR Associates, 1997); Frank R. Kemerer, Valerie Martinez, and Kenneth Godwin, *Comparing Public and Private Schools: Teacher Survey Results* (Denton, TX: University of North Texas, Center for the Study of Education Reform, 1996).

26   Bryk, Lee, and Holland, *Catholic Schools and the Common Good.*

27   Choy, "Public and Private Schools"; Frank R. Kemerer, Valerie Martinez, Kenneth Godwin, and C. Ausbrooks, *Comparing Public and Private Schools: Student Survey Results* (Denton, TX: University of North Texas, Center for the Study of Education Reform, 1997; Muller, "Parent Involvement in Education and School Sector."

28   Muller, "Parent Involvement in Education and School Sector."

29   Choy, "Public and Private Schools."

30 Kemerer, Martinez, Godwin, and Ausbrooks, *Comparing Public and Private Schools.*

31 Richard Rothstein, Martin Carnoy, and Luis Benveniste, *Can Public Schools Learn from Private Schools?* (Washington, DC: Economic Policy Institute and the Aspen Institute, 1999).

32 James W. Fraser, "Time to Cut the Link between Teacher Preparation and Certification?" *Education Week,* January 31, 2001, 56.

33 E.g., Kate Walsh, *Teacher Certification Reconsidered: Stumbling for Quality* (Baltimore, MD: Abell Foundation, 2001).

34 Frederick M. Hess, *Tough Love for Schools: Essays on Competition, Accountability, and Excellence* (Washington, DC: AEI Press, 2006); Terry M. Moe, "A Highly Qualified Teacher in Every Classroom," in *Within Our Reach: How America Can Educate Every Child,* ed. J. E. Chubb (Lanham, MD: Rowman & Littlefield, 2005).

35 Darling-Hammond, "Teacher Quality and Student Achievement: A Review of State Policy Evidence."

36 Dan D. Goldhaber and Dominic J. Brewer, "Does Teacher Certification Matter? High School Teacher Certification Status and Student Achievement," *Educational Evaluation and Policy Analysis* 22, no. 2 (2000): 129–45; see also Linda Darling-Hammond, Barnett Berry, and Amy Thoreson, "Does Teacher Certification Matter? Evaluating the Evidence," *Educational Evaluation and Policy Analysis* 23, no. 1 (2001): 57–77.

37 E.g., Eric A. Hanushek, "A More Complete Picture of School Resource Policies," *Review of Educational Research* 66, no. 3 (1996): 397–409.

38 R. Greenwald, L. Hedges, and R. Laine, "The Effect of School Resources on School Achievement," *Review of Educational Research* 66 (1996): 361–96.

39 S. Loucks-Horsley and C. Matsumoto, "Research on Professional Development for Teachers of Mathematics and Science: The State of the Scene," *School Science and Mathematics* 99, no. 5 (1999): 258–71.

40 Thomas P. Carpenter, Elizabeth Fennema, Penelope Peterson, Chi-Pang Chiang, and Megan Loef, "Using Knowledge of Children's Mathematics Thinking in Classroom Teaching: An Experimental Study," *American Educational Research Journal* 26 (1989): 499–531; David K. Cohen and Heather C. Hill, *Learning Policy: When State Education Reform Works* (New Haven, CT: Yale University Press, 2001); Heather C. Hill, Brian Rowan, and Deborah Lowenberg Ball, "Effects of Teachers' Mathematical Knowledge for Teaching on Student Achievement," *American Educational Research Journal* 42, no. 2 (2005): 371–406.

41 National Council of Teachers of Mathematics, *Curriculum and Evaluation Standards for School Mathematics* (Reston, VA: NCTM, 1989); National Council of Teachers of Mathematics, *Assessment Standards for School Mathematics* (Reston, VA: NCTM, 1995); National Council of Teachers of Mathematics,

Principles and Standards for School Mathematics (Reston, VA: NCTM, 2000);
National Council of Teachers of Mathematics, and Commission on Teach-
ing Standards for School Mathematics, *Professional Standards for Teaching
Mathematics* (Reston, VA: The Council, 1991).

42   E.g., R. Reys, B. Reys, R. Lapan, G. Holliday, and D. Wasman, "Assessing
the Impact of Standards-Based Middle Grades Mathematics Textbooks
on Student Achievement," *Journal for Research in Mathematics Education*
34, no. 1 (2003): 74–95; J. E. Riordan and P. E. Noyce, "The Impact of Two
Standards-Based Mathematics Curricula on Student Achievement in Massachusetts," *Journal for Research in Mathematics Education* 32, no. 4 (2001):
368–98; Alan H. Schoenfeld, "Making Mathematics Work for All Children:
Issues of Standards, Testing, and Equity," *Educational Researcher* 31, no. 1
(2002): 13–25; Sharon L. Senk and Denisse R. Thompson, *Standards-Based
School Mathematics Curricula: What Are They? What Do Students Learn? Studies in Mathematical Thinking and Learning* (Mahwah, N.J.: Lawrence Erlbaum
Associates, 2003).

43   Tom Loveless and P. Diperna, "How Well Are American Students Learning? Focus on Math Achievement," in *Brown Center Report* (Washington,
DC: Brookings Institution, 2000).

44   Sarah T. Lubienski, "Examining Instruction, Achievement, and Equity
with NAEP Mathematics Data," *Educational Policy Analysis Archives* 14,
no. 14, http://epaa.asu.edu/epaa/v14n14/; Stephen Raudenbush, R. Fotiu,
and Y. F. Cheong, "Inequality of Access to Educational Opportunity: A National Report Card for Eighth Grade Math," *Educational Evaluation & Policy
Analysis* 20 (1998): 253–68.

45   Sarah T. Lubienski, "Instruction, Achievement and Equity: Intersections
of Race and SES in NAEP data" (paper, American Educational Research
Association, San Diego, CA, 2004).

46   Chandler, *Traditional Schools, Progressive Schools*.

47   Katerina Bodovski and George Farkas, "Do Instructional Practices Contribute to Inequality in Achievement? The Case of Mathematics Instruction in Kindergarten," *Journal of Early Childhood Research* 5, no. 3 (2007):
301–22; C. Guarino, Laura Hamilton, J. R. Lockwood, and A. Rathburn,
*Teacher Qualifications, Teaching Practices, and Reading and Mathematics Gains
of Kindergartners* (Washington, DC: National Center for Education Statistics,
2006); E. G. Hausken and A. Rathbun, "Mathematics Instruction in Kindergarten: Classroom Practices and Outcomes" (paper, annual conference of
the American Educational Research Association, San Diego, CA, 2004).

48   Bryk, Lee, and Holland, *Catholic Schools and the Common Good*, 309.

49   Alt and Peter, *Private Schools*.

50   Similar teacher-reported data were not available in the NAEP 2003 data
set for grade 8.

51   In the raw NAEP data, there appear to be no consistent differences in stu-
      dent beliefs about mathematics across the school types. However, beliefs
      have been found to consistently correlate with student SES and race/
      ethnicity, with more advantaged students tending to espouse less rigid,
      traditional beliefs about mathematics. Given the marked decrease in the
      private school coefficients in Model 10 of the grade 4 NAEP hierarchical
      linear modeling tables (see Table A9), it is clear that private elementary
      school students hold more rigid, traditional beliefs about mathematics
      than their demographically similar peers in public schools. It is also worth
      noting that the changes in private school coefficients are less marked in
      grade 8, suggesting a weaker pattern of instructional disparities by sector
      at that grade level, perhaps due to the fact that the eighth grade curricu-
      lum has traditionally emphasized more than computation-related topics;
      Sarah Theule Lubienski, "A Closer Look at Black-White Mathematics Gaps:
      Intersections of Race and SES in NAEP Achievement and Instructional
      Practices Data," *Journal of Negro Education* 71, no. 4 (2002): 269–87; Marilyn
      Strutchens, Sarah T. Lubienski, R. McGraw, and S.K. Westbrook, "NAEP
      Findings Regarding Race/Ethnicity: Students' Performance, School Expe-
      riences, Attitudes/Beliefs and Family Influences," in *Results and Interpreta-
      tions of the 1990 through 2000 Mathematics Assessments of the National As-
      sessment of Educational Progress*, ed. P. Kloosterman and F. K. Lester (Reston,
      VA: National Council of Teachers of Mathematics, 2004).

52   National Council of Teachers of Mathematics, *Curriculum and Evalua-
      tion Standards for School Mathematics* (Reston, VA: NCTM, 1989); National
      Council of Teachers of Mathematics, *Principles and Standards for School
      Mathematics* (Reston, VA: NCTM, 2000).

53   Greeley, *Catholic High Schools and Minority Students.*

54   E.g., William Carbonaro, "Public-Private Differences in Achievement among
      Kindergarten Students: Differences in Learning Opportunities and Stu-
      dent Outcomes," *American Journal of Education* 113, no. 1 (2006): 31–65;
      Reardon, Cheadle, and Robinson, "The Effects of Catholic School Atten-
      dance on Reading and Math Achievement in Kindergarten through Fifth
      Grade."

55   E.g., some differences include the creation of instruction-related com-
      posite variables in our ECLS-K analysis, the use of logistic regression to
      screen out variables that do not differ by sector after controlling for
      demographics, and the specific order in which we entered variables in the
      models.

56   This finding seems inconsistent with earlier research using the ECLS-K
      kindergarten data, in which Guarino and colleagues found that teacher-
      reported emphases on traditional practices and computation (as well as
      measurement and advanced topics, advanced numbers and operations,
      and student-centered instruction) were positively associated with

mathematics test score gains in kindergarten. However, their methods differed in several key ways from our ECLS-K analyses. First, their focus was on kindergarten students, so their results may indicate a difference in effectiveness based on the age of the students. Second, while we examined teaching practices and curricular content separately, they grouped these items together when creating composites, thereby possibly masking meaningful differences; Guarino, Hamilton, Lockwood, and Rathburn, *Teacher Qualifications, Teaching Practices, and Reading and Mathematics Gains of Kindergarteners.*

57 National Council of Teachers of Mathematics, *Principles and Standards for School Mathematics.*

CHAPTER SEVEN

1 Robert Kuttner, *Everything or Sale: The Virtues and Limits of Markets* (New York: University of Chicago Press, 1999), 163.

2 Michael J. Sandel, *What Money Can't Buy: The Moral Limits of Markets* (New York: Farrar, Straus and Giroux, 2012).

3 Eric A. Hanushek, "Comments in Response to Grogger and Neal's 'Further Evidence on the Effects of Catholic Secondary Schooling,'" in *Brookings-Wharton Papers on Urban Affairs 2000*, ed. W. G. Gale and J. R. Pack (Washington, DC: Brookings Institution Press, 2000), 196.

4 Erica Frankenberg, Genevieve Siegel-Hawley, and Jia Wang. "Choice without Equity: Charter School Segregation," *Educational Policy Analysis Archives* 19, no. 1 (2011); Erica Frankenberg and Chungmei Lee, "Charter Schools and Race: A Lost Opportunity for Integrated Education," *Educational Policy Analysis Archives*, no. 32 (2003), http://epaa.asu.edu/epaa/v11n32/; Jin Lee and Christopher Lubienski, "Is Racial Segregation Changing in Charter Schools?" *International Journal of Educational Reform* 20, no. 3 (2011): 192–209; Christopher Lubienski, "Privatizing Form or Function? Equity, Outcomes and Influence in American Charter Schools," *Oxford Review of Education* 39, no. 4 (2013); Christopher Lubienski, Liz Gordon, and Jin Lee. "Self-Managing Schools and Access for Disadvantaged Students: Organizational Behavior and School Admissions in Auckland," *New Zealand Journal of Educational Studies* 48, no. 1 (2013).

5 While some will note that the disadvantaged are underrepresented in private schools because of tuition barriers, which could be overcome through vouchers, recent research on organizational behavior suggests that, given greater autonomy, schools often use that autonomy to avoid serving such students; Erica Frankenberg, Genevieve Siegel-Hawley, and Jia Wang, "Choice without Equity: Charter School Segregation," *Educational Policy Analysis Archives* 19, no. 1 (2011), http://epaa.asu.edu/ojs/article/view/779; Natalie Lacireno-Paquet, Thomas T. Holyoke, Michele Moser, and Jeffrey R.

Henig, "Creaming versus Cropping: Charter School Enrollment Practices in Response to Market Incentives," *Educational Evaluation and Policy Analysis* 24, no. 2 (2002): 145–58; Christopher Lubienski, "School Choice as a Civil Right: District Responses to Competition and Equal Educational Opportunity," *Equity and Excellence in Education* 38, no. 4 (2005): 331–41; Christopher Lubienski, "The Decile Delusion: Innovation, Equity and Incentives," *Education Review* 2, no. 3 (2011): 16–18; Christopher Lubienski, Charisse Gulosino, and Peter Weitzel, "School Choice and Competitive Incentives: Mapping the Distribution of Educational Opportunities across Local Education Markets," *American Journal of Education* 115, no. 4 (2009): 601–47.

6   Martin Carnoy, "National Voucher Plans in Chile and Sweden: Did Privatization Reforms Make for Better Education?" *Comparative Education Review* 42, no. 3 (1998): 309–38; Martin Carnoy and Patrick J. McEwan, "Does Privatization Improve Education? The Case of Chile's National Voucher Plan," in *Choosing Choice: School Choice in International Perspective*, ed. D. N. Plank and G. Sykes (New York: Teachers College Press, 2003); Tomas Englund, "Communities, Markets and Traditional Values: Swedish Schooling in the 1990s," *Pedagogy, Culture and Society* 2, no. 1 (1994): 5–29; Edward B. Fiske and Helen F. Ladd, *When Schools Compete: A Cautionary Tale* (Washington, DC: Brookings Institution Press, 2000); Liz Gordon and Geoff Whitty, "Giving the 'Hidden Hand' a Helping Hand? The Rhetoric and Reality of Neoliberal Education Reform in England and New Zealand," *Comparative Education* 33, no. 3 (1997): 453–68; Chang-Ta Hsieh and Miguel Urquiola, *When Schools Compete, How Do They Compete? An Assessment of Chile's Nationwide School Voucher Program* (New York: National Center for the Study of Privatization in Education, 2002); Hugh Lauder, David Hughes, Sue Watson, Sietske Waslander, Martin Thrupp, Rob Strathdee, Ibrahim Simiyu, Ann Dupuis, Jim McGlinn, and Jennie Hamlin, *Trading in Futures: Why Markets in Education Don't Work* (Buckingham, UK: Open University Press, 1999); Patrick J. McEwan, "The Effectiveness of Public, Catholic, and Non-religious Private Schools in Chile's Voucher System," *Education Economics* 9, no. 2 (2001): 103–28; Patrick J. McEwan and Martin Carnoy, "The Effectiveness and Efficiency of Private Schools in Chile's Voucher System," *Educational Evaluation and Policy Analysis* 22, no. 3 (2000): 213–39; Marie-Andree Somers, Patrick J. McEwan, and J. Douglas Willms, "How Effective Are Private Schools in Latin America?" *Comparative Education Review* 48, no. 1 (2004): 48–69; Geoffrey Walford, "Diversity, Choice, and Selection in England and Wales," *Educational Administration Quarterly* 33, no. 2 (1997): 158–69.

7   For example, Karl L. Alexander and Aaron M. Pallas, "School Sector and Cognitive Performance: When Is a Little a Little?" *Sociology of Education* 58, no. 2 (1985): 115–28; J. Douglas Willms, "Catholic-School Effects on

Academic Achievement: New Evidence from the High School and Beyond Follow-up Study," *Sociology of Education* 58, no. 2 (1985): 98–114.

8   James S. Coleman, Thomas Hoffer, and Sally Kilgore, *Public and Private Schools: A Report to the National Center for Educational Statistics* (Chicago, IL: National Opinion Research Center, 1981).

9   See also Anthony S. Bryk, "Disciplined Inquiry or Policy Argument?" *Harvard Educational Review* 51, no. 4 (1981): 497–510; Richard J. Murnane, "Evidence, Analysis, and Unanswered Questions," *Harvard Educational Review* 51, no. 4 (1981): 483–90.

10   Valerie E. Lee and Anthony S. Bryk, "Science or Policy Argument? A Review of the Quantitative Evidence in Chubb and Moe's *Politics, Markets, and America's Schools*," in *School Choice: Examining the Evidence*, ed. M. E. Rasell and R. Rothstein (Washington, DC: Economic Policy Institute, 1993); see also Anthony S. Bryk and Valerie E. Lee, "Science or Policy Argument? A Rejoinder to Chubb and Moe," in *School Choice: Examining the Evidence*, ed. M. E. Rasell and R. Rothstein (Washington, DC: Economic Policy Institute, 1993); Kevin B. Smith and Kenneth J. Meier, *The Case against School Choice: Politics, Markets, and Fools* (Armonk, NY: M.E. Sharpe, 1995); Marla E. Sukstorf, Amy Stuart Wells, and Robert L. Crain, "A Re-Examination of Chubb and Moe's *Politics, Markets, and America's Schools*," in *School Choice: Examining the Evidence*, edited by M. E. Rasell and R. Rothstein (Washington, DC: Economic Policy Institute, 1993).

11   Agence France-Presse, "Global Assets Go into Private Hands at a Lively Pace," *Washington Times*, July 20, 2000, http://www.ncpa.org/pi/internat/intdex7.html; Stephen J. Ball, *Education Plc: Understanding Private Sector Participation in Public Sector Education* (New York: Routledge, 2007); Michelle Celarier, "Privatization: A Case Study in Corruption," *Journal of International Affairs* 50, no. 2 (1997): 531–44; C. Chitty, "Privatisation and Marketisation," *Oxford Review of Education* 23, no. 1 (1997): 45–62; CQ Researcher, "Private Prison Capacity Rising," *CQ Researcher*, August 9, 1996, 711; Harvey B. Feigenbaum and Jeffrey R. Henig, "Privatization and Political Theory," *Journal of International Affairs* 50, no. 2 (1997): 338–56; Ahmed Galal, Leroy Jones, Pankaj Tandoon, and Ingo Vogelsang, *Welfare Consequences of Selling Public Enterprises: An Empirical Analysis* (Oxford, UK: Oxford University Press, 1994); International Finance Corporation, "Privatization: Principles and Practice," in *Lessons of Experience* (Washington, DC: International Finance Corporation, World Bank, 1995).

12   Harvey B. Feigenbaum, Jeffrey R. Henig, and Chris Hamnett, *Shrinking the State: The Political Underpinnings of Privatization* (Cambridge, UK: Cambridge University Press, 1999); David Osborne and Ted Gaebler, *Reinventing Government: How the Entrepreneurial Spirit Is Transforming the Public Sector* (New York: Plume, 1992).

13   Janelle T. Scott and Catherine DiMatrino, "Hybridized, Franchised,

Duplicated, and Replicated: Charter Schools and Management," in *The Charter School Experiment: Expectations, Evidence, and Implications*, ed. C. Lubienski and P. Weitzel (Cambridge, MA: Harvard Education Press, 2010).

14   Steve Barr, Frederick Hess, Vanessa Kirsch, Joel I. Klein, Tom Vander Ark, and Paul Tough, "How Many Billionaires Does It Take to Fix a School System?" *New York Times*, March 9, 2008.

15   For example, A+ Denver, *School Achievement in Denver: The Impact of Charter Schools* (Denver, CO: A+ Denver, 2012); Center for Education Reform, *What the Research Reveals about Charter Schools* (Washington, DC: Center for Education Reform, 2000).

16   For example, Friedman Foundation, *The ABCs of School Choice, 2007–2008 Edition* (Indianapolis, IN: Friedman Foundation, 2008).

17   Barr, Hess, Kirsch, Klein, Ark, and Tough, "How Many Billionaires Does It Take to Fix a School System?"

18   Naomi Oreskes and Erik M. Conway, *Merchants of Doubt: How a Handful of Scientists Obscured the Truth on Issues from Tobacco Smoke to Global Warming* (New York: Bloomsbury Press, 2010).

19   Dale Mezzacappa, "Market Forces: Professor Paul Peterson's Influential Proteges," April 18, 2006, http://www.educationsector.org/publications /market-forces-professor-paul-petersons-influential-protégés.

20   For example, Jay P. Greene, "Vouchers in Charlotte," *Education Next* 1, no. 2 (2001): 55–60; Jay P. Greene, Paul E. Peterson, and J. Du, *The Effectiveness of School Choice in Milwaukee: A Secondary Analysis of Data from the Program's Evaluation* (Cambridge, MA: Program on Education Policy and Governance, Harvard University, 1996); Jay P. Greene, William G. Howell, and Paul E. Peterson, *An Evaluation of the Cleveland Scholarship Program* (Cambridge, MA: Program on Education Policy and Governance, Harvard University, 1997); William G. Howell, Patrick J. Wolf, Paul E. Peterson, and David E. Campbell, *Test-Score Effects of School Vouchers in Dayton, Ohio, New York City, and Washington, D.C.: Evidence from Randomized Field Trials* (Cambridge, MA: Harvard Program on Education Policy and Governance, 2000).

21   Christopher Lubienski, Peter Weitzel, and Sarah T. Lubienski, "Is There a 'Consensus' on School Choice and Achievement? Advocacy Research and the Emerging Political Economy of Knowledge Production," *Educational Policy* 23, no. 1 (2009): 161–93; e.g., Alan B. Krueger and Pei Zhu, "Another Look at the New York City School Voucher Experiment," *American Behavioral Scientist* 47, no. 5 (2004): 658–98; Kim K. Metcalf, "Commentary—Advocacy in the Guise of Science: How Preliminary Research on the Cleveland Voucher Program Was 'Reanalyzed' To Fit a Preconception," *Education Week*, September 23, 1998, 34, 39; John F. Witte, *Reply to Greene, Peterson and Du: "The Effectiveness of School Choice in Milwaukee: A Secondary*

Analysis of Data from the Program's Evaluation" (Madison, WI: Department of Political Science and The Robert La Follette Institute of Public Affairs, University of Wisconsin-Madison, 1996); John F. Witte, "The Milwaukee Voucher Experiment: The Good, the Bad, and the Ugly," *Phi Delta Kappan*, September, 1999, 59–64.

22 Katie Ash, "K–12 Marketplace Sees Major Flow of Venture Capital," *Education Week*, February 1, 2012, 1, 10–11.

23 Oreskes and Conway, *Merchants of Doubt*.

24 Oreskes and Conway, *Merchants of Doubt*.

25 For example, Henry Braun, Frank Jenkins, and Wendy Grigg, *A Closer Look at Charter Schools Using Hierarchical Linear Modeling* (Washington, DC: National Center for Education Statistics, 2006); Henry Braun, Frank Jenkins, and Wendy Grigg, *Comparing Private Schools and Public Schools Using Hierarchical Linear Modeling* (Washington, DC: National Center for Education Statistics, 2006); Sarah Theule Lubienski and Christopher Lubienski, "School Sector and Academic Achievement: A Multi-Level Analysis of NAEP Mathematics Data," *American Educational Research Journal* 43, no. 4 (2006): 651–98; Christopher Lubienski, Corinna Crane, and Sarah T. Lubienski, "What Do We Know about School Effectiveness? Academic Gains in a Value-Added Analysis of Public and Private Schools," *Phi Delta Kappan*, May, 2008, 689–95; Margaret E. Raymond and Center for Research on Education Outcomes, *Multiple Choice: Charter School Performance in 16 States* (Stanford, CA: Stanford University, 2009).

26 For example, Greg Forster, "'F' Is for Failure," *National Review Online*, May 12, 2005; Caroline M. Hoxby, *Achievement in Charter School and Regular Public Schools in the United States: Understanding the Differences* (Cambridge, MA: Harvard University and National Bureau of Economic Research, 2004); Caroline M. Hoxby, *A Straightforward Comparison of Charter Schools and Regular Public Schools in the United States* (Cambridge, MA: Department of Economics, Harvard University, 2004); Caroline M. Hoxby, *A Serious Statistical Mistake in the CREDO Study of Charter Schools* (Stanford, CA: Stanford University, 2009); Shanea Watkins, "Are Public or Private Schools Doing Better? How the NCES Study Is Being Misinterpreted," *Heritage Foundation Backgrounder*, September 1, 2006, 1–4.

27 For example, Paul E. Peterson and Elena Llaudet, *On the Public-Private School Achievement Debate* (Cambridge, MA: Program on Education Policy and Governance, Harvard University, 2006).

28 Shanea Watkins, "Are Public or Private Schools Doing Better?"

29 John E. Chubb and Terry M. Moe, *Politics, Markets, and America's Schools* (Washington, DC: Brookings Institution, 1990), 217.

30 Christopher Lubienski, "Innovation in Education Markets: Theory and Evidence on the Impact of Competition and Choice in Charter Schools," *American Educational Research Journal* 40, no. 2 (2003): 395–443.

31   Joseph L. Bast and Herbert J. Walberg, "Can Parents Choose the Best
      Schools for Their Children?" *Economics of Education Review* 23, no. 4 (2004):
      431–40.

32   Courtney A. Bell, "Social Class Differences in School Choice: The Role
      of Preferences," in *School Choice Policies and Outcomes: Philosophical and
      Empirical Perspectives*, ed. W. Feinberg and C. Lubienski (Albany, NY: State
      University of New York Press, 2008); Michele Moser et al., *The Demand
      for Information for Educational Decision Making in the District of Columbia: A
      Public Discourse* (Washington, DC: District of Columbia State Education
      Office, 2003); David Dodenhoff, *Fixing the Milwaukee Public Schools: The
      Limits of Parent-Driven Reform* (Thiensville, WI: Wisconsin Policy Research
      Institute, 2007); Paul Teske, Jody Fitzpatrick, and Gabriel Kaplan, "The In-
      formation Gap?" *Review of Policy Research* 23, no. 5 (2006): 969–81; Virginia
      R. Weidner, "Information and Information Use for School Choice under
      a Statewide Voucher Program," *Politics of Education Association Bulletin* 29,
      no. 2 (2005): 1–5; Amy Stuart Wells, "The Sociology of School Choice: Why
      Some Win and Others Lose in the Educational Marketplace," in *School
      Choice: Examining the Evidence*, ed. M.E. Rasell and R. Rothstein (Washing-
      ton, DC: Economic Policy Institute, 1993).

33   For example, Robert Bifulco and Helen F. Ladd, "School Choice, Racial
      Segregation, and Test-Score Gaps: Evidence from North Carolina's Charter
      School Program," *Journal of Policy Analysis and Management* 26, no. 1 (2006):
      31–56; Sam Dillon, "Ohio Goes After Charter Schools That Are Failing,"
      New York Times, November 8, 2007, http://www.nytimes.com/2007/11/08
      /us/08charter.html.

34   Justine S. Hastings, Thomas J. Kane, and Douglas O. Staiger, *Parental Prefer-
      ences and School Competition: Evidence from a Public School Choice Program*
      (Cambridge, MA: National Bureau of Economic Research, 2005); Bretten
      Kleitz, Gregory R. Weiher, Kent Tedin, and Richard Matland, "Choice,
      Charter Schools, and Household Preferences," *Social Science Quarterly* 81,
      no. 3 (2000): 846–54; Christopher Lubienski, "Incentives for School Di-
      versification: Competition and Promotional Patterns in Local Education
      Markets," *Journal of School Choice* 1, no. 2 (2006): 1–31; Christopher Lubien-
      ski, "Marketing Schools: Consumer Goods and Competitive Incentives
      for Consumer Information," *Education and Urban Society* 40, no. 1 (2007):
      118–41.

35   David Arsen and Yongmei Ni, "The Effects of Charter School Competition
      on School District Resource Allocation," *Educational Administration Quar-
      terly* 48, no. (1): 3–38; Fiske and Ladd, *When Schools Compete*; Christopher
      Lubienski, "Public Schools in Marketized Environments: Shifting Incen-
      tives and Unintended Consequences of Competition-Based Educational
      Reforms," *American Journal of Education* 111, no. 4 (2005): 464–86; Christo-
      pher Lubienski, Matthew Linick, and Justin York, "Marketing Schools and
      Equitable Access in the United States," in *The Management and Leadership*

of Educational Marketing: Research, Practice and Applications, ed. I. Oplatka and J. Hemsley-Brown (Bingley, UK: Emerald, 2012): 109–35.

36   For example, Gary Becker, "Competition" (paper, the Heritage Foundation 25th Anniversary Leadership for America Lectures, Chicago, IL, September 12, 1999); Milton Friedman, "The Promise of Vouchers," *Wall Street Journal*, December 5, 2005, A20; Virginia Gilder, "Want Better Public Education? Support Private Vouchers," *Imprimis* 28, no. 9 (1999): 5–6; Herbert J. Walberg and Joseph L. Bast, *Education and Capitalism: How Overcoming Our Fear of Markets and Economics Can Improve America's Schools* (Stanford, CA: Hoover Institution Press, 2003).

37   Caroline M. Hoxby, *Do Private Schools Provide Competition for Public Schools?* (Cambridge, MA: National Bureau of Economic Research, 1994); Caroline M. Hoxby, "The Effects of Private School Vouchers on Schools and Students," in *Holding Schools Accountable: Performance-Based Reform in Education*, ed. H. F. Ladd (Washington, DC: Brookings Institution, 1996); Caroline M. Hoxby, "Does Competition among Public Schools Benefit Students and Taxpayers?" *American Economic Review* 90, no. 5 (2000): 1209–38.

38   For example, Jesse Rothstein, "Does Competition among Public Schools Benefit Students and Taxpayers? A Comment on Hoxby (2000)," *American Economic Review* 97, no. 5 (2007): 2026–37; Joydeep Roy and Lawrence Mishel, *Advantage None: Re-Examining Hoxby's Finding of Charter School Benefits* (Washington, DC: Economic Policy Institute, 2005).

39   For example, Hsieh and Urquiola, *When Schools Compete, How Do They Compete?*; Fiske and Ladd, *When Schools Compete*; Rosalind Levacic and Philip A. Woods, "The Impact of Quasi-Markets and Performance Regulation on Socially Disadvantaged Schools" (draft paper, annual meeting of the American Educational Research Association, New Orleans, LA, April, 2000); Matthew Linick, "A Study of the Effects of Charter School Policy on Public School District Resource Allocation Using Multiple Quasi-Experimental Designs," Ph.D. Dissertation, Department of Education Policy, Organization and Leadership," 2013, University of Illinois, Champaign, IL; Taryn Rounds Parry, "How Will Schools Respond to the Incentives of Privatization? Evidence from Chile and Implications for the United States," *American Review of Public Administration* 27, no. 3 (1997): 248–69; S. Waslander and M. Thrupp, "Choice, Competition and Segregation: An Empirical Analysis of a New Zealand Secondary School Market, 1990–93," *Journal of Education Policy* 10, no. 1 (1995): 1–26; Sue Watson, David Hughes, and Hugh Lauder, " 'Success' and 'Failure' in the Education Marketplace: An Example from New Zealand," *Journal of Educational Change* 4, no. 1 (2003): 1–24; Wells, "The Sociology of School Choice."

40   Peter Davies, Nick Adnett, and Jean Mangan, "The Diversity and Dynamics of Competition: Evidence from Two Local Schooling Markets," *Oxford Review of Education* 28, no. 1 (2002): 91–107; Fiske and Ladd, *When Schools Compete*; Lacireno-Paquet, Holyoke, Moser, and Henig, "Creaming Versus

Cropping"; Lauder et al., *Trading in Futures*; Lubienski, "Incentives for
School Diversification"; Lubienski, Linick, and York, "Marketing Schools
and Equitable Access in the United States"; Yongmei Ni and David Arsen,
"The Competitive Effects of Charter Schools on Public School Districts," in
The Charter School Experiment: Expectations, Advocacy and Implications, ed. C.
Lubienski and P. Weitzel (Cambridge, MA: Harvard Education Press, 2010);
Parry, "How Will Schools Respond to the Incentives of Privatization?";
Izhar Oplatka, "The Emergence of Educational Marketing: Lessons from
the Experiences of Israeli Principals," *Comparative Education Review* 46,
no. 2 (2002): 211–33; Geoff Whitty, Sally Power, and David Halpin, *Devolu-
tion and Choice in Education: The School, the State, and the Market* (Bristol, PA:
Open University Press, 1998).

41   Christopher Lubienski, "Privatising Form or Function? Equity, Outcomes,
and Influence in American Charter Schools," *Oxford Review of Education* 39,
no. 4 (2013); Christopher Lubienski, "The Decile Delusion: Innovation,
Equity and Incentives," *Education Review* 2, no. 3 (2011): 16–18.

42   For example, David Arsen and Yongmei Ni. "The Effects of Charter School
Competition on School District Resource Allocation," *Educational Ad-
ministration Quarterly* 48, no. 1 (2011): 3–38; Fiske and Ladd, *When Schools
Compete*; Lauder et al., *Trading in Futures*; Lubienski, "Public Schools in
Marketized Environments."

43   Frankenberg, Siegel-Hawley, and Wang, "Choice without Equity"; Jin Lee
and Christopher Lubienski, "Is Racial Segregation Changing in Charter
Schools?" *International Journal of Educational Reform* 20, no. 3 (2011); Lubienski, Gulosino, and Weitzel, "School Choice and Competitive Incentives"; Lubienski, Linick, and York, "Marketing Schools and Equitable
Access in the United States"; Kelly E. Rapp and Suzanne E. Eckes, "Dispel-
ling the Myth of 'White Flight': An Examination of Minority Enrollment
in Charter Schools," *Educational Policy* 21, no. 4 (2007): 615–61; Linda A.
Renzulli and Vincent J. Roscigno, "Charter Schools and the Public Good,"
Contexts 6, no. 1 (2007): 31–36; Christian P. Wilkens, "Students with Disabilities in Urban Massachusetts Charter Schools," *Teachers College Record*
(2011).

44   K. Polanyi, *The Great Transformation* (New York: Rinehart & Company,
1944); Sandel, *What Money Can't Buy*.

APPENDIX A

1   National Council of Teachers of Mathematics, *Curriculum and Evalua-
tion Standards for School Mathematics* (Reston, VA: NCTM, 1989); National
Council of Teachers of Mathematics, *Principles and Standards for School
Mathematics* (Reston, VA: NCTM, 2000).

2   For example, we reran the HLM models with an expanded sample by

deleting student lunch eligibility at the student and school level, as well as by deleting the school-level LEP indicator (given that these variables contributed the majority of missing data). The samples were then 185,681 students in 7,321 schools at grade 4, and 149,127 students across 5,965 schools at grade 8. Although the public school advantage weakened, as would be expected, the general finding that private school coefficients were statistically equal to or less than 0 after controlling for demographics and school location did not change.

3   For more information, see E. G. Johnson, "The Design of the National Assessment of Educational Progress," *Journal of Educational Measurement* 29, no. 2 (1992): 95–110; E.G. Johnson and K. F. Rust, "Population Inferences and Variance Estimation for NAEP Data," *Journal of Educational Statistics* 17, no. 2 (1992): 175–90.

4   Donald B. Rubin, *Multiple Imputation for Nonresponse in Surveys* (New York: Wiley, 1987).

5   Given the many complexities of NAEP, when questions about variables or procedures arose, NAEP experts at NCES, ETS, and Westat were consulted.

6   Steven W. Raudenbush, Anthony S. Bryk, Y. F. Cheong, R. Congdon, and M. du Toit, *HLM 6: Linear and Nonlinear Modeling* (Lincolnwood, IL: Scientific Software International, 2004).

7   NCES recommends the use of AM for running cross-tabulations of NAEP data. The standard errors obtained with AM were slightly more conservative than those on the NAEP Data Explorer (http://nces.ed.gov/nations reportcard/nde). More information about AM is available at (http://am .air.org).

8   Stephen W. Raudenbush and Anthony S. Bryk, *Hierarchical Linear Models: Applications and Data Analysis Methods* (Thousand Oaks, CA: Sage Publications, 2002).

9   National Assessment Governing Board, *National Assessment of Educational Progress: Design 2000–2010* (Washington, DC: National Assessment Governing Board, 1999).

10   We recognize the disagreements about the appropriate categories and terms to use when discussing racial and ethnic subgroups. To be consistent with the NAEP data, we use the designations employed by NAEP.

11   There may be differences in IEP use in public and private schools. Hence, we ran models both with and without this variable. Although removing this variable slightly elevated the private school coefficients, it did not change the general finding that those coefficients were statistically equal to or less than 0 after controlling for demographics and school location.

12   To preserve data, students who reported that they did not know whether they had a particular resource were recoded to "no," with the logic that even if the resource was present in his/her home, it was not (directly) enriching the student's home experiences. The six variables were positively

correlated at grades 4 and 8, and a factor analysis produced only one factor with an eigenvalue greater than 1. Given a high correlation (roughly .9)
between the sum of the six variables and the resulting composite from
the factor analysis, we chose to use the sum for ease in reporting to broad
audiences.

13   These were the four categories used on the NAEP survey, and the intent
was to simply convert this "books" variable to a 0–1 scale to match the
remaining five home resources variables.

14   For example, 95% of private school students in schools "not participating" in the lunch program had higher than average scores on the home
resources composite

15   Another important socioeconomic indicator, parent education level, was
in the 2003 NAEP data, but roughly one-third of fourth graders and one-
fifth of eighth graders responded, "I don't know" to the question. To limit
missing data, we ultimately decided not to include parent education level.
However, the HLM models were run at grade 8 with parent education included, and the results were very similar to the final models reported here.
Additionally, NAEP includes student- and school-level Title 1 information, but inconsistencies in the ways schools determine students' Title 1
eligibility prompted us to exclude these variables from analyses.

16   To preserve data, race/ethnicity information regarding sampled students
from the school was used as a proxy when administrator-reported school
information was missing. Also, the resulting variable was divided by 100
so that the HLM coefficients would be more accurate when rounded to
one decimal place (e.g., 1.2 instead of 0.012).

17   For example, National Council of Teachers of Mathematics, *Principles and
Standards for School Mathematics*.

18   These standard deviations were calculated by taking the square root of
the variance between schools in the study's null HLM models (following
the methods of Clare E. Von Secker and Robert W. Lissitz, "Estimating the
Impact of Instructional Practices on Student Achievement in Science,"
Journal of Research in Science Teaching 36, no. 10 (1999): 1110–26).

19   We performed the usual regression diagnostics for the final fourth- to
eighth-grade models, and no problems were identified. Specifically, we
examined the means, standard deviations, and plots of fitted and residual
values by school type, and no group appeared to be substantially better
predicted than others. The means of residuals were close to 0 for each
school type, and the standard deviations were similar.

20   For example, Anthony S. Bryk, Valerie E. Lee, and Peter B. Holland, *Catholic
Schools and the Common Good* (Cambridge, MA: Harvard University Press,
1993).

21   The term "comparable" here indicates that the schools are similar on all
measures entered into the HLM models thus far.

22   Consistent with Sarah Theule Lubienski, "Examining Instruction, Achievement, and Equity with NAEP Mathematics Data," *Educational Policy Analysis Archives* 14, no. 14 (2006), http://epaa.asu.edu/epaa/v14n14/.

23   Issues of multiple comparisons merit consideration owing to the inclusion of over a dozen different school- and instruction-related variables in Models 4–10. Given that variables were included at two different levels (student and school) and at two different grades (fourth and eighth), there are likely differing opinions regarding exactly how the issue of multiple comparisons should be addressed. For this reason, the common standard of .05 is used, but three different significance levels are denoted (.05, .01, and .001), and in drawing conclusions from this study, we emphasize those variables that consistently showed significance at both the fourth and eighth grades (when possible).

APPENDIX B

1   National Center for Education Statistics, *User's Manual for the ECLS-K Third Grade Public-Use Data File and Electronic Code Book* (Washington, DC: U.S. Department of Education – Office of Educational Research and Improvement, 2004).

2   We decided to keep students who changed schools but remained in the same sector in the analysis because the sample bias introduced from eliminating these students in the sample would be more harmful than the extra school-level noise added from the effect of having been in a different school. The t-tests indicated that those 1,714 students (or 14.4% of the sample) who would have been dropped have a significantly lower average SES than the rest of the sample. In addition, a significantly smaller percentage is white (50% vs. 58%), while a significantly larger percentage are black (18% vs. 12%). Still, we ran the full HLM model using the reduced sample in order to confirm that there were no major differences found in the results.

3   K. Denton and Jerry West, *Children's Reading and Mathematics Achievement in Kindergarten and First Grade* (Washington, DC: National Center for Education Statistics, 2002), 28.

4   National Center for Education Statistics, *User's Manual for the ECLS-K Third Grade Public-Use Data File and Electronic Code Book.*

5   National Council of Teachers of Mathematics, *Curriculum and Evaluation Standards for School Mathematics* (Reston, VA: NCTM, 1989); National Council of Teachers of Mathematics, *Principles and Standards for School Mathematics* (Reston, VA: NCTM, 2000).

6   National Center for Education Statistics, *Early Childhood Longitudinal Study-Kindergarten Class of 1998-99 (ECLS-K), Psychometric Report for Kindergarten through First Grade* (Washington, DC: U.S. Department of Education, Office of Educational Research and Improvement, 2002).

7   We also included three other SES-related variables that have been found
to relate to student achievement growth from kindergarten through fifth
grade (Sarah T. Lubienski and Corinna C. Crane, "Beyond Free Lunch:
Which Family Background Measures Matter?" *Education Policy Analysis
Archives* 18, no. 11 [2010]), including the number of siblings, how many
books the child has, and if there is a computer in the home. However,
their coefficients were either not significant or were only marginally
significant when added after the ECLS-K SES composite variable and the
other student demographics. In addition, they did not have any effect on
the school sector coefficient, so they were left out of the analysis for the
sake of simplicity.

8   For more details, see Corinna Crane, "Mathematics Performance in Public
and Catholic Elementary Schools: Explaining the Disparity" (Ph.D. diss.,
University of Illinois, 2010).

9   Daniel P. Mayer, "Do New Teaching Standards Undermine Performance
on Old Tests?" *Educational Evaluation and Policy Analysis* 20, no. 2 (1998):
53–73; Daniel P. Mayer, "Measuring Instructional Practice: Can Policymakers Trust Survey Data?" *Educational Evaluation and Policy Analysis* 21, no. 1
(1999): 29–45; D. Stipek and P. Byler, "The Early Childhood Classroom
Observation Measure," *Early Childhood Research Quarterly* 19, no. 3 (2004):
375–97.

10   ECLS-K also included a variable measuring time on mathematics. Unfortunately, teachers were asked how much time they spent per day (1–30 minutes, 31–60 minutes, 61–90 minutes, etc.) and then were asked in a separate variable how many days they spent per week, with response options
of "daily," "three or four times a week," "once or twice a week," and so on.
These variables did not allow for an accurate comparison of time actually
spent per week for any cases except for those who reported daily math
instruction (which was about 92% of teachers who answered this question). We ran HLM models with these 92% of cases and found that time
on math was not significantly associated with mathematics test score
gains either before or after demographic information was entered into the
models. This is likely because the vast majority reported 31 to 60 minutes
per day, and this does not differentiate between teachers who spend about
half an hour versus ones who spend an hour per day. Because of the lack
of relationship found and the problems with the time on mathematics
variables, they were not included in the final analysis.

11   Partial correlations were run examining the relationship between initial
first-grade math t-score and third-grade teacher instructional practice
composite variables to determine whether initial student ability is a confounding variable that influences the type of instruction students receive.
There was no significant correlation between prior ability and the reform-
oriented practices composite and a slightly positive correlation between
prior ability and the traditional practices composite ($r = .02$, $p < .05$), indi-

cating that students who score higher have teachers who report a slightly greater frequency of traditional practices. In addition, there were no significant correlations between a student's SES and either the reform-oriented or traditional practices composite variables.

12   The low Cronbach's alpha reliability score was concerning, but we chose to keep these items together in the composite for several reasons. First, initial exploratory principal components factor analysis with Varimax rotation broke these three items into one component. Second, the items were all positively correlated, and the removal of any of the items would not have improved the alpha score by more than .02. Finally, all three had responses that differed similarly by school type. We also ran a full model with the three traditional practices variables separately and found that this did not change the results (none of the variables were significant on their own or in the composite, and including them separately did not significantly alter other coefficients in the model).

13   Charles T. Clotfelter, Helen F. Ladd, and Jacob L. Vigdor, "Teacher Credentials and Student Achievement: Longitudinal Analysis with Student Fixed Effects," *Economics of Education Review* 26, no. 6 (2007): 673–82; R.G. Croninger, J. K. Rice, A. Rathbun, and M. Nishio, "Teacher Qualifications and Early Learning: Effects of Certification, Degree, and Experience on First-Grade Student Achievement," *Economics of Education Review* 26, no. 3 (2007): 312–24; Brian Rowan, R. Correnti, and R.J. Miller, "What Large-Scale, Survey Research Tells Us about Teacher Effects on Student Achievement: Insights from the Prospects Study of Elementary Schools," *Teachers College Record* 104, no. 8 (2002): 1525–67; M.W. Stuhlman and R.C. Pianta, "Profiles of Educational Quality in First Grade," *Elementary School Journal* 109, no. 4 (2009): 323–42; Z. Xu and Charisse A. Gulosino, "How Does Teacher Quality Matter? The Effect of Teacher-Parent Partnership on Early Childhood Performance in Public and Private Schools," *Education Economics* 14, no. 3 (2006): 345–67.

14   Clotfelter, Ladd, and Vigdor, "Teacher Credentials and Student Achievement"; Steven G. Rivkin, Eric A. Hanushek, and John F. Kain, "Teachers, Schools, and Academic Achievement," *Econometrica* 73, no. 2 (2005): 417–58.

15   M.V. Borland and R.M. Howsen, "An Examination of the Effect of Elementary School Size on Student Academic Achievement," *International Review of Education* 49, no. 5 (2003): 463–74; Craig B. Howley and R. Bickel, "The Matthew Project: National Report. ERIC Document Reproduction Service" (ERIC Document Reproduction Service No. ED 478 058, 1999); I. Kuziemko, "Using Shocks to School Enrollment to Estimate the Effect of School Size on Student Achievement," *Economics of Education Review* 25, no. 1 (2006): 63–75; Valerie E. Lee and Susanna Loeb, "School Size in Chicago Elementary Schools: Effects on Teachers' Attitudes and Students' Achievement," *American Educational Research Journal* 37, no. 1 (2000): 3–31.

16   For more details, see Crane, "Mathematics Performance in Public and Catholic Elementary Schools."

17   Aggregated student SES was not included as a control when running the binary logistic regressions at the class and school levels because this would only have been based on an average of two or three students in the classroom.

18   Reardon et al. and Carbonaro examined school sector differences in the ECLS-K data using both propensity-score matching and ordinary least squares regressions and obtained similar results with both methods. Hence, we did not use propensity score matching in our analyses; William Carbonaro, "Public-Private Differences in Achievement among Kindergarten Students: Differences in Learning Opportunities and Student Outcomes," *American Journal of Education* 113, no. 1 (2006): 31–65; Sean F. Reardon, Jacob E. Cheadle, and Joseph P. Robinson, "The Effects of Catholic School Attendance on Reading and Math Achievement in Kindergarten through Fifth Grade," *Journal of Research on Educational Effectiveness* 2, no. 1 (2009): 45–87.

19   Stephen W. Raudenbush and Anthony S. Bryk, *Hierarchical Linear Models: Applications and Data Analysis Methods* (Thousand Oaks, CA: Sage Publications, 2002); Steven W. Raudenbush, Anthony S. Bryk, Y.F. Cheong, R. Congdon, and M. du Toit, *HLM 6: Linear and nonlinear modeling* (Lincolnwood, IL: Scientific Software International, 2004).

20   Leaving the binaries uncentered makes results interpretable as deviations from a specific student in a particular classroom and school (in this case a black female with no learning problem diagnosed in a large-city public school, etc.) rather than deviations from a nonexistent "average" student.

21   National Council of Teachers of Mathematics, *Curriculum and Evaluation Standards for School Mathematics*; National Council of Teachers of Mathematics, *Principles and Standards for School Mathematics*.

22   National Center for Education Statistics, *User's Manual for the ECLS-K Third Grade Public-Use Data File and Electronic Code Book*, 3–15.

23   National Center for Education Statistics, *User's Manual for the ECLS-K Third Grade Public-Use Data File and Electronic Code Book*, 3–12.

24   Karen M. Anderson and Michael A. Resnick, *Careful Comparisons: Public and Private Schools in America* (Alexandria, VA: National School Boards Association, 1997); K.J. Gruber, S.D. Wiley, S.P. Broughman, G.A. Strizek, and M. Burian-Fitzgerald, *Schools and Staffing Survey, 1999–2000: Overview of the Data for Public, Private, Public Charter, and Bureau of Indian Affairs Elementary and Secondary Schools* (Washington, DC: National Center for Education Statistics, 2002); Xu and Gulosino, "How Does Teacher Quality Matter?"

25   The average of 49.38 is below the expected *t*-score mean of 50 owing in part to the fact that other private school students are not included in the

sample. Those students are likely to have higher t-scores on average so removing them would lower the overall t-score mean.

26 James S. Coleman, E.Q. Campbell, C.J. Hobson, J. McPartland, A.M. Mood, F.D. Weinfeld, and R.L. York. 1966. *Equality of Educational Opportunity*. Washington, DC: National Center for Educational Statistics.

27 Some researchers argue that the percentage of students with disabilities is underreported in Catholic schools because these schools have different obligations and incentives to do so. Paul E. Peterson and Elena Llaudet, *On the Public-Private School Achievement Debate* (Cambridge, MA: Program on Education Policy and Governance, Harvard University, 2006). In order to determine whether this variable might be biased in the ECLS-K sample, we compared the percentage of public school students whose parents reported that they have been diagnosed with a learning, speech, or hearing problem with the percentage of Catholic school parents who report this and found that 1.8 times more public school parents reported this (8.8% vs. 4.9%). We then compared this with the average percentage of children with disabilities as reported by teachers in each sector and found that the percentage of special education students reported in public school classrooms was 2.1 times that reported in Catholic school classrooms (or 11.2% vs. 5.3%). This difference in ratios does indicate a possible slight underreporting in Catholic schools. To confirm that the results of the study were not biased by this, we reran the final reduced model in the analysis (Model 15 in Table 84) and found that the Catholic coefficient was slightly larger −2.35 vs. −2.48) but still highly significantly negative.

28 A large portion of the variation has already been explained by Model 3, when students' first-grade test score was added to the model. A substantial portion of the remaining unexplained variation is likely due to students' experiences in second grade, which we do not have information on, as well as to unexplained variation in the data from things that have not been measured.

29 James S. Coleman, Thomas Hoffer, and Sally Kilgore, *High School Achievement: Public, Catholic, and Private Schools Compared* (New York: Basic Books, 1982); Thomas Hoffer, Andrew M. Greeley, and James S. Coleman, "Achievement Growth in Public and Catholic Schools," *Sociology of Education* 58, no. 2 (1985), 74–97; Stephen Raudenbush and Anthony S. Bryk, "A Hierarchical Model for Studying School Effects," *Sociology of Education* 59, no. 1 (1986): 1–17.

30 Similarly, Reardon, Cheadle, and Robinson (2009) found no significant race x sector interactions in their analysis of the ECLS-K data but noted that small sample sizes for some subgroups limited their analysis.

31 Donald A. Rock and Judith M. Pollack, *Early Childhood Longitudinal Study-Kindergarten Class of 1998-99 (ECLS-K): Psychometric Report for Kindergarten*

through First Grade (Washington, DC: National Center for Education Statistics, 2002), 2–7.

32   Donald Rock and Judith M. Pollack, *Early Childhood Longitudinal Study-Kindergarten Class of 1998–99 (ECLS-K)*, 2–8.

33   For more information on this analysis, as well as additional analyses involving student proficiency on particular subscales, see Crane, "Mathematics Performance in Public and Catholic Elementary Schools."

Index